ADVANCE WARS
DUAL STRIKE

THE OFFICIAL NINTENDO PLAYER'S GUIDE

PREPARE FOR WAR!

The motley crew of misfits and miscreants known as the Black Hole Army has resurfaced in Omega Land, and it's brought trouble. Pockets of the once-lush countryside are transforming overnight into desolate wastelands. This time, it's up to you and the members of the allied forces to get to the bottom of the conspiracy once and for all. Control the intense action on two fronts using the Nintendo DS's dual screens. Call the shots with your hand-picked cadre of COs, or let one do the work for you. Either way, it'll take all the skill you can muster to fend off the dual strike.

CONTENTS

CAMPAIGN

⭐ Bonus missions (marked with a star) are available only if you find the map or secret document hidden in the level that precedes it. Playing bonus levels is not necessary for completing the campaign, but they will give your CO additional experience and give you the opportunity to build new weapons.

KINDLE

CONTROLS

You've got an entire arsenal at your fingertips. Learn to use the controls and harness the strength of your military on two screens.

CONTROL SCHEMATIC

The following pages detail every method of input you'll use to direct your armies.

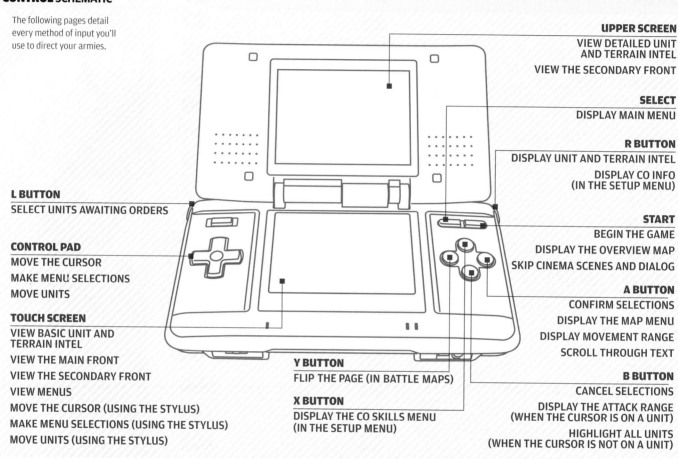

UPPER SCREEN
VIEW DETAILED UNIT
AND TERRAIN INTEL
VIEW THE SECONDARY FRONT

SELECT
DISPLAY MAIN MENU

R BUTTON
DISPLAY UNIT AND TERRAIN INTEL
DISPLAY CO INFO
(IN THE SETUP MENU)

START
BEGIN THE GAME
DISPLAY THE OVERVIEW MAP
SKIP CINEMA SCENES AND DIALOG

A BUTTON
CONFIRM SELECTIONS
DISPLAY THE MAP MENU
DISPLAY MOVEMENT RANGE
SCROLL THROUGH TEXT

B BUTTON
CANCEL SELECTIONS
DISPLAY THE ATTACK RANGE
(WHEN THE CURSOR IS ON A UNIT)
HIGHLIGHT ALL UNITS
(WHEN THE CURSOR IS NOT ON A UNIT)

L BUTTON
SELECT UNITS AWAITING ORDERS

CONTROL PAD
MOVE THE CURSOR
MAKE MENU SELECTIONS
MOVE UNITS

TOUCH SCREEN
VIEW BASIC UNIT AND
TERRAIN INTEL
VIEW THE MAIN FRONT
VIEW THE SECONDARY FRONT
VIEW MENUS
MOVE THE CURSOR (USING THE STYLUS)
MAKE MENU SELECTIONS (USING THE STYLUS)
MOVE UNITS (USING THE STYLUS)

Y BUTTON
FLIP THE PAGE (IN BATTLE MAPS)

X BUTTON
DISPLAY THE CO SKILLS MENU
(IN THE SETUP MENU)

DUAL SCREENS

As if controlling combat on one front weren't enough to keep you busy, you now have the benefit of two screens on which to view intel and fight your battles.

THE UPPER SCREEN

During gameplay, the upper screen will display detailed information about selected units or terrain. Some missions will involve a secondary front that takes place on the upper screen. You can watch the action play out automatically, or in some instances you can take full control of the battle. In these situations, the action on the secondary front will shift to the lower screen during your turn, and return to the upper screen afterward.

THE TOUCH SCREEN

The touch-sensitive lower screen is where most of the action takes place. You can use the stylus to control your armies during battle, or employ the Control Pad and buttons to direct the action. Most of the in-game menus and detailed information will appear on the touch screen. During battle, combat animations will play out on the lower display unless you disable this feature.

STYLUS CONTROLS

You can order your armies into action with a few simple taps and strokes of the stylus. The pen is indeed mightier than the sword.

TAP THE SCREEN TO MAKE A SELECTION

Touch the stylus to the screen to make your unit selection, and hold the stylus on a unit to display its range. Tapping the stylus on any terrain feature will display detailed information about that type of terrain on the upper screen. Tapping on enemy units will display detailed unit information on the upper screen. You can hold the stylus on enemy units to display their firing range, just as you would your own units.

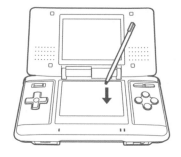

SEND YOUR TROOPS INTO ACTION

Hold the stylus on a unit to display its range. Then select a space within its range of movement to have the unit move there. As soon as you lift the stylus from the touch screen, your unit will move to the chosen space and the action menu will appear.

★ TOUCH WITH CARE

Be careful when wielding the stylus. Like in chess, once you let go of a unit, it will be too late to change your mind.

BUTTON CONTROLS

You can also control the action through conventional means by pressing the appropriate button for the job.

BUTTON TAPS ARE STYLUS SUBSTITUTES

If using the stylus isn't your thing, you can easily manage the action via the Control Pad and the A Button. Use the Control Pad to move the cursor to any unit or terrain feature. Push the A Button to select the unit or terrain feature and so on. The button control scheme may be the more forgiving way to wage war in Omega Land, especially when playing in a bumpy environment such as a bus or car.

NOW TO WAR

Your units are capable of performing a wide range of actions, depending on the situation at hand. Know your options before issuing an order.

TAKE COMMAND AND ISSUE YOUR ORDERS

The battles in *Advance Wars: Dual Strike* follow a specific flow. Become familiar with the duties you'll need to perform each day to keep your units alive and well. We've listed a basic day's actions below. Once you've selected and moved a unit, you must give it a command before moving into action with another unit. These commands are listed to the right; depending on the situation, your unit will have a variety of options.

SELECT A COMMANDING OFFICER FOR THE BATTLE AHEAD

For some missions you will need to choose one or more COs to lead the fight.

SURVEY THE FIELD AND REVIEW YOUR OPTIONS

Don't charge into each day blindly and simply move your units as far as possible. Select each unit and move it carefully, being sure to think about the possible outcomes of each movement.

ISSUE COMMANDS CAREFULLY FOR MAXIMUM BENEFIT

Once you've moved a unit, you'll need to give it orders. Many times you'll have multiple options to choose from. Be sure to command your units wisely. If you move a Mech or Infantry unit onto a property next to an enemy, you may want to attack the enemy before you capture the real estate.

REVIEW YOUR UNITS BEFORE ENDING EACH DAY

Be sure to check the battlefield before ending each day; you don't want to leave any units idle and vulnerable.

CAPTURE
Moving Infantry or Mech units onto properties allows you to capture them.

DIVE
Submarines can dive beneath the surface to hide from enemy attack.

DROP
Once you've loaded a unit, you can drop it off on suitable terrain after each movement.

FIRE
Select Fire to attack enemy units within your firing range.

JOIN
You can combine units of the same type if each unit's HP is below 10.

LOAD
Some units can hold and carry other units. Choose Load to load them up.

REPAIR
You may gain the ability to repair units along the way, restoring HP.

RISE
Select Rise to return a Sub to the surface of the water.

SEND
In missions with a secondary front, you may be able to send units from the main front to help with the fight.

SUPPLY
Some units have the ability to supply other units with fuel and ammo.

WAIT
This finishes your turn with the selected unit, where it will wait until the next day.

STRATEGY BRIEFING

Success in battle will depend on your skill and efficiency in managing the battlefield. Here are a few things to consider during each mission to gain an advantage over your enemies.

- **CAPTURE PROPERTIES**
  Your cities supply your army with funds each day, and you'll need money to expand your army. The more property you control, the more money you'll make. You'll also need bases, airports and other specialized properties to manufacture units.

- **PRODUCE LOGICAL UNITS**
  Don't always build the biggest, baddest weapons you can afford. You may want save money for later in the battle, so spend wisely.

- **MOVE STRATEGICALLY**
  Carefully plan each of your movements. Keeping your troops out of harm's way is crucial to success. Sometimes, however, sacrifices are necessary.

- **PLAN OFFENSIVE AND DEFENSIVE MANEUVERS**
  Not all battles are won with purely offensive maneuvers. In some situations, setting up a defensive front in one area while sneaking a small assault team unnoticed into another area is the best option.

GAME MODES

You've got five gameplay modes to explore, each featuring multitudes of maps, weapons and difficulty settings to satisfy your inner tyrant.

CAMPAIGN MODE

OMEGA WAR

The story of the Omega war unfolds during Campaign mode. Here, you'll advance the plot as you defeat the Black Hole Army each mission. Rid the land of the evil scourge once and for all.

COMMANDER IN CHIEF

During every battle, you'll deploy military units and earn points according to how well you perform in three categories: speed, technique and power. Points are tallied at the conclusion of each battle, and you'll be awarded a rank depending on your total score. Your COs will also advance in rank as they earn battle experience.

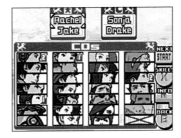

★ HARD CAMPAIGN

Once you've fought your way through the Normal Campaign, you'll have the opportunity to really challenge your battle skills in the Hard Campaign. As you might expect, the harder version is brutal.

WAR ROOM

MULTIPLE CHOICE

In the War Room, you'll select from a variety of battle situations and settings to further test your command worthiness. Go against a crowd of able-bodied officers as you fight on a host of maps. Tweak the settings to suit your tastes, and see what you're made of.

CO SETTINGS

You can decide the number of COs you'll fight against here and set up a Dual Strike battle against the CPU.

SKILL SETTINGS

Like a clean, simple fight? You can turn skills on or off at your whim, which will affect how much experience you earn.

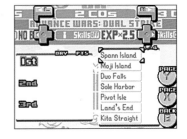

VERSUS MODE

FRIENDLY FIRE

Duke it out with up to three of your closest friends (or enemies) in Versus mode. Tailor the battle conditions to your liking and make it as punishing or forgiving as you want. You can even fight the CPU for some solo action.

WAR AMONG FRIENDS

Settle a score the old-fashioned way—through military might! Choose your favorite COs, equip them with up to four different skill sets and send them into the fray.

FIELDER'S CHOICE

There are seven map categories to choose from, so the possibilites are virtually limit-less. Fight on a variety of battlefields designed for two to four officers. War Room maps are available in Versus mode as are Classic maps from previous Advance Wars games. Want a totally original way to settle the score? Design your own map and take it to Versus mode.

★ NORMAL AND DS

You can play on tons of different maps in standard play, but certain maps will be off-limits when you choose a dual-front encounter in DS Battle.

SURVIVAL MODE

SKILL TEST

Survival mode gives you three submodes to test your mettle. You can limit battle funds, the amount of turns you take, or the time available to run a gauntlet of 11 missions in a row. Once you breeze through a submode, you can purchase a harder version of it.

MANAGEMENT POSITION

Each Survival submode is about managing different aspects of battlefield operations. If you can master each of the three submodes, you'll have no problem restoring peace to the world, no matter what Black Hole throws at you.

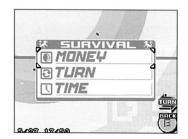

MONEY

The Mondy submode tests your ability to manage the funds involved in running an army. Producing just enough of the right type of unit to win each battle is crucial to conserving cash and earning a great rank.

TURN

In the Turn submode, you'll have a finite number of days to complete all 11 missions. Each move must count, as every fight will cause your turn reserves to drain.

TIME

It's a race against the clock in Time mode. Speed through every scenario in under 25 minutes to finish.

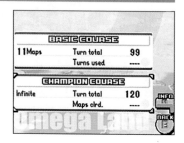

★ CHAMPION COURSE

Once you've cleared the normal Survival mode, take on the Champion Course. The maps are infinite, so the game will continue until you run out of steam.

COMBAT MODE

REAL TIME

Tired of turn-based battle strategies? Try Combat mode for some nonstop, fast-paced action in real time. Choose your units before the battle and send them into action. It's an entirely new spin on classic Advance Wars gameplay.

DIFFICULT DECISIONS

In Combat mode, you'll have to give some thought to which CO you want commanding your forces. Consider your officer's strengths and weaknesses when purchasing units. If you lose a unit in combat, it will be gone for the remainder of the game. Capture bases to gain additional forces.

SYSTEM MENU

BATTLE MAPS

The Battle Maps area is where you'll find new maps to purchase for use in the various gameplay modes. Visit Hachi for all your battlefield needs. Don't forget to check back often, as you may find some new items for sale once you meet certain gameplay conditions.

HISTORY

Like your own personal captain's log, the History feature lets you review an extensive list of your battlefield accomplishments and performance statistics. You can earn 300 medals and five trophies during your military career. Check back often to see what you've amassed.

SOUND ROOM

The Sound Room lets you sample the music from Advance Wars: Dual Strike, including CO themes, Team themes and music from the Omega War.

DESIGN ROOM

The Design Room allows you to personalize your Advance Wars experience. Build your own battle maps or change your CO's appearance. You can even change the background displays with new wallpaper. See page 9 for further details.

GALLERY

In the Gallery you'll find special wallpapers of the characters and scenes from the game. Check back often—new artwork will become viewable once you've reached various gameplay milestones.

WIRELESS LINK

You can battle against several of your friends in various gameplay modes, exchange custom maps and message each other via the wireless link. Up to eight players can partake in Combat mode. Only one game card is required.

WIRELESS LINK

Clobber your friends via the marvels of wireless communication, and see once and for all who's the toughest.

GET CONNECTED

Wireless mode allows two or more Nintendo DS units to connect wirelessly so you can battle against your friends, message each other and trade user-created content.

MULTIPLAYER ACTION

Each player will need his own Nintendo DS and copy of Advance Wars: Dual Strike in order to play against each other using the various multiplayer modes available, except when using Download mode to send Combat to other players.

★ GAME CARD

Although you need only one Advance Wars: Dual Strike game card to play Combat, you may experience slightly different gameplay if all players have their own copy of the game.

NORMAL BATTLE

Two to four players can battle against one another in Normal Battles. Each player will need his own Nintendo DS and copy of Advance Wars: Dual Strike to play the Normal Battle mode.

DS BATTLE

Two players can engage in a Dual Strike Battle. Each combatant will need a Nintendo DS and copy of Advance Wars: Dual Strike.

TRADE MAPS

This mode allows you to send a user-created map to another player. On the map-trading screen, player one will select the tradeable creation, then choose where to send it. The player receiving the map must choose a place to save the data.

COMBAT

Up to eight players wreak havok in Combat mode. Fight it out with friends and customize the settings however you want. Only one player needs an Advance Wars: Dual Strike game card.

DOWNLOAD

Use the wireless functionality of the Nintendo DS to wage war against up to seven other players. Each player must have his own copy of the game.

SENDING DATA

The player sending data must first insert the game card into the DS, then select Advance Wars: Dual Strike from the DS menu screen. When the Wireless menu appears, choose the Download option. Make sure all systems are turned on before you send data.

RECEIVING DATA

To receive data, select DS Download Play from the DS menu screen then choose Advance Wars: Dual Strike and highlight "Yes" when the correct software appears on the game-confirmation screen. Once the download from the game card-equipped DS is complete, you'll see all available play modes.

MESSAGING

You can assign personal messages to each of the system buttons and send them to opponents during battle. Break your foe's concentration with a well-timed joke or scathing barb.

DESIGN ROOM

Craft custom playgrounds of destruction and stage your own battlefield scenarios in the Design Room.

MAP DESIGN

CUSTOM CREATION

Create your own battlefields to use in Versus mode and the wireless modes, or simply trade your works with friends.

SETTING THE SCENE

You'll want to consider a few things when building your own battlefield. To make it an interesting and enjoyable challenge, plan ahead and follow the guidelines presented here.

1 START THE FIGHT RIGHT

Each Versus map will need at least two different-colored HQs to be playable, with one unit or base.

2 EASY MONEY

Create occupied cities for each team to encourage unit-building.

3 NEUTRAL TEMPTATIONS

Include plenty of neutral properties to entice players to compete over land.

4 PRODUCTION POSITIONS

Scatter bases around the map to foster exploration.

5 PIPELINE PRECAUTIONS

If you place a pipeline on the battlefield, be sure to leave ample room to navigate around it, or include joints.

6 HIDE AND SEEK

Placing forests and reefs on your maps will provide great cover for units during Fog of War scenarios.

7 MOUNTAIN MEN

Mountainous maps provide strategic havens for ground troops to shine.

8 EQUAL OPPORTUNITY

Balance each side with comparable forces to avoid lopsided conflicts.

CO DESIGN

FASHION DESIGNER

Gussy up your COs in CO Design mode. You can change the color of the standard outfits and unlock civilian attire for your officers to wear after they reach level 10. (The shirt icon allows you to change into something more comfortable.) Creativity, as always, is encouraged.

DISPLAY DESIGN

WALLPAPER CHOICES

Switch out the background displays for something a little different. Use the Display Design mode to choose your favorite design. You'll earn new wallpapers as you progress through the campaign.

COMMANDING OFFICERS

Commanding officers come in all shapes, sizes and genders (not to mention a robot). Get to know each one's strengths, weaknesses and powers.

TAKE COMMAND

Each CO has an individual personality, along with diverse skills and abilities. The following pages provide some insight into how best to use each one as the game progresses.

MISSION CONTROL

Victory won't come easy, especially for inexperienced COs. With each win, you'll earn points depending upon how well you perform in the field. A good CO will always think ahead and play his strengths against the enemy's weaknesses.

⭐ CO RANKING

You can improve a CO's skill set by using him often. As your officer racks up the points and climbs the ranks, you can equip him with specialized skills. During Dual Strike battles, if you use only one CO your experience is doubled.

INDIVIDUAL STRENGTHS

Knowing an individual CO's strengths and vulnerabilities is crucial when assigning a leader to your forces. Choose wisely.

ATTRIBUTE ADJUSTMENTS

Take a look at the unit data and skills information for each CO when preparing for battle. Equipping skills is a great way to enhance a CO's strengths or counter known weaknesses.

WORKING IN TANDEM

During Dual Strike battles, some CO pairs work better than others. You may want to assign COs with complementary strengths and weaknesses, each countering the other's soft spots. During the fight, switch COs whenever you can play to their strengths.

MIXED SIGNALS

Keep your friends close, and your enemies closer. You'll meet up with some wicked opponents who just might join your ranks out of necessity.

SWITCHING TEAMS

Pairing up COs from different teams creates combinations that give you special CO Powers and firepower or defensive strength. Consider the task at hand and the units in your arsenal before picking your officers.

SPECIAL POWERS

Each CO has powerful skills he can activate in a battle. These CO Powers will build slowly as you attack, defend and capture properties. Using the powers at just the right time can turn the battle from a hopeless quagmire into a landslide victory.

CO POWERS

A CO's default power will become available first in combat. Fill the small stars in the power meter to charge your CO Power, then unleash it at the right moment to inflict widespread damage on your opponent or to boost certain stats of your own squad temporarily.

SUPER CO POWERS

The Super CO Powers are stronger versions of the regular CO Powers. It'll take longer to fill up the power meter, but the result will be worth the effort.

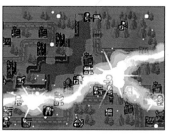

TAG BATTLES

You can activate a Tag Battle during battles in which you're using two COs. The incredible strength of the Tag Battle comes from taking advantage of each commander's Super CO Power, allowing you to move both COs in a single day. This feature can completely change the face of the battle, so use it prudently.

ORANGE STAR

You can purchase Nell, Andy and Hachi in the store. You must complete the Normal Campaign before they become available.

RACHEL

A young Orange Star CO, she strives to follow in the footsteps of her big sister, Nell. She brings a breath of fresh air to her units.

Her troops are quite hardworking, and they increase base resupplies by one.

LUCKY LASS Improves her chance to strike with massive firepower and destroy her enemies. Lucky!

COVERING FIRE Provides covering fire by launching three missiles from Orange Star HQ in Omega Land.

MAX

A brave and loyal friend, not to mention a strong fighter, Max hates any kind of treachery, preferring a good, old-fashioned brawl instead.

Non-Infantry direct-combat units are tops. Indirect-combat troops are reduced in range and firepower.

MAX FORCE Firepower of non-Infantry direct-combat units rises.

MAX BLAST Firepower of non-Infantry direct-combat units rises greatly.

NELL

Rachel's big sister and the supreme commander of Orange Star, Nell is an able commanding officer with a superb sense of fashion.

Nell sometimes strikes with more force than expected. She is the first to tell you she was born lucky.

LUCKY STAR Improves her chance to strike with increased firepower and destroy her enemies. Lucky!

LADY LUCK Improves her chance to strike with massive firepower and destroy her enemies. Very lucky!

ANDY

A whiz with a wrench, this mechanical boy wonder earned fame as the hero who saved Macro Land in the last great war.

Andy has no real weaknesses. He is proficient with air, sea and land units, and is ready to fight wherever and whenever.

HYPER REPAIR Restores 2 HP to all units.

HYPER UPGRADE Restores 5 HP to all units. Firepower rises, and unit movement increases by one space.

JAKE

A young, energetic Orange Star CO, Jake is a top-notch tank commander.

Jake fights well in the open, where the firepower of all of his units are increased on the plains.

BEAT DOWN Firing range of vehicles is increased by one. Firepower of all units is increased on plains.

BLOCK ROCK Firing range of vehicles is increased by one, and movement range by two. Firepower of all units is greatly increased on plains.

SAMI

Sami is a strong-willed Orange Star special forces captain who loves long hair.

Sami's an infantry specialist, so her foot soldiers do more damage and capture faster. Her non-Infantry direct-combat units have weaker firepower.

DOUBLE TIME Infantry units receive a movement bonus of one space. Their attack also increases.

VICTORY MARCH Increases all foot soldiers' movement by two spaces and gives them an attack bonus. They can capture in one turn even if they're not at full HP.

HACHI

Owner of the Battle Maps shop, Hachi is rumored to be Orange Star's former commander in chief.

Hachi uses secret trade routes to get lower deployment costs for all units.

BARTER Speaks with such authority that he obtains even lower deployment costs.

MERCHANT UNION Deployment costs drop. Merchant pals gather from around the globe and help him deploy ground units from any allied property.

BLUE MOON

Olaf can be purchased from Hachi in the store.

SASHA

Colin's sister. Normally ladylike, but becomes daring when she gets angry.

Being the heir to a vast fortune, she gets an additional 100 funds from allied bases.

MARKET CRASH The more funds she has, the more she can decrease the enemy's power meter.

WAR BONDS Earns funds when she inflicts damage on a foe. The greater the damage, the more she earns.

COLIN

Blue Moon's rich boy CO and Sasha's little brother. A gifted CO with a sharp if insecure mind.

Colin is the heir to a vast fortune who can purchase units at bargain-basement prices. His troops' low firepower stems from his lack of experience.

GOLD RUSH Increases deployment funds by one and a half times.

POWER OF MONEY Uses wealth to increase the strength of weapons. The more funds available, the stronger the weapons become.

GRIT

A laid-back style masks his dependability. A peerless marksman. Works well with Olaf.

Grit's range for distance weapons is one space greater than other COs'. They cause more damage, too. Weak in non-Infantry direct combat.

SNIPE ATTACK Increases range of distance weapons by one space. Attack strength of these weapons also increases.

SUPER SNIPE Distance weapons can shoot two spaces farther than normal. They also receive a firepower bonus.

OLAF

Olaf may be a pompous braggart, but his tactical prowess has earned him the respect of his peers and the admiration of his people.

Winter weather poses no problem for Olaf or his troops. Snow causes his firepower to rise, and his troops can move through it with no fuel or movement penalty.

BLIZZARD Causes snow to fall for two days, forcing his foe to consume more fuel.

WINTER FURY A mighty blizzard causes 2 HP of damage to all deployed enemy troops. The snow will also force the foe to use more fuel.

GREEN EARTH

Drake can be purchased from Hachi in the store.

JESS

A gallant tank-driving CO who excels at analyzing information. A hero of the last war.

Under Jess, vehicular units have superior firepower. Air and naval units are comparatively weak.

TURBO CHARGE Movement range of vehicular units goes up by one space. Attack increases, and fuel and ammo supplies are also replenished.

OVERDRIVE Movement range of vehicular units goes up by two spaces. Attack dramatically increases, and fuel and ammo supplies are also replenished.

JAVIER

A Green Earth CO who values chivalry and honor above all else. Often commands his units to charge.

Increased defense versus indirect attacks. When he captures Com Towers, his defense also goes up.

TOWER SHIELD Improves defense versus indirect attacks and doubles the effect of Com Towers.

TOWER OF POWER Improves defense versus indirect attacks and triples the effect of Com Towers.

EAGLE

Green Earth's daring pilot hero. Joined the air force to honor his father's legacy.

Air units use less fuel than those of other armies and also have superior firepower. Naval units have weaker firepower.

LIGHTNING DRIVE Able to move non-Infantry units twice during a turn, but their firepower is cut in half.

LIGHTNING STRIKE Able to move non-Infantry units twice during a turn. No firepower penalty.

DRAKE

A bighearted former pirate who hates fighting. Also a great surfer. Dude!

Naval units have superior firepower, but air units have weaker attacks.

TSUNAMI Causes a tidal wave that does 1 HP of damage to all enemy units and reduces their fuel by half.

TYPHOON Causes a giant tidal wave that does 2 HP of damage to all enemy units and reduces their fuel by half. Produces rain for one full day.

YELLOW COMET

Kanbei can be purchased from Hachi in the store.

SENSEI

A former paratrooper rumored to be quite the CO in his day.

Sensei offers powerful Infantry and high transport movement range. Superior firepower for copters, but naval units have weaker attacks.

COPTER COMMAND Attack-copter firepower increases. Infantry units with 9 HP appear in all allied cities, ready to be moved.

AIRBORNE ASSAULT Attack-copter firepower increases. Mech units with 9 HP appear in all allied cities, ready to be moved.

GRIMM

A Yellow Comet CO with a dynamic personality. Couldn't care less about the details. Nicknamed "Lightning Grimm."

Firepower of all units is increased, thanks to his daredevil nature, but their defense is a little weak.

KNUCKLEDUSTER Increases the attack of all units.

HAYMAKER Greatly increases the attack of all units.

SONJA

Kanbei's cool and collected daughter who likes to plan before acting. She excels in information warfare.

All units have extended vision range in Fog of War. Sonja keeps HP intel hidden from foes. She manipulates info to reduce enemy terrain effects by one.

ENHANCED VISION Increases the vision range of all units by one space and allows them to see into woods and reefs. Reduces enemy terrain effects by two.

COUNTER BREAK Increases the vision range of all units by one space and allows them to see into woods and reefs. Counterattacks are stronger. Reduces enemy terrain effects by three.

KANBEI

The emperor of Yellow Comet. A skilled CO who has a soft spot for his daughter.

All units have high offensive and defensive abilities, but are expensive to deploy.

MORALE BOOST Increases firepower of all units.

SAMURAI SPIRIT Greatly strengthens offensive and defensive abilities of all units. Firepower doubles when inflicting damage in counterattacks.

BLACK HOLE

These Black Hole COs can be purchased from Hachi in the store. You must first finish the Normal Campaign to unlock them for purchase.

VON BOLT

New commander in chief of the Black Hole forces. A mysterious old man who has been alive a very, very long time. The mastermind of the Omega war.

All units have superior firepower and defense.

EX MACHINA Fires shockwaves that paralyze electrical systems and cause 3 HP of damage to all forces in range. Damaged units must skip their next turn.

KINDLE

Jugger and Koal's commanding officer. Has a blunt, queen-like personality.

An upper-crust CO who excels at urban warfare. Firepower of all on-base units is increased.

URBAN BLIGHT Increases the attack of all units on a base. Also inflicts 3 HP of damage to enemy units on bases.

HIGH SOCIETY Greatly increases the attack of all units on a base. The more bases she controls, the more firepower she gains.

ADDER

A self-absorbed CO who believes his skills are matchless. Second to Hawke in rank.

Adept at making quick command decisions, he stores up energy for his CO Power more rapidly than other COs.

SIDESLIP Movement range for all units is increased by one.

SIDEWINDER Movement range for all units is increased by two.

FLAK

The strongman of the Black Hole Army. Promoted from private by Hawke, who was impressed by his natural ability.

Flak has high firepower, but he relies solely on strength. His shoddy technique sometimes reduces the damage his units deal.

BRUTE FORCE Increases dispersion of fire. There is a chance of getting a super-strong blow, but units' firepower might suddenly drop instead.

BARBARIC BLOW Attack power increases dramatically, but so does the dispersion rate, which affects the amount of damage targets take.

JUGGER

A robotlike CO with the Black Hole Army. No one knows his true identity! Gets a little bit smarter when he uses his CO Power.

Jugger has high firepower, but he relies solely on strength. His shoddy technique sometimes reduces the damage his units deal.

OVERCLOCK Increases dispersion of fire. There is a chance of getting a super-strong blow, but units' firepower might suddenly drop instead.

SYSTEM CRASH Attack power increases dramatically, but so does the dispersion rate, which affects the amount of damage targets take.

HAWKE

A CO of the Black Hole Army who will stop at nothing to achieve his goals.

All units possess superior firepower. His CO Power builds up more slowly than those of other COs.

BLACK WAVE All damaged units recover 1 HP. In addition, all enemy units suffer 1 HP of damage.

BLACK STORM All damaged units recover 2 HP. In addition, all enemy units suffer 2 HP of damage.

CLONED COs

Black Hole has managed to clone a few of your allies. Though these doppelgangers resemble your friends, give them no quarter.

Olaf may be a pompous braggart, but his tactical prowess has earned him the respect of his peers and the admiration of his people.
Hit: Warm boots
Miss: Rain clouds

Winter weather poses no problem for Olaf or his troops. Snow causes his firepower to rise, and his troops can move through it with no fuel penalty.

EVIL TWINS

The cloned COs share the same skills as their nonclone counterparts. You can read a CO's dossier in-game by selecting CO from the command list.

OLAF

You'll go up against Olaf's clone in the Dark Ambition mission. See page 68.

KANBEI

Kanbei's evil twin is brought into battle during the Ring of Fire confrontation (page 72).

ANDY

Andy's pasty-faced counterpart shows up in the Surrounded! debacle. You can read about it on page 74.

DRAKE

Drake's clone surfaces in the Pincer Strike mission (see page 70).

KOAL

A CO of the Black Hole Army who is always planning his next destructive act.

Adept at making quick decisions, he stores up energy for his CO Power at a faster rate than other COs. He's a master of road-based battles.

FORCED MARCH Movement range for all units is increased by one space. Units have more firepower on roads.

TRAIL OF WOE Movement range for all units is increased by two spaces. Units have more firepower on roads.

LASH

The wunderkind of the Black Hole forces, she's small but fierce. She invented most of Black Hole's new weapons.

Lash is skilled at taking advantage of terrain features. She can turn terrain effects into firepower bonuses.

TERRAIN TACTICS In addition to using terrain effects to increase firepower, movement cost for all units drops to one.

PRIME TACTICS Terrain effects are doubled and used to increase attack strength. Additionally, movement cost for all units drops to one.

⭐ THE GOOD, THE BAD AND THE UGLY

With so many choices in front of you, picking the right CO for the job is a daunting task. Always assess the combat situation before making your picks. When weighing your options, consider the terrain and the units that both you and your opponent have at your disposal.

TAG BATTLES

Double your pleasure. Double your fun. For the advantage in combat, two COs are better than one!

DOUBLE TROUBLE

Certain missions require you to lead your military with two or more COs. In such events, you have the benefit of pairing up officers whose skills complement each other, and when their CO Power meters are filled to capacity, you can unleash an astonishing Tag Battle attack to really sock it to your enemies.

TEAM UP, TAKE TURNS

Dual Strike battles force you to split up your officers across two fronts. At the beginning of the mission, weigh your options when choosing your pair, especially when the action on the secondary front involves specialized combat (such as an aerial battle). In standard missions, which take place on a single front, you should rotate COs periodically to charge their CO Power meters evenly.

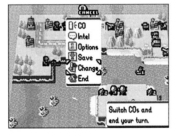

Switch COs and end your turn.

Lander units load and unload units here.

CO SELECTION

Don't toss any pair of officers together unless you have a good reason. Consult the charts on page 15 to see if their skills are compatible or complementary. Examine the battlefield and refer to the Black Hole Intel to get a firm grasp on the situation, then make your CO selection. Whether or not you go with our suggested pairings, it's always a good idea to size up the situation in advance, as having the right COs for the job is crucial to running a smooth military.

STAR POWER

As you lay waste to your enemies and conquer properties across the battlefield, you will fill your current CO's power meter. The more you charge up a CO's meter, the stronger his attack will be when you activate his CO Power or engage him in a Tag Battle. Knowing when to exercise your special attacks can swiftly turn the tide of battle in your favor. On the flip side, squandering your CO Power on frivolous fireworks displays is a bad idea.

Block Rock

TAG-TEAM TIMING

Once your team of officers is rarin' to go with ample CO Power, you're ready for a full-on Tag Battle. When you initiate a Tag Battle, each of your COs will have a turn to attack the enemy. The key to using this special double attack is timing. Don't execute a Tag Battle unless the situation warrants it. If your opponent beats you to the punch, your Tag Battle may counteract the effects by healing some of your units or increasing your units' firepower.

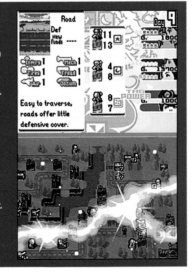

Easy to traverse, roads offer little defensive cover.

COMMAND COMPATIBILITY

Not all COs play nice together. Some possess skills and special attacks that work well individually but lower your military's attack strength. If you want to venture out on your own rather than follow our officer suggestions, get a leg up and refer to the charts on this page.

SUPERIOR STARS

The list below shows various beneficial pairings between different COs. Some couples work together better than others. The more stars you see next to a name, the better the match.

CO	COMBINATIONS		
■ JAKE	■ JESS ✪	■ RACHEL ✪✪	
■ RACHEL	■ JAKE ✪✪	■ NELL ✪✪✪	
■ MAX	■ ANDY ✪	■ GRIT ✪✪	
■ SAMI	■ SONJA ✪	■ EAGLE ✪✪✪	
■ NELL	■ RACHEL ✪✪✪		
■ HACHI	■ SENSEI ✪✪		
■ ANDY	■ MAX ✪	■ HAWKE ✪	■ EAGLE ✪✪
■ SASHA	■ COLIN ✪✪		
■ COLIN	■ SASHA ✪✪✪		
■ GRIT	■ OLAF ✪	■ MAX ✪✪	
■ OLAF	■ GRIT ✪		
■ GRIMM	■ SENSEI ✪		
■ SENSEI	■ GRIMM ✪	■ HACHI ✪✪	
■ SONJA	■ SAMI ✪	■ LASH ✪	■ KANBEI ✪✪✪
■ KANBEI	■ JAVIER ✪	■ SONJA ✪✪✪	
■ JAVIER	■ JESS ✪	■ KANBEI ✪	
■ JESS	■ JAVIER ✪	■ JAKE ✪	
■ EAGLE	■ DRAKE ✪✪	■ ANDY ✪✪	■ SAMI ✪✪✪
■ DRAKE	■ EAGLE ✪✪		
■ LASH	■ HAWKE ✪	■ FLAK ✪	■ SONJA ✪
■ HAWKE	■ LASH ✪	■ ANDY ✪	
■ JUGGER	■ KINDLE ✪	■ KOAL ✪✪	
■ KOAL	■ KINDLE ✪	■ ADDER ✪	■ JUGGER ✪✪
■ KINDLE	■ JUGGER ✪	■ KOAL ✪	
■ VON BOLT			
■ FLAK	■ LASH ✪		
■ ADDER	■ KOAL ✪		

NEGATIVE COMBINATIONS

Certain CO selections result in unhappy marriages. If you match the following COs together, your army will be penalized with weaker attacks during Tag Battles, as indicated by each combination's value percentage. A normal matchup will yield a value of 100%, but a bad matchup can dip as low as 65%. Avoid these combinations unless you encounter a situation in which each CO's individual strength outweighs the Tag Battle penalty.

COs		VALUE %
RACHEL	KOAL	65
EAGLE	HAWKE	70
OLAF	LASH	80
HAWKE	KINDLE	80
VON BOLT	NON-BLACK HOLE	90
EAGLE	LASH	90
DRAKE	HAWKE	90
LASH	COLIN	90
JESS	HAWKE	90
JAKE	KINDLE	90

ADDITIONAL ATTACK VALUE

These CO pairings boost your army's attack power. When matched, these COs have a combined attack value of 105% during Tag Battles.

COs			COs	
NELL	ANDY		SASHA	JAKE
NELL	MAX		SASHA	RACHEL
NELL	SAMI		SASHA	GRIMM
SAMI	ANDY		JAVIER	SENSEI
SAMI	MAX		JAVIER	GRIMM
COLIN	OLAF		ADDER	FLAK
COLIN	GRIT		ADDER	HAWKE *
SENSEI	KANBEI		ADDER	LASH *
SENSEI	SONJA			
JESS	DRAKE			
JESS	EAGLE			

*For these two pairs, the Attack value increases only when Adder activates the Tag Battle.

SPECIAL TAG POWERS

The CO pairings listed below have a unique Tag Battle attack available only to them. These special Tag Battle attacks can devastate your opponent and turn your army into an unstoppable force.

CO COMBINATIONS		VALUE %	POWER NAME
HACHI	SENSEI	100	GRIZZLED VETS
ANDY	HAWKE	105	SHAKY ALLIANCE
SONJA	LASH	105	BRAINSTORM
JUGGER	KOAL	105	POWER SURGE
JAKE	JESS	110	HEAVY METAL
JAVIER	KANBEI	110	CODE OF HONOR
SENSEI	GRIMM	110	ROLLING THUNDER
HAWKE	LASH	110	REBEL YELL
JUGGER	KINDLE	110	FIREWORKS
ANDY	MAX	110	POWER WRENCH
MAX	GRIT	110	BIG COUNTRY
SAMI	SONJA	110	GIRL POWER
JESS	JAVIER	110	GREEN FLASH
KINDLE	KOAL	110	FLASH POINT
FLAK	LASH	110	BRUISE CRUISE
KOAL	ADDER	110	CREEPY CRAWLY
OLAF	GRIT	115	SNOW PATROL
DRAKE	EAGLE	115	STORMWATCH
ANDY	EAGLE	115	AIR LIFT
JAKE	RACHEL	120	ORANGE CRUSH
SAMI	EAGLE	120	EARTH AND SKY
COLIN	SASHA	130	TRUST FUND
RACHEL	NELL	130	WINDFALL
KANBEI	SONJA	130	BATTLE STANDARD

RANKS & SKILLS

Earn valuable rewards as you gain battle experience and rack up points with every victory.

MISSION RANKING

Each mission you complete will earn you points, which you can redeem to purchase items in the Battle Maps store. You'll be judged on the speed at which you complete the mission, the amount and efficiency of damage you deal to your enemies, and the amount of damage your troops receive during the fight.

THE POINTS ADD UP

Your points are tallied at the conclusion of battle, and you'll be awarded one of four ranks (shown on the right). You may also receive bonus points for destroying certain types of enemy units or objects. The bonus points do not count toward your rank.

S RANK
280-300 PTS

A RANK
250-279 PTS

B RANK
200-249 PTS

C RANK
0-199 PTS

INCREASING RANK

The points you earn in each battle also affect the COs who led the fight. After a mission, points are added to a CO's EXP. The more a CO is used in combat, the more experience he will gain and the more skills he will earn.

UP THROUGH THE RANKS

Although it might seem advantageous to use the same CO continually to raise his level faster, it's a good idea to switch officers periodically. That way you can increase his skills and experience evenly with those of his colleagues. Otherwise, you run the risk of having one or two powerful officers, and a whole stable of weaklings.

BATTLE SKILLS

As your COs move up the ranks, they'll earn battle skills that they can equip (up to four at a time) before a battle. The skills are powerful modifiers that enhance an officer's strengths or compensate for weaknesses. Consider the battle conditions and the enemies present when you're equipping skills.

★ EQUIPPING SKILLS

You'll get the opportunity to assign available CO skills (up to four per CO) during CO selection. Examine the available modifiers, then equip the skill(s) of your choice to each officer before you deploy him into combat. Choose carefully—you will be unable to change skills after the mission starts.

SKILLS: RANK 1

 BRUISER
Direct attack +5%

 SHARPSHOOTER
Indirect attack +5%

 SLAM GUARD
Direct-fire defense +8%

 SNIPE GUARD
Indirect-fire defense +8%

 COMBAT PAY
Damage foes to earn cash

LUCK
Random higher damage

SKILLS: RANK 2

 APC GUARD
APC defense +10%

 TOWER POWER
Com Tower effect +5%

 SNEAKY
Dive/Hide fuel cost -1

SKILLS: RANK 3

 TEAMWORK
Tag CO's attack +5%

 SCOUT
Vision +1

 MECHANIC
Base repair +1

 INVADER
Capture +1

 SALE PRICE
Production cost -5%

SKILLS: RANK 4

 ROAD RAGE
Road attack +10%

 RANGER
Woods attack +10%

 URBAN FIGHTER
City attack +10%

 MOUNTAINEER
Mountain attack +10%

 SEAMANSHIP
Sea attack +10%

 BACKSTAB
Dive/Hide attack +15%

SKILLS: RANK 5

 APC BOOST
APC movement +1

 MISSILE GUARD
Damage from silos -1

 CANNON GUARD
Damage from cannons -2

 STAR POWER
Power meter fills quickly

SKILLS: RANK 6

 BODYGUARD
Tag CO's defense +10%

PRAIRIE DOG
Plain movement +1

PATHFINDER
Woods movement +1

 STEALTHY
Dive/Hide fuel cost -2

 GOLD RUSH
Funds from bases +100

SKILLS: RANK 7

HIGH AND DRY
Attack in rain +20%

ICEBREAKER
Attack in snow +20%

SAND SCORPION
Attack in sandstorm +20%

SKILLS: RANK 8

 BRAWLER
Direct attack +8%

 SNIPER
Indirect attack +8%

 SLAM SHIELD
Direct-fire defense +12%

 SNIPE SHIELD
Indirect-fire defense +12%

SKILLS: RANK 9

 SYNERGY
Tag CO's attack +8%

 FIRE SALE
Production cost -8%

SKILLS: RANK ★

 EAGLE EYE
Vision +2

 GEAR HEAD
Base repair +2

 CONQUERER
Capture +2

 MISTWALKER
Hide units during Super CO

 **SOUL OF HACHI**
Deploy in cities in Super CO

TERRAIN INTEL

You'll fight in every environment and weather condition under the sun. Although you can't beat Mother Nature, you can use her to your advantage.

BATTLE GROUNDS

The battlefield can be an ugly, unforgiving place. Combat will have your forces slogging through mud, snow, water, fog, and rocky mountain trails, not necessarily in that order. But it's not all bad—many of Omega Land's natural wonders can give you an advantage in the heat of battle.

THE LAY OF THE LAND

Before you ramp up production at a base, take note of the battlefield. Certain units can harness the environment for a boost in firepower and defense. This holds especially true when duking it out under the Fog of War, where climbing to a mountaintop can greatly increase visibility and the forests can cloak your numbers as you move through enemy territory undetected.

FORECAST FOR DISASTER

Put away that sunscreen, because contrary to the pictures in the recruitment brochure, you won't always fight in ideal conditions. Snow, sandstorms, rain and fog turn the battlefield into a nasty, brutal mess. From decreased visibility to increased fuel consumption, Mother Nature won't hesitate to throw misfortune your way.

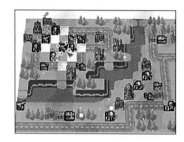

TERRAIN FEATURES

Below is a list of terrain features you will encounter on the battlefields of Omega Land. Each environment has an effect on unit movement, and can provide extra cover that could save you costly losses during a firefight.

AREA FACILITIES

In addition to the natural features of Omega Land, each battlefield contains various manmade structures such as cities and airports. These properties generate funds each day, giving you the ability to manufacture and deploy units. They even provide defensive cover during skirmishes.

 BRIDGE & ROAD
Ground forces travel at top speed on roads and bridges. Bridges are choke points and great spots to make defensive stands.

 FOREST
Offering twice as much cover as plains, forests also slow vehicles down. Units can hide here during the Fog of War.

 MOUNTAIN
On the ground, only Mech and Infantry units can cross mountains, and they are twice as protective as forests.

 PLAINS
Plains will slow vehicle movement slightly and offer little defensive cover.

 REEF
Reefs provide naval units defensive cover during the Fog of War, allowing them to pass unseen.

 RIVER
The shallow water of rivers allows Infantry and Mech units to cross easily, but vehicles must use bridges.

 SEA
The deep water of the seas is open to naval units. The sea won't impede travel and offers little defense.

 SHOAL
The shallow water of shoals can be crossed with any ground unit and offer a loading point for Landers.

⭐ CLIMATE CHANGE

The climates of Omega Land are diverse. While the look and feel of many terrain features will change as you travel the lands, their effect on units will remain constant. Some COs are better suited to certain climate conditions than others, and some, like Olaf, are unaffected by bad weather. Consider the conditions when making your officer selections at the start of a mission.

 AIRPORT
Airports have a great effect on a battle's outcome. Air units will change the face of the war.

 BASE
Bases can produce all types of ground units. Use them to churn out forces for the duration of the battle.

 CITY
Cities generate revenue, provide defensive cover and refuel and repair ground units.

 COM TOWER
Com Towers boost your ground units' attack power. The more you control, the greater the effect.

 HQ
Your HQ is like a king in a chess game: lose it and you lose the battle.

 MISSILE SILO
Missile Silos will allow Infantry or Mech units to launch a missile to damage all units within their blast radius.

 PIPELINE & JOINT
Pipelines will figure prominently into your strategies whenever they appear. You can cross them by blasting through their joints.

 RESEARCH LAB
Research labs often contain plans for new weapons being developed by Black Hole.

 SEAPORT
Seaports are like airports and bases, allowing you to build, repair and refuel naval units.

⭐ FACILITY FUNDS

Each piece of real estate under your control generates income on a daily basis. You'll need these funds to produce reinforcements and supply your existing forces. Capture neutral and enemy properties to boost your net worth and output capacity.

UNIT SPECIFICATIONS

In addition to making tactical decisions, you'll have to stay within budget when cranking out units to augment your army.

LAND UNITS

Throughout the course of the game, you'll have the opportunity to build a variety of land-based units. Some, like the Piperunner, are quite specialized. Others, like Mechs, are great all-purpose fighters. Nothing in war comes free, so consider the benefit versus cost for each unit you intend to produce.

ANTI-AIR

These specialized units are strong against air units, Infantry and Mech units. However, they are ineffective against tanks.

	COST	8,000
WEAPON ONE		**AMMO**
VULCAN CANNON		9
WEAPON TWO		**AMMO**
-		-

| ATTACK | 1 | FUEL | 60 | MOVE | 6 | VISION | 2 |

APC

These units can transport Infantry and Mechs. They can also deliver fuel and ammo to other units. APCs are not armed and therefore can't fire on enemy units.

	COST	5,000
WEAPON ONE		**AMMO**
-		-
WEAPON TWO		**AMMO**
-		-

| ATTACK | - | FUEL | 70 | MOVE | 6 | VISION | 1 |

ARTILLERY

These basic indirect-combat units are relatively inexpensive. They pound enemy forces from a distance.

	COST	6,000
WEAPON ONE		**AMMO**
CANNON		9
MACHINE GUN		INFINITE
WEAPON TWO		**AMMO**
-		-

| ATTACK | 2-3 | FUEL | 50 | MOVE | 5 | VISION | 1 |

INFANTRY

Infantry units are the cheapest to deploy. They can capture properties, but they have scant firepower.

	COST	1,000
WEAPON ONE		**AMMO**
MACHINE GUN		INFINITE
WEAPON TWO		**AMMO**
-		-

| ATTACK | 1 | FUEL | 99 | MOVE | 3 | VISION | 2 |

MECH

These units can capture properties and have high attack power. They are also effective at moving through difficult terrain.

	COST	3,000
WEAPON ONE		**AMMO**
BAZOOKA		3
WEAPON TWO		**AMMO**
MACHINE GUN		INFINITE

| ATTACK | 1 | FUEL | 70 | MOVE | 2 | VISION | 2 |

MEDIUM TANK

Medium Tanks have high offensive and defensive capabilities.

	COST	16,000
WEAPON ONE		**AMMO**
MEDIUM TANK CANNON		8
WEAPON TWO		**AMMO**
MACHINE GUN		INFINITE

| ATTACK | 1 | FUEL | 50 | MOVE | 5 | VISION | 1 |

MEGATANK

The Megatank is the most powerful land unit ever developed. It was designed by the Green Earth army. Its size makes it the slowest of the tanks.

	COST	28,000
WEAPON ONE		**AMMO**
MEGACANNON		3
WEAPON TWO		**AMMO**
MACHINE GUN		INFINITE

| ATTACK | 1 | FUEL | 50 | MOVE | 4 | VISION | 1 |

MISSILE LAUNCHER

The powerful Missle Launchers wreak havoc on air units. Additionally, their vision range on Fog of War maps is also quite large.

	COST	12,000
WEAPON ONE		**AMMO**
SURFACE-TO-AIR MISSILES		6
WEAPON TWO		**AMMO**
-		-

| ATTACK | 3-5 | FUEL | 50 | MOVE | 4 | VISION | 5 |

NEOTANK

A unit based on tank technology and developed by the Black Hole Army, the Neotank is significantly more powerful than a Md. Tank.

	COST	22,000
WEAPON ONE		**AMMO**
NEOCANNON		9
WEAPON TWO		**AMMO**
MACHINE GUN		INFINITE

| ATTACK | 1 | FUEL | 99 | MOVE | 6 | VISION | 1 |

PIPERUNNER

These devastating indirect-combat units were developed by the Black Hole army. They can move only along pipes.

	COST	20,000
WEAPON ONE		**AMMO**
PIPE CANNON		9
WEAPON TWO		**AMMO**
-		-

| ATTACK | 2-5 | FUEL | 99 | MOVE | 9 | VISION | 4 |

RECON

These units are designed for reconnaissance. They are effective against Infantry units and have a large movement range.

	COST	4,000
WEAPON ONE		**AMMO**
MACHINE GUN		INFINITE
WEAPON TWO		**AMMO**
-		-

| ATTACK | 1 | FUEL | 80 | MOVE | 8 | VISION | 5 |

ROCKET LAUNCHER

These powerful units are capable of firing on both ground and naval units from a great distance. Their range of fire exceeds that of standard Artillery units.

	COST	15,000
WEAPON ONE		**AMMO**
ROCKETS		6
WEAPON TWO		**AMMO**
-		-

| ATTACK | 3-5 | FUEL | 50 | MOVE | 5 | VISION | 1 |

TANK

These small, inexpensive tanks have a substantial range of movement, making them easy to deploy in large numbers.

	COST	7,000
WEAPON ONE		**AMMO**
TANK CANNON		9
WEAPON TWO		**AMMO**
MACHINE GUN		INFINITE

| ATTACK | 1 | FUEL | 70 | MOVE | 6 | VISION | 3 |

NAVAL UNITS

Sporting a powerful navy can drastically improve your army's effectiveness, even against land units. Each unit has its share of strengths and weaknesses, which you'll have to consider when deploying your aquatic force.

AIR UNITS

Death from above! You have a host of powerful and agile aircraft at your disposal. While having a superior air force might seem like a major goal, you need to take in to consideration that what goes up must come down. Keep your birds well-fueled and well-armed if you want them to guard the skies.

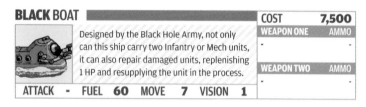

CARRIER

This humongous ship can shelter up to two air units at a time, resupplying them in the process. It also boasts extremely long-range indirect attack capabilities against air units.

	COST	30,000
WEAPON ONE		AMMO
MISSILES		9
WEAPON TWO		AMMO
-		-

ATTACK **3-8** FUEL **99** MOVE **5** VISION **4**

BATTLE COPTER

These copters can fire on many types of units, which makes them invaluable in the field.

	COST	9,000
WEAPON ONE		AMMO
AIR-TO-SURFACE MISSILES		6
WEAPON TWO		AMMO
MACHINE GUN		INFINITE

ATTACK **1** FUEL **99** MOVE **6** VISION **3**

BATTLESHIP

These powerful ships have a tremendous range of fire. Their cannon does incredible amounts of damage to other naval units.

	COST	28,000
WEAPON ONE		AMMO
CANNON		9
WEAPON TWO		AMMO
-		-

ATTACK **2-6** FUEL **99** MOVE **5** VISION **2**

BLACK BOMB

These unmanned aerial weapons were developed by the Black Hole Army. When they explode, all units within three spaces take damage.

	COST	25,000
WEAPON ONE		AMMO
-		-
WEAPON TWO		AMMO
-		-

ATTACK **-** FUEL **45** MOVE **9** VISION **1**

BLACK BOAT

Designed by the Black Hole Army, not only can this ship carry two Infantry or Mech units, it can also repair damaged units, replenishing 1 HP and resupplying the unit in the process.

	COST	7,500
WEAPON ONE		AMMO
-		-
WEAPON TWO		AMMO
-		-

ATTACK **-** FUEL **60** MOVE **7** VISION **1**

BOMBER

Bombers can inflict heavy damage to both ground and naval units.

	COST	22,000
WEAPON ONE		AMMO
BOMBS		9
WEAPON TWO		AMMO
-		-

ATTACK **1** FUEL **99** MOVE **7** VISION **2**

CRUISER

Cruisers can do heavy damage to both Submarine and air units. They can also transport up to two copters at a time.

	COST	18,000
WEAPON ONE		AMMO
ANTI-SUB MISSILES		INFINITE
WEAPON TWO		AMMO
ANTI-AIR MACHINE GUN		INFINITE

ATTACK **1** FUEL **99** MOVE **6** VISION **3**

FIGHTER

Fighters rule the skies, inflicting heavy damage on other air units.

	COST	20,000
WEAPON ONE		AMMO
MISSILES		9
WEAPON TWO		AMMO
-		-

ATTACK **1** FUEL **99** MOVE **9** VISION **2**

LANDER

These transport units can carry up to two ground units at a time. They carry no weapons, but can take a beating.

	COST	12,000
WEAPON ONE		AMMO
-		-
WEAPON TWO		AMMO
-		-

ATTACK **-** FUEL **99** MOVE **6** VISION **1**

STEALTH FIGHTER

Only a unit directly adjacent to a cloaked Stealth Fighter can detect it.

	COST	24,000
WEAPON ONE		AMMO
MISSILES		6
WEAPON TWO		AMMO
-		-

ATTACK **1** FUEL **60** MOVE **6** VISION **4**

SUBMARINE

Only Cruisers and other Subs can attack this unit when it's submerged.

	COST	20,000
WEAPON ONE		AMMO
TORPEDO		6
WEAPON TWO		AMMO
-		-

ATTACK **1** FUEL **60** MOVE **5** VISION **5**

TRANSPORT COPTER

These copters can transport both Mech and Infantry units. They carry no weapons so get them out of the hot zone fast.

	COST	5,000
WEAPON ONE		AMMO
-		-
WEAPON TWO		AMMO
-		-

ATTACK **-** FUEL **99** MOVE **6** VISION **2**

★ OOZIUMS ARE ICKY

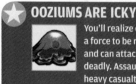

You'll realize on your first encounter with them that Ooziums are a force to be reckoned with. Though they move at a snail's pace and can attack only directly adjacent opponents, Ooziums are deadly. Assault the slimy foes with a large group, or you'll suffer heavy casualties.

★ DIFFERENT BY DESIGN

You may notice differences in the way the same units appear from battle to battle. This is due to the teams' different designs and cultures. Don't worry though; an APC from Yellow Comet will protect troops just as well as an APC from Orange Star or any other force.

STRATEGIC COMMAND

The battlefield is a dynamic war zone where anything can happen. Even so, if you follow these basic strategies, you'll come out on top.

MISSION STATEMENT

Though battles and missions will vary, if you stick to these basic principles you'll remain one step ahead of your foes. Winning the war is a long and arduous task, but each victory will bring you closer to achieving your goal.

- **CAPTURE PROPERTIES**
  Securing properties is an important task in each battle. Properties supply you with daily income and act as "recharge stations" to heal and supply your units.

- **PRODUCE LOGICAL UNITS**
  Knowing which units to produce is a key factor to an efficient victory. Before you build, you must consider the terrain and what enemy units are being deployed.

- **MOVE STRATEGICALLY**
  Every movement on the battlefield will have an effect on what your enemy does, and in turn affects the outcome of the battle. Plot your moves carefully.

- **PLAN OFFENSIVE AND DEFENSIVE MANEUVERS**
  Although it may look great in war movies, charging your enemy with guns blazing isn't always the most effective tactic. You'll need to set up strong defensive lines to prevent your foes from capturing your HQ while you're out in the field, so consider stationing a few units for guard duty.

FIELD STUDY

Consider the terrain features of each battlefield when planning your attacks and setting up a defensive perimeter.

THE HIGH ROAD

Seek cover on mountaintops and in the thick of forests. You'll not only reduce your visibility to the enemy, but increase your defenses, as well. When fighting in the Fog of War, you can gain visibility from on high.

HIGHWAY CRUISIN'

Ground-based units travel the farthest (and fastest) on smooth roads, though they'll be most vulnerable to attack while out in the open. If you take the road less traveled, such as through woods or water, you may incur movement penalties.

LOOK FOR CHOKE POINTS

To reach an objective, you might have to funnel your units through narrow valleys. The same is true for your enemy, so consider staging an ambush or completely blocking access through areas by setting up a choke point.

UNIT INTERACTION

Keep your units strong and well-supplied throughout the battle. This is especially important for missions in which you can't build reinforcements.

UNITED WE STAND

Units of the same type can be combined when they've suffered damage. Joining units will keep your HP high, affording you a better chance of survival.

SUPPLY AND DEMAND

As the battles wear on, fuel and ammo supplies will dwindle. Be sure to keep APCs on hand to resupply any units in need of munitions or gas.

DROPPED AND LOADED

Transport vehicles such as the APC and Transport Copter provide quick, safe travel for your ground troops, and can even tote tanks. Additionally, they provide a temporary diversion, so when your capture team is in danger of getting creamed, place your APC in the line of fire to give the team time to complete its task. When dropping units off, be sure to leave them in the safest space available.

PROPERTY VALUE

Building units takes money, and to fill your coffers you'll need to capture as many properties as you can.

OCCUPIED CITIES

Cities generate daily funds, but they also provide a safe haven where units can replenish fuel and ammo supplies and recover a small amount of HP each day. Units parked in cities are not invincible, but they have elevated defense.

PRODUCTION FACILITIES

Bases, airports and seaports are necessary to manufacture units. Make it a priority to capture as many as you can throughout a mission, unless time is of the essence. Remember that your enemy will likely pursue these pieces of real estate as well.

COUNTERINTELLIGENCE

The Black Hole Army will throw all manner of units at you. While you'll frequently be outgunned, you can still get the upper hand by deploying your equipment astutely.

TANK TOPS

Tanks are highly armored heavy-hitters. Fight fire with fire, sending your own tanks after your enemies. Artillery and Rockets are also effective against the iron beasts, as are Battle Copters and Bombers.

AERIAL ACTION

Aerial units are potent weapons. They can be shot down by other aerial units, Anti-air guns or Missiles. These high flyers have incredible range, so steer your units clear of them unless you're on the offensive.

WATERSPORTS

Naval weapons can turn the tide of a battle, but you can attack them with a variety of ground, aerial and naval units of your own. It's often a good idea to eliminate the enemy's navy early in the fight.

INTRODUCTION

OFFENSIVE STRATEGY

You'll need to follow some simple rules when engaging the enemy in offensive maneuvers if you want to win each battle with minimal casualties. The boxes below detail some simple yet effective concepts that will help you come out on top.

COVERING FIRE
Stage your attacks from the cover of trees, city streets or mountains. You'll not only get the "first to fire" advantage, but your surroundings will boost your defenses against counterattacks.

DOUBLE TEAM
Most times, you'll find it difficult to wipe out an enemy unit in one fell swoop. In that case, weaken your opponent with a unit of equal or greater strength, then stage another assault to finish the job.

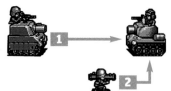

MIX UP YOUR FORCES
Send out small teams of mixed units to ensure you'll have the right equipment available to meet any situation. You won't always be able to see what your opponent has waiting in the wings, so it pays to be prepared.

MOVE IN UNISON
You'll greatly amplify your military strength if you cluster your units in small groups. Try to keep slower units in step with your faster ones when driving through hot zones.

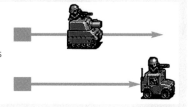

ESCORT SERVICE
Since transport units have no weapons of their own, they're sitting ducks for enemy fire. It's best to escort them whenever possible, keeping them safe from attack as they move troops across the battlefield.

OCCUPY FACILITIES
You can temporarily shut down an enemy's production facility by parking one of your units on top of it. You can convert the facility by capturing it with Infantry or Mechs.

DEFENSE DEPARTMENT

Good defensvie skills are essential on the battlefield. If the bad guys snatch your HQ from under your feet, it's game over. Keep your enemy contained, your units intact and your properties safe from capture. Maintaining a solid defense might sound difficult, but if you follow these guidelines you'll be in good shape.

UNDER COVER
Whether you are the one attacking or being attacked, your defensive stats are increased when you're hiding in the woods, roaming a city or climbing a mountain. It's a good idea to hunker down in one of these spots when the flak gets thick.

PROTECT YOUR ASSETS
Keep your army's economy healthy by retaining (or expanding) your empire. Don't let your enemy steal your real estate, or you'll lose precious income, and limit your manufacturing capabilities and access to convenient safe havens.

PASS DEFENSE
Narrow passes are great places to hold off enemy assaults. Station a few powerful indirect-combat units near the entrance; you can easily destroy your foes as they advance.

SACRIFICIAL STRATEGY
There will be times when you are forced to make the difficult decision of sacrificing a unit to accomplish an objective. Weigh your options fully before giving up one of your own.

COVER FROM A DISTANCE
Protect your Artillery and other indirect-fire units by keeping a Tank or Missiles nearby. If your opponent sends a Tank in to attack, shell it with your guardian unit from a distance.

BEYOND REACH
Check the movement and firing range of enemy units before moving your own. You can delay and sometimes completely avoid unnecessary conflict by moving outside of their reach.

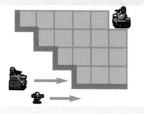

MISSION BRIEFING

To make your job easier, we've broken down each part of a typical mission's walk-through so you'll know how to interpret the mission data.

CAMPAIGN CONTRIBUTIONS

This strategy guide arms you with the information necessary to thwart the Black Hole Army's plans for world domination. How you play the game is up to you, but the following pages will give you a good basis on which to build your attack plans. Each mission is laid out in a format that corresponds with the details on this page.

1 MISSION TERMS

Each mission has conditions for success. You'll find the mission terms and related tips here.

2 OMEGA LAND OVERVIEW

This map shows the location where each battle will take place.

3 VS. BOX

The COs fighting for each side appear here. For battles in which you can choose which CO you wish to use, we've inserted our recommendation for that mission. You may choose to use a different CO or CO combination, depending upon your own strategy style.

4 AREA PROPERTIES

This chart shows the number of each type of property available at the start of the mission. The colored circles indicate which team controls the properties listed, and the Ⓐ column shows a tally of allied properties. You'll also find all neutral (Ⓝ) and Black Hole-controlled (▓) properties listed here.

NOTE: The funds earned from properties owned by different teams are not combined; they count toward that team.

5 BONUS POINTS

Some missions will offer bonus points for destroying certain objects. We'll list the number and type of objects and the total number of bonus points available in each mission.

NOTE: Bonus points do not count toward mission rankings.

6 BLACK HOLE INTEL

It's good to know what to expect from your enemy. That's why we've provided the Black Hole Intel box. It gives you detailed tips on Black Hole's tendencies in each mission.

NOTE: In Hard Campaign mode, these boxes note changes to the Black Hole Army's forces.

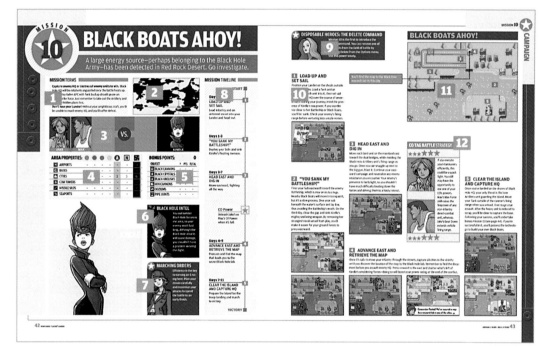

7 MARCHING ORDERS

You'll need to perform well to receive the S ranking at the end of a mission. The Marching Orders box will offer helpful strategies and tips.

NOTE: In Hard Campaign, this box gives details on how your forces have changed since the Normal Campaign.

8 MISSION TIMELINE

The mission timeline gives you an overview of the goals and strategies for each mission. We've specified a range of days in which you should be able to complete each goal and receive a good Speed score at the mission's end. Here you'll also find recommendations for when to use your CO Powers.

NOTE: In Hard Campaign mode, the mission timeline will contain additional strategy.

9 SPECIAL FEATURES

Whenever you come across a new feature or object on the battlefield, we'll give you the lowdown. The more informed you are, the better you'll be at commanding your forces to victory.

10 NUMBERED TIPS

The numbered tips are expanded explanations of the mission timeline. Each corresponds to a location on the map. Since most of the action plays out on the DS's lower screen, we usually include screenshots of only the bottom screen.

NOTE: In Hard Campaign, there are no expanded tips. Numbers on the timeline correspond to ones on the map.

11 BATTLEFIELD MAPS

Every campaign map is included, and we've eliminated all units and Fog of War to give you a clear representation of each area. Note that the allied HQ you see onscreen may differ from what is shown in the guide, because the icon the game displays depends on which CO you used in the previous mission.

NOTE: The maps in the Hard Campaign differ from those in the Normal Campaign.

12 CO POWER STRATEGY

Take advantage of each CO's full powers with the CO Power strategy boxes. You'll find detailed information and tips on when and how to use each CO Power to the utmost effectiveness.

NOTE: In Hard Campaign mode, the CO Power strategy appears only in the mission timeline.

ADVANCE WARS DUAL STRIKE

★ CAMPAIGN

BATTLE FOR OMEGA LAND

There are 28 missions in the Normal Campaign—three of which you can access only by finding secret documents or capturing a particular laboratory. It's a good idea to skim through a mission walk-through before you jump into combat, if only to gain basic intelligence on your opponent or to remind yourself of current objectives. Good luck out there!

JAKE'S TRIAL

It's time for your first lesson in field combat. Get ready to school commanding officer Rachel with a speedy victory.

MISSION TERMS

Destroy all of Rachel's units to win. Though your forces are evenly matched with your opponent's, you have the first-move advantage. The key to a speedy victory is to destroy Rachel's Tanks off the bat. From there, you can shift your attention to her Infantry units. Don't bother capturing any cities just yet, since you won't be able to build units or carry funds into the next mission.

MISSION TIMELINE

START

Days 1-2
ELIMINATE THE TANK UNIT
1

 VS.

JAKE   RACHEL

AREA PROPERTIES:

	●	●	●	○	A	N	✖
✈ AIRPORTS	-	-	-	-	-	-	-
🏠 BASES	-	-	-	-	-	-	-
🏙 CITIES	1	1	-	-	2	3	-
COM TOWERS	-	-	-	-	-	-	-
MISSILE SILOS	-	-	-	-	-	-	-
SEAPORTS	-	-	-	-	-	-	-

BONUS POINTS: 0

OBJECT	#	PTS	TOTAL
BLACK CANNONS	-	-	-
BLACK CRYSTALS	-	-	-
BLACK OBELISKS	-	-	-
MINICANNONS	-	-	-
OOZIUMS	-	-	-
PIPE JOINTS	-	-	-

🌙 BLUE MOON INTEL

Your opponent is a seasoned CO, but since this is your first mission she'll give you some breathing room. You'll face a Tank and some ground troops in the field—hardly a formidable force. Since both armies are evenly matched, this battle will be a quick one.

⭐ MARCHING ORDERS

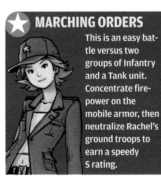

This is an easy battle versus two groups of Infantry and a Tank unit. Concentrate firepower on the mobile armor, then neutralize Rachel's ground troops to earn a speedy S rating.

Days 2-4
DESTROY THE INFANTRY UNITS
2

VICTORY

1 ELIMINATE THE TANK UNIT

Position your Tank unit to the north of Rachel's. You'll deal out more damage as the attacker than as the defender and weaken her unit for your Mechs. Move your Mech unit to the woods south of the enemy Tanks and deal the finishing blow, thus eliminating the armored threat.

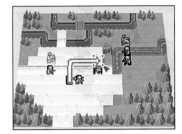

JAKE'S TRIAL

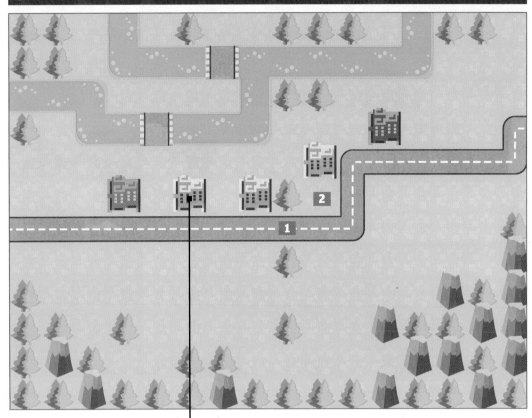

Capturing the cities is optional in this battle. Keep your Infantry moving and on the attack instead.

2 DESTROY THE INFANTRY UNITS

After you've wiped out Rachel's Tanks, head north and target her Mech and Infantry units. They'll likely seek refuge in a nearby city, thus giving them the home-field advantage. Your armored unit and Mech squad should have no problem dispatching your foes within a couple of rounds, though.

★ MAN AGAINST MACHINE: LEVELING THE FIELD

Infantry against Tanks—it's the classic David vs. Goliath scenario. Use Mechs against mobile armor whenever possible, and attack from the cover of woods or from higher ground. You'll get a morale boost as the attacker, so always be the first to initiate such a conflict to increase your chances of survival.

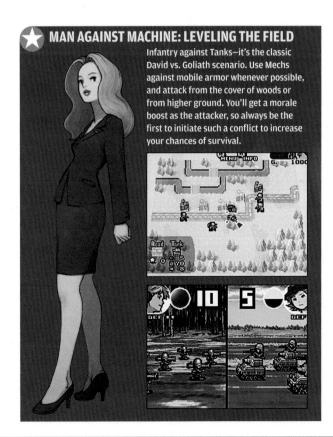

THE NEW BLACK

You encounter the Black Hole Army as its grip tightens over Omega Land. Confront and defeat the enemy.

MISSION TERMS

Destroy all enemy units to win. Use your Artillery to decimate the Black Hole Tank units.

Keep your Infantry unit alive! At the start of the battle, your Infantry is only one man strong. Protect your soldier at all costs. Load your Infantry unit into the APC and head to the city in the southeast for shelter and supplies.

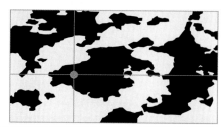

VS.

JAKE

JUGGER

AREA PROPERTIES:

	●	●	●	●	Ⓐ	Ⓝ	✳
AIRPORTS	-	-	-	-	-	-	-
BASES	3	-	-	-	3	-	-
CITIES	-	-	-	-	-	-	-
COM TOWERS	-	-	-	-	-	-	-
MISSILE SILOS	-	-	-	-	-	-	-
SEAPORTS	-	-	-	-	-	-	-

BONUS POINTS: 0

OBJECT	#	PTS	TOTAL
BLACK CANNONS	-	-	-
BLACK CRYSTALS	-	-	-
BLACK OBELISKS	-	-	-
MINICANNONS	-	-	-
OOZIUMS	-	-	-
PIPE JOINTS	-	-	-

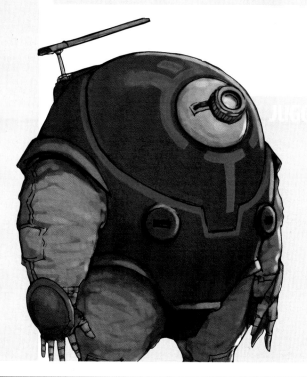

JUGGER

BLACK HOLE INTEL

The Black Hole Tank forces will be bogged down in the woods with limited movement for several days. Use this to your advantage.

MARCHING ORDERS

Exploit the limited mobility of enemy Tanks while they're moving through the forest. Pound them mercilessly with Artillery fire from the south.

MISSION TIMELINE

START ▪

Days 1-2
MOVE THE INFANTRY UNIT TO SAFETY 1

Days 1-4
DESTROY THE ENEMY TANKS 2
Shell them from afar with your Artillery.

VICTORY ▪

1 MOVE THE INFANTRY UNIT TO SAFETY

Your Infantry is in critical shape. March your lone soldier south and load him into the APC. The armored personnel carrier can cover greater distance than other units, provided that it's not moving through mountains and forests. Head to the city in the southeast and unload your troop. A few days in civilization will add reinforcements to this once-ailing unit, far from harm's way.

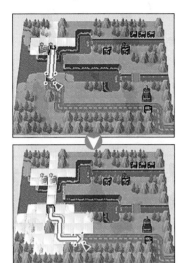

THE NEW BLACK

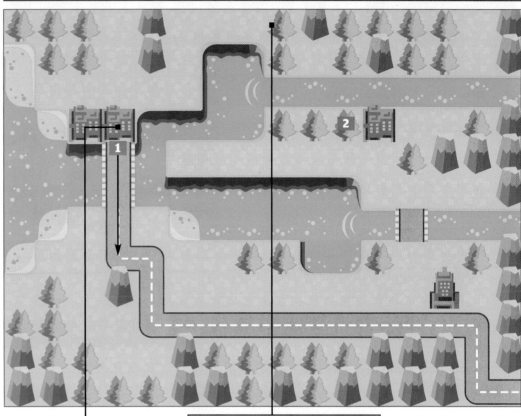

Use your Tank unit to block enemy Tanks from advancing at this choke point.

Your Infantry should flee this location, as it's not far from enemy forces.

2 DESTROY THE ENEMY TANKS

Blast the enemy Tank column from across the river with your Artillery. You should reduce most of them to scrap metal before they move out of range, though some remnants may escape to the west. Position your Tank at the forest entrance to block their escape.

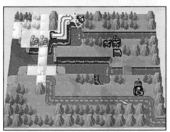

★ **INDIRECT ATTACKS: FURY FROM AFAR**

Indirect fire is a beautiful thing. Though Artillery cannot move and attack on the same turn, it can unleash massive mayhem on enemy units from afar. Familiarize yourself with each unit's firing range, and plan your movement accordingly.

Indirect combat? Cool. Does that mean I can hit those tanks across the river?

MISSION 3

MAX ATTACKS

Big man Max steps up to the plate to help you out, but does he have the guts to withstand Black Hole's newest weapon?

MISSION TERMS

Capture the HQ or destroy all enemy units to win. Given the strength of Lash's armored forces, your easiest path to victory is by capturing enemy HQ. Airlift an Infantry unit inside a Transport Copter, but avoid the Black Bomb at all costs. When it detonates, it'll severely damage all units in the vicinity.

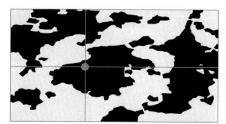

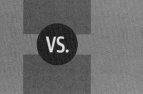

MAX   VS.   LASH

AREA PROPERTIES:

	●	●	●	●	A	N	✕
AIRPORTS	-	-	-	-	-	-	-
BASES	-	-	-	-	-	-	-
CITIES	1	-	-	-	1	-	1
COM TOWERS	-	-	-	-	-	-	-
MISSILE SILOS	-	-	-	-	-	-	-
SEAPORTS	-	-	-	-	-	-	-

BONUS POINTS: 0

OBJECT	#	PTS	TOTAL
BLACK CANNONS	-	-	-
BLACK CRYSTALS	-	-	-
BLACK OBELISKS	-	-	-
MINICANNONS	-	-	-
OOZIUMS	-	-	-
PIPE JOINTS	-	-	-

BLACK HOLE INTEL

Black Hole forces will aggressively attack your cities in the northeast, leaving their HQ wide open for capture.

MARCHING ORDERS

Capturing enemy HQ is your top priority. To do it, you'll need to keep an Infantry unit on the move, preferably inside a Transport Copter or APC.

MISSION TIMELINE

START

Days 1-2
SECURE THE BRIDGES — 1

Days 1-2
DETONATE THE BLACK BOMB — 2
Sacrifice some helicopters and clear the route to enemy HQ.

Days 2-4
MOVE TROOPS TO BLACK HOLE HQ — 3
Fly your loaded Transport Copter to the enemy base.

Days 3-6
ATTACK ENEMY MD. TANK UNITS — 4
Combine your units if necessary and attack the enemy's Md. Tanks.

Days 4-7
CAPTURE BLACK HOLE HQ — 5

VICTORY

1 SECURE THE BRIDGES

Keep your HQ protected at all times. Move an Infantry unit to the city to improve defenses. Relocate your Artillery south of the city to give yourself a good vantage point from which to fire on enemy units as they approach. Lastly, cover the bridge with a Battle Copter.

2 DETONATE THE BLACK BOMB

The Black Bomb can reduce your air force by half if you're not careful. Position your air units to the northwest part of the harbor and coax the bomb to explode from there. Once the Black Bomb is gone, the skies will be cleared for travel, though you will have undoubtedly suffered some casualties. Consider joining multiple helicopter units to concentrate unit strength.

MAX ATTACKS

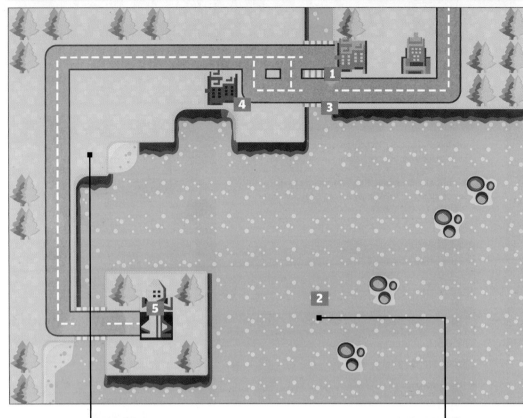

> Black Hole Md. Tanks are no match against a Battle Copter unit at full strength.

> Detonate the Black Bomb early to clear passage to enemy HQ.

3 MOVE TROOPS TO BLACK HOLE HQ

Position your air transport next to your Infantry, then load your ground forces inside. Fly your Transport Copter to enemy HQ and drop off a small invasion force over the course of several turns. Combine your Battle Copters to boost their strength if they were weakened from the Black Bomb's blast. You'll need healthy air units to take on Lash's Tank brigade.

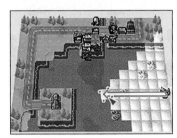

4 ATTACK ENEMY MD. TANK UNITS

Initiate combat with enemy Md. Tank units to retain the "first to fight" advantage. Your air units should have no problem reducing Lash's Tanks to smoldering wreckage, provided you've combined damaged units to boost unit strength. If an enemy Md. Tank retreats to a city, continue the assault and prevent the enemy from receiving reinforcements.

5 CAPTURE BLACK HOLE HQ

The lights are on but nobody's home at Black Hole HQ. Bust down the door and capture the city while the rest of Lash's forces are occupied in the northeast. It'll take your invasion party several turns to claim the base, but by now Lash's forces will be too far off to intervene. Victory is yours!

RECLAIM THE SKIES

A Black Hole missile is headed your way, and time is running out. Destroy the enemy forces before impact.

MISSION TERMS

The missile is closing in! Keep your eye on the clock ticking away on the upper screen. Pause the game if you need time to think.

Destroy all enemy units within 30 minutes to win! A speedy victory is the order of the day. Deploy your forces swiftly and effectively to beat the clock.

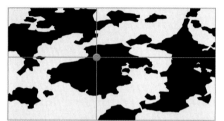

RACHEL   VS.   JUGGER

AREA PROPERTIES: ● ● ● ● Ⓐ Ⓝ ✖

	●	●	●	●	Ⓐ	Ⓝ	✖
✖ AIRPORTS	-	-	-	-	-	-	-
🏠 BASES	-	-	-	-	-	-	-
🏙 CITIES	4	-	-	-	4	-	-
📡 COM TOWERS	-	-	-	-	-	-	-
◪ MISSILE SILOS	-	-	-	-	-	-	-
🚢 SEAPORTS	-	-	-	-	-	-	-

BONUS POINTS: 0

OBJECT	#	PTS	TOTAL
🔲 BLACK CANNONS	-	-	-
🔲 BLACK CRYSTALS	-	-	-
🔲 BLACK OBELISKS	-	-	-
🔲 MINICANNONS	-	-	-
🔲 OOZIUMS	-	-	-
🔲 PIPE JOINTS	-	-	-

BLACK HOLE INTEL

Heavily outnumbered, the Black Hole forces don't stand a chance against you. They'll attack, but won't do much damage.

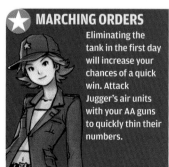

★ MARCHING ORDERS

Eliminating the tank in the first day will increase your chances of a quick win. Attack Jugger's air units with your AA guns to quickly thin their numbers.

MISSION TIMELINE

START ■

Day 1
DESTROY THE
ENEMY TANK UNIT   **1**

Day 1
HIT THE BLACK HOLE   **2**
AIR UNITS

Day 2
FINISH OFF   **3**
YOUR FOES

VICTORY ■

① DESTROY THE ENEMY TANK UNIT

Target your rockets at the Black Hole Tank unit near the bridge. You'll seriously thin the numbers in their armored unit, giving yourself the opportunity to finish them off with your Tank unit from the north. By destroying Jugger's tanks early on, you'll reduce the enemy's offensive power while forging your own path to a quick victory and an S rating.

RECLAIM THE SKIES

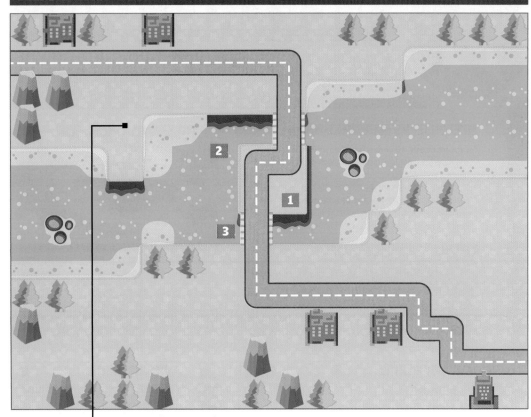

Keep your APC and Infantry units away from enemy fighters—they're defenseless against superior firepower.

② HIT THE BLACK HOLE AIR UNITS

Destroy the Black Hole Battle Copter in one fell swoop with your Missile unit positioned to the north. With the chopper force out of commission, you can concentrate your anti-aircraft fire on the remaining Fighters and Bomber by the bridge. Load your Infantry into the APC and drive away from the firefight, just in case one of Jugger's remaining forces goes on the offensive.

③ FINISH OFF YOUR FOES

Destroy what's left of Jugger's crippled forces with your AA guns, rockets and missiles. The remaining units will turn tail and try to escape, but you should have no problem wasting the cowards before they get to sea.

⭐ DOUBLE TROUBLE: TWO SCREENS OF ACTION

This is the first mission to display combat information (rather than statistics) on the upper screen. While the action rages on the lower screen, you can track the location of the inbound missile above. Check the impact timer periodically so you know just how long you have before it detonates on your city.

NEVERENDING WAR

Black Hole forces have been spotted entering the Tahira Range. Now it's time for a little reconnaissance. . . .

MISSION TERMS

Capture enemy HQ or destroy all enemy units to win.
You'll start this battle at a severe disadvantage, so producing the appropriate units right away is essential for success. The Black Hole units are concentrated largely in the northeast. Focus on capturing the city and the base to the south and producing a few Artillery units with the northern base. Once your army is up to snuff, you can go on the offensive.

VS.

JAKE

KOAL

AREA PROPERTIES: ● ● ● ● Ⓐ Ⓝ ✶

	●	●	●	●	Ⓐ	Ⓝ	✶
🛫 AIRPORTS	-	-	-	-	-	-	-
🏠 BASES	2	-	-	-	2	1	-
🏙 CITIES	4	-	-	-	4	4	4
📡 COM TOWERS	-	-	-	-	-	-	-
🚀 MISSILE SILOS	-	-	-	-	-	-	-
⚓ SEAPORTS	-	-	-	-	-	-	-

BONUS POINTS: 0

OBJECT	#	PTS	TOTAL
🔫 BLACK CANNONS	-	-	-
💎 BLACK CRYSTALS	-	-	-
🗿 BLACK OBELISKS	-	-	-
🔫 MINICANNONS	-	-	-
🦠 OOZIUMS	-	-	-
🔧 PIPE JOINTS	-	-	-

BLACK HOLE INTEL

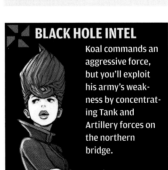

Koal commands an aggressive force, but you'll exploit his army's weakness by concentrating Tank and Artillery forces on the northern bridge.

★ MARCHING ORDERS

Manufacturing the right units is crucial. Start pumping out Artillery and Tank units to defend the northern front. Keep capturing cities with your Mechs to increase your daily earnings.

KOAL

MISSION TIMELINE

START ■

Days 1-3 ①
FIRE UP THE WAR MACHINE

Days 2-5 ②
SECURE THE NORTHERN BRIDGE

Days 3-6 ③
FORTIFY AND DEFEND YOUR POSITIONS
Beef up your military might to stave off the Black Hole forces.

CO Power ★
Beat Down is Jake's weaker power, but it's effective here.

Days 5-8 ④
ENVELOP AND DESTROY FORCES
Sneak some units through the southern region to ensure victory.

CO Power ★
Use Beat Down again, or Block Rock if you've got the energy.

Days 9-12 ⑤
STORM THE BLACK HOLE HQ
If you haven't defeated Koal's forces already, capture the enemy HQ.

VICTORY ■

MULTIPLE CHOICE: COs TO GO

You'll have the option during certain missions to select one or more COs to send into battle. Each commanding officer has unique powers that, when used effectively, can turn the tide of battle. Consider the layout of enemy forces and the local terrain when choosing your officer.

NEVERENDING WAR

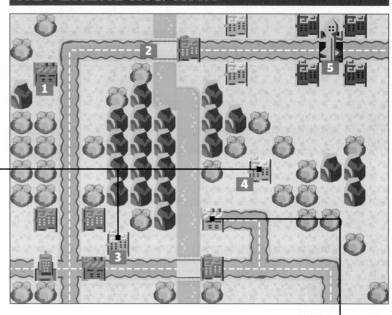

Increase your daily earnings by capturing neutral cities. Added revenue equals increased production.

Capture the southern base and start cranking out Mech units and an APC.

1 FIRE UP THE WAR MACHINE

You begin the battle at a disadvantage, but that doesn't mean you can't turn it around. Manufacture a Tank at the northern base. Move your Mech south to capture the neutral city near HQ. Koal's units will move westward and attempt a power grab—position your newly minted armor on the northern bridge. During the next round, pump out some Artillery. You'll eventually perform a "bait and switch" maneuver by luring enemy units into Artillery range with your Tank as you nudge eastward.

FACTORY FRESH: SMART UNIT PRODUCTION

Don't blindly manufacture random units. Remember, you have only limited daily income and resources, so make your units count. Examine your enemy's forces and crank out units that you can employ strategically and effectively against him to maximize your bang per buck.

CO POWER STRATEGY

★★★☆☆☆

Jake's Beat Down CO power will boost your artillery's firing range, making it easier to waste Koal's forces from afar while you defend the bridge. You should be able to use Beat Down twice during the battle.

5 STORM THE BLACK HOLE HQ

With most of Koal's forces in ruins, make your move on Black Hole HQ. Assuming you have several Tanks and Artillery in the vicinity, you should be able to surgically remove the final stragglers from the battlefield without suffering any casualties of your own. Doing so will boost your Power rating. Truck your Mech landing party to Koal's house and kick in his front door. You're only a couple of turns from imminent victory.

2 SECURE THE NORTHERN BRIDGE

After you push your Tank east to the northern bridge, manufacture an Artillery unit during your next turn. As your Tank moves closer to hostile territory, your enemy's forces will spring to life. Roll your Artillery toward the bridge. As Koal's forces move in, they'll be within prime shelling range of your mighty cannon. Don't stop production at just these two units, however. Continue pumping out Tanks and Mechs while you can, as they will be in the vicinity of the action. Place your Mech and Infantry units in the cover of the forest or atop nearby mountains. This will increase their Defensive rating and protect them against Koal's heavy rollers.

3 FORTIFY AND DEFEND YOUR POSITIONS

Produce a Tank unit at your southern base once you've secured the bridge to the north. Consider manufacturing an APC to deliver supplies to your troops in the field. After you've created a small force consisting of a Tank, APC, and several Mechs, you should have ample coverage in the south. Don't go crazy with production, but learn to use your existing forces effectively. The action in the north is hot by now, with Black Hole forces engaging your Tanks and Mechs by the bridge. Protect your artillery from direct attacks and lay waste to Koal's evil forces from afar. You'll cripple his army in a matter of days.

4 ENVELOP AND DESTROY FORCES

Sweep your southern forces east, destroying any Black Hole opposition you encounter. Capture the base and city in the region to boost your daily income and provide nearby units with reinforcements. Load an assault team (Mechs, preferably) into your APC, and truck north to Black Hole HQ, but be wary of stray Tank or Artillery forces in the area.

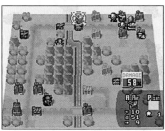

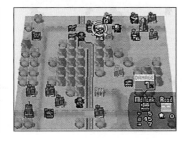

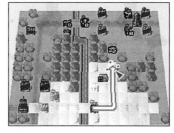

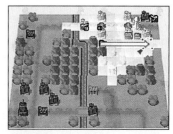

MISSION 6

THE OCEAN BLUE

Not far from the allied forces headquarters, Blue Moon has assembled to meet the advancing Black Hole threat head-on.

MISSION TERMS

Capture enemy HQ or destroy all enemy units to win.
You're up against a strong Black Hole presence here, so the quickest path to victory lies in capturing enemy HQ. To reach their home base, you'll need to transport a landing party across dangerous waters. If you attempt to wipe out Lash's forces, you'll need to keep a constant eye on your force's fuel and ammunition levels.

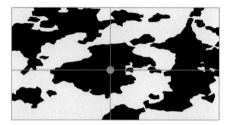

COLIN VS. LASH

AREA PROPERTIES:

	●	●	●	●	A	N	✴
AIRPORTS	-	-	-	-	-	-	-
BASES	-	-	-	-	-	-	-
CITIES	2	-	-	-	2	2	-
COM TOWERS	-	-	-	-	-	-	-
MISSILE SILOS	-	-	-	-	-	-	-
SEAPORTS	-	-	-	-	-	-	-

BONUS POINTS: 0

OBJECT	#	PTS	TOTAL
BLACK CANNONS	-	-	-
BLACK CRYSTALS	-	-	-
BLACK OBELISKS	-	-	-
MINICANNONS	-	-	-
OOZIUMS	-	-	-
PIPE JOINTS	-	-	-

COLIN

✴ BLACK HOLE INTEL

Lash will likely exercise her naval muscle during this fight. Her Battleship is a powerful floating weapon that will cripple any units within firing range.

★ MARCHING ORDERS

A focused, tactical strike against the Black Hole Army should open up its HQ to your landing party. Protect your Infantry at all costs, or risk losing the battle.

MISSION TIMELINE

START ■

Day 1
ELIMINATE THE ENEMY CRUISER ❶
The cruiser is the biggest threat to your Battle Copter. Destroy it first.

Days 1-3
TRANSPORT YOUR INFANTRY ❷
Speed troop transport via Lander and APC.

Days 1-3
ADVANCE AND SECURE A PERIMETER ❸
Contain Lash's naval units and secure a path for your Lander.

Days 2-5
CLEAR THE WAY FOR YOUR LANDING ❹
Protect your troop transport while in transit, and clear the shores.

Days 3-7
SINK THE BATTLESHIP ❺
The Battleship is the deadliest unit here. Be wary of its capabilities.

Days 5-8
CAPTURE BLACK HOLE HQ ❻
Storm enemy shores and claim the Black Hole HQ as your own.

VICTORY ■

■1 ELIMINATE THE ENEMY CRUISER

Lob a salvo of rockets at the enemy Cruiser, then finish it off with an assault from your own. By eliminating the Cruiser first, you'll drastically reduce Lash's ability to attack your Battle Copter. Lash's Rocket unit on shore can target only land and sea units, so your whirlybird is safe from harm.

THE OCEAN BLUE

Load a Tank or Artillery into the APC as support for your landing team bound for enemy HQ.

Blast the enemy navy with rockets, but pay mind to the Battleship's firing range.

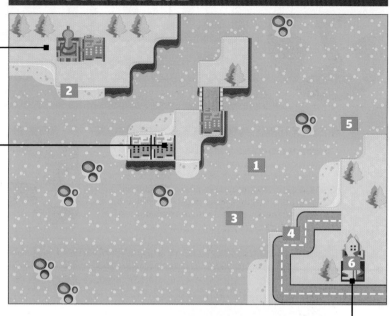

You'll need your Infantry unit intact to conquer Black Hole HQ, so keep your men alive at all costs.

■2 TRANSPORT YOUR INFANTRY

Your Lander can ferry two units at a time. Load your Infantry into the APC, then load the APC into the Lander. You've got space for one more passenger, so consider lugging a Tank or Artillery unit along for the ride. Once on land, the APC can bring supplies to units in the field, whereas the Artillery can protect your soldiers on the ground.

■3 ADVANCE AND SECURE A PERIMETER

Sail your Cruiser and Submarine units east, while keeping them out of firing range of the deadly Battleship. The enemy sub might make a move against either of your vessels, but it's a worthy sacrifice for the greater good. Pound Lash's forces daily until you've reduced them to nothingness.

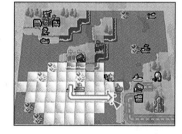

■4 CLEAR THE WAY FOR YOUR LANDING

Fly your Battle Copter onto enemy soil and waste the Black Hole Rocket battery, Tank and Infantry unit. Once the shores are clear, your landing party will have no trouble capturing Lash's HQ. It should take you only two turns once your men have stormed the city gates.

■5 SINK THE BATTLESHIP

Once your landing crew is safely ashore, surround Lash's Battleship with direct-attack units and start pounding. You can lock it between the shoreline and your sea units and chip away at its ample health over the course of several days.

■6 CAPTURE BLACK HOLE HQ

The Black Hole Army's forces are nearly decimated, though you've likely taken some heavy casualties yourself. Move your men to enemy HQ and start your assault. Remember, as long as you keep your Infantry in one piece, success is virtually guaranteed. If you've got firepower to spare, send your Battle Copter after the tattered remnants of Lash's forces.

FOG ROLLS IN

A rolling fog enshrouds the Black Hole forces as the Allied Army approaches....

MISSION TERMS

Capture the HQ or destroy all enemy units to win. The battlefield is cloaked in the Fog of War, obscuring enemy unit locations. You'll need to progress slowly, creeping across the battlefield in a strong, tight-knit formation. Reveal enemy positions before they can ambush you, while keeping an eye on their every movement. Use forests and reefs to conceal your position, but be wary of ambushes from these areas.

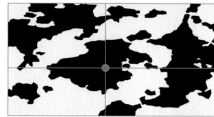

SASHA **VS.** KOAL

AREA PROPERTIES:

	●	●	●	◐	Ⓐ	Ⓝ	✴
✈ AIRPORTS	-	-	-	-	-	-	-
🏠 BASES	-	-	-	-	-	-	-
🏙 CITIES	2	-	-	-	2	2	2
📡 COM TOWERS	-	-	-	-	-	-	-
◪ MISSILE SILOS	-	-	-	-	-	-	-
🚢 SEAPORTS	-	-	-	-	-	-	-

BONUS POINTS: 0

OBJECT	#	PTS	TOTAL
🔲 BLACK CANNONS	-	-	-
🔲 BLACK CRYSTALS	-	-	-
🔲 BLACK OBELISKS	-	-	-
🔲 MINICANNONS	-	-	-
🔲 OOZIUMS	-	-	-
🔲 PIPE JOINTS	-	-	-

✴ BLACK HOLE INTEL

The Black Hole Infantry will capture your cities in the northeastern sector—let them fall. Your immediate focus should be on the several hidden units scattered on the battlefield.

★ MARCHING ORDERS

Patience is key to victory. Note the locations of all known Black Hole units—even those in hiding. Destroy Koal's Artillery and use the Fog of War and environmental cover to your advantage.

MISSION TIMELINE

START ■

Days 1-3 ❶
EXPOSE AND ATTACK NEARBY ENEMY UNITS
Black Hole Artillery is the immediate threat that must be destroyed.

Days 2-6 ❷
CAPTURE THE SOUTHERN CITIES
Your own cities will fall, so even the score with new real estate.

Days 3-7 ❸
SEEK AND DESTROY (WITH CAUTION)
Proceed methodically, as the Fog of War hides Black Hole forces.

Days 4-9 ❹
HEAD NORTH AND EXTERMINATE
Continue routing Koal's units methodically.

Days 7-11 ❺
DROP YOUR TROOPS AND CAPTURE HQ
Destroy Koal's Artillery before invading Black Hole HQ with troops.

VICTORY ■

LIMITED VISIBILITY: THE FOG OF WAR

The Fog of War clouds battlefield visibility, so you must plan your moves carefully. Each unit's range of vision varies. Terrain such as woods and reefs conceal forces, hiding them from view until an opponent reaches an adjacent square. Be wary when moving forces near these locations—an ambush could strike at any time.

You can only see stuff that's in a lighted area. It's the same deal for the enemy. ▽

FOG ROLLS IN

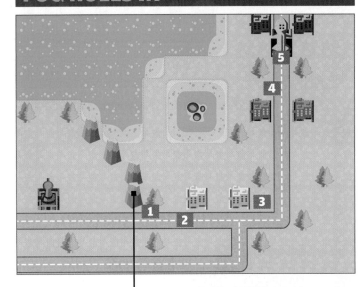

Climb the mountain to gain a high-ground advantage while exposing the Artillery in the forest nearby.

1 EXPOSE AND ATTACK NEARBY ENEMY UNITS

Position your Infantry unit in the mountain range and expose the enemy Artillery hiding in the adjacent forest. Once it's exposed, move in and attack swiftly, thus destroying one of Koal's most powerful (and valuable) units on the battlefield. Load your Mech into the APC and head to the southeast sector.

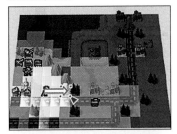

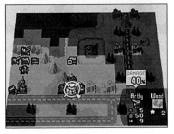

2 CAPTURE THE SOUTHERN CITIES

With Koal's Artillery gone, you're clear to invade the southern-central cities. Hold your ground for a day or two, using the buildings and forests for cover. Koal will send in reinforcements, but you'll have the upper hand. Your Artillery and Rocket units can blast them from afar as they approach. Keep your APC safely hidden in the trees and cities, exposing it only when necessary to supply units with fuel or ammunition.

3 SEEK AND DESTROY (WITH CAUTION)

Creep eastward, securing the large south-eastern area of the battlefield as you go. A Black Hole Tank unit will pose a minor threat. Eliminate it quickly. Other enemy units will show up to the party, including a landing force inside an APC. Deal with them swiftly and clear the area. Sweep the forests and smoke out Koal's units as you prepare for your final push to enemy HQ.

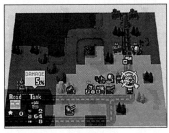 

4 HEAD NORTH AND EXTERMINATE

Truck your Recon unit north and expose the remainder of the battlefield. Enemy Artillery waits in the forest near Koal's HQ. Expose it quickly and move in for the kill. The reef in the small pond hides an enemy Lander. Although it poses no threat, its heavy armor makes it tough to destroy. Just ignore it for now. Continue the push on HQ and hit Koal where it hurts!

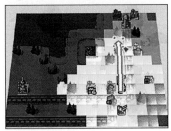 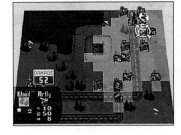

5 DROP YOUR TROOPS AND CAPTURE HQ

After you lay waste to Koal's Artillery, swing your APC into town and unload your troops. By this point, it's up to you to decide how to score a win. You can concentrate fire on the Lander parked in the reef and wipe out Koal's entire force, or you can capture HQ and raise your flag over the capitol. Either way, victory is in the bag.

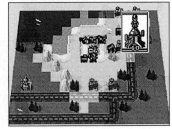

TAG BATTLE

Intelligence reports show Black Hole movement in the area. Expect fierce fighting and a new unit from the enemy.

MISSION TERMS

Capture the HQ or destroy all enemy units to win. This will be your most challenging fight to date. Assemble your forces and attack from several key locations to pierce the Black Hole fronts and capture its HQ. Destroying every enemy unit will be a tough task, since they'll likely have at least two bases cranking out units early on. Furthermore, you'll be up against the duo of destruction—Jugger and Lash.

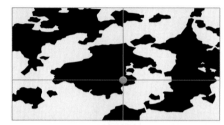

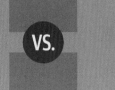

VS.

JAKE — JUGGER — LASH

AREA PROPERTIES:

		●	●	●	●	A	N	✖
✖	AIRPORTS	-	-	-	-	-	1	-
⌂	BASES	2	-	-	-	2	4	1
⌂	CITIES	3	-	-	-	3	10	1
✖	COM TOWERS	-	-	-	-	-	-	-
◢	MISSILE SILOS	-	-	-	-	-	-	-
⬚	SEAPORTS	-	-	-	-	-	-	-

BONUS POINTS: 0

OBJECT	#	PTS	TOTAL
BLACK CANNONS	-	-	-
BLACK CRYSTALS	-	-	-
BLACK OBELISKS	-	-	-
MINICANNONS	-	-	-
OOZIUMS	-	-	-
PIPE JOINTS	-	-	-

BLACK HOLE INTEL

Neutralize the Piperunner early—it will aggressively police the areas near the western bases during the first few days of combat.

★ MARCHING ORDERS

Cripple the Black Hole Army's manufacturing ability to ensure a speedy win. Protect your Infantry and Mechs with Tanks or Rockets to keep them safe.

MISSION TIMELINE

START ■

Days 1-4
BUILD FORCES AND ATTACK THE PIPERUNNER 1
A single Tank unit can eliminate the Piperunner in the first four days.

Days 3-6
HEAD SOUTH AND SNATCH THE AIRPORT 2
Claim the skies and gain the advantage; just watch for enemy AA guns.

CO Power ★
Jake's Beat Down power works well here.

Days 3-9
SECURE THE CENTRAL BATTLEFIELD AREA 3
Claim the bases and secure the bridges to fortify your position.

Days 5-8
SECURE A STRONG PERIMETER 4
Secure the eastern and western flanks to surround your enemies.

CO Power ★

Days 7-13
OUTFLANK THE ENEMY FORCES 5
Move in several strong units from the flank.

Days 11-18
DECIMATE THE OPPOSITION 6
Wipe out the remainder of the Black Hole forces or capture enemy HQ.

VICTORY ■

1 BUILD FORCES AND ATTACK THE PIPERUNNER

Build two Infantry units the first day and conserve some funds to build a Tank the next. Capture the neutral properties to the north and east of your HQ. The city to the south of HQ is in range of the Piperunner, so ignore it for now. Conceal your Tank in the forest at point 1 on the map and bide your time for the impending assault on the fourth day. Crank out additional Infantry and a Tank on days three and four to bolster your expansion plans—just be sure to stay out of the Piperunner's firing range when moving your units. The eastern zone is devoid of enemy forces, so move in and claim all neutral bases and cities. Once you destroy the Piperunner, head south with Infantry. Send along a Tank to support your troops.

3 SECURE THE CENTRAL BATTLEFIELD AREA

Move a capture team consisting of Infantry and a Tank in the vicinity of the base by the bridge. Its central location will allow you to produce units and move them to the front line, hastening your capture of Black Hole HQ dramatically. Enemy forces have their eye on the strategically located property, so grab it before the opposition does. Once you've got the cash, produce several Rocket units to guard the bridges. Hold enemy forces at bay as you continue to build up your forces. Continue capturing the cities and base in the northeast while you produce Tank and Rocket units to bolster your defenses against the advancing Black Hole forces.

TAG BATTLE

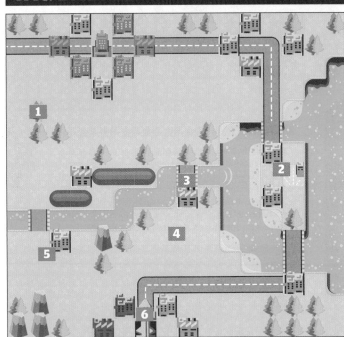

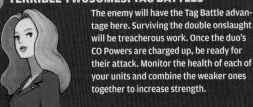

2 HEAD SOUTH AND SNATCH THE AIRPORT

Load Infantry into an APC and head toward the airport. Escort your transport with a Tank, just in case you run into hostile forces. Capturing the airport gives you a huge tactical advantage that allows you to produce air units. Produce a Bomber to gain air superiority and shorten the fight.

With that airport we just captured, we can now build air units.

CO POWER STRATEGY

★★★★★★

Jake's CO Power, Beat Down, will boost your Artillery's firing range, which will help you defend the bridges from the advancing Black Hole threat. You should be able to unleash Beat Down twice during the conflict.

⭐ TERRIBLE TWOSOMES: TAG BATTLES

The enemy will have the Tag Battle advantage here. Surviving the double onslaught will be treacherous work. Once the duo's CO Powers are charged up, be ready for their attack. Monitor the health of each of your units and combine the weaker ones together to increase strength.

5 OUTFLANK THE ENEMY FORCES

When you've whittled the enemy army down a notch, position some units in the southeastern zone (see the image below). Catch your foes off guard while they are distracted to the west. Hold your ground near the center base, and move a few units from the west farther south to stave off any units birthed from Black Hole bases. Continue to envelop your enemy, sending some indirect-fire units for added strength. Have an APC loaded with a landing party trail behind. When the opportunity presents itself, your strike force will be ready to act on HQ.

6 DECIMATE THE OPPOSITION

Escort your APC with some heavy firepower; a Bomber, Tank and Rocket unit should suffice. Once you've ensured your Infantry's safety, unload your troops and make your move on Black Hole headquarters. It's possible that during your final push you can wipe out the remainder of Jugger's and Lash's forces. Capture Black Hole HQ or eliminate all enemy units—either path to victory is fine, as long as you ultimately drive the enemy from the region. Keep an eye open for stray Black Hole Infantry units as you advance each day—if any sneak their way to your HQ, the tide of battle could turn quickly against you.

4 SECURE A STRONG PERIMETER

After you've secured the central bases and airport, bulk up your defenses to ward off the incoming Black Hole forces. You must maintain control of this region if you want to win easily.

VICTORY OR DEATH!

The Black Crystal is bleeding the planet dry. Take down the Black Arc flying fortress and destroy the sinister gem.

MISSION TERMS

Take out the Black Crystal to win. A narrow pass through the mountains is your only land route to the heavily protected Black Crystal. You'll need to win the air battle on the secondary front to have any chance of flying through the pass unscathed. You can't control the action high in the sky, but you can establish a general strategy. When Rachel joins you on the main front, you can do some Tag Battle damage.

JAKE RACHEL **VS.** KOAL LASH

AREA PROPERTIES:

	●	●	●	●	Ⓐ	Ⓝ	✖
🛫 AIRPORTS	-	-	-	-	-	1	-
🏠 BASES	1	-	-	-	1	3	-
🏙 CITIES	4	-	-	-	4	12	-
📡 COM TOWERS	-	-	-	-	-	-	-
🚀 MISSILE SILOS	-	-	-	-	-	-	-
⚓ SEAPORTS	-	-	-	-	-	-	-

BONUS POINTS: 20

OBJECT	#	PTS	TOTAL
🔲 BLACK CANNONS	-	-	-
🔲 BLACK CRYSTALS	1	20	20
🔲 BLACK OBELISKS	-	-	-
🔲 MINICANNONS	-	-	-
🔲 OOZIUMS	-	-	-
🔲 PIPE JOINTS	-	-	-

✖ BLACK HOLE INTEL

Black Hole forces outnumber yours, and they'll have the upper hand at first. You'll need to build units and defend yourself from their advances until you blast the Black Arc from the sky.

★ MARCHING ORDERS

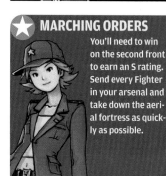

You'll need to win on the second front to earn an S rating. Send every Fighter in your arsenal and take down the aerial fortress as quickly as possible.

MISSION TIMELINE

START

Day 1
1
SPLIT YOUR FORCES, FIGHT TWO FRONTS
Send some aerial units skyward in a bid to win the second front quickly.

Days 1-3
2
DEFEND YOUR TURF AND SUPPORT THE AIR
Send a Bomber to the second front while you prepare for ground assault.

Days 4-8
3
STAGE AN ASSAULT TEAM NEAR THE PASS
When it's safe, produce a few Md. Tanks for a raid.

CO Power ★
Save your CO Power until you can use it in a Tag Battle.

Days 4-10
4
WEAKEN YOUR ENEMY
Attack the units that are guarding the Black Crystal.

Days 9-12
5
DESTROY THE BLACK CRYSTAL
Once you have a few Md. Tanks at the ready, it's clobberin' time.

VICTORY

1 SPLIT YOUR FORCES, FIGHT TWO FRONTS

Send every available Fighter to the secondary front. You'll need to concentrate your air power to thwart the Black Arc and its guardian aircraft. Prioritize the capture of the airport and base near your HQ. Weaken the enemy AA gun with your Tank, then finish it off with a strike from one of your Bombers.

VICTORY OR DEATH!

SECONDARY FRONT

Beware of additional Fighters patrolling the skies behind the aerial fortress—they'll eventually attack you.

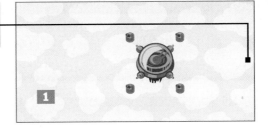

MAIN FRONT

Capture this airport and produce a Fighter, which you'll send to the secondary front.

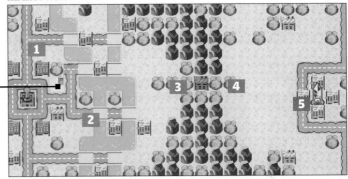

2 DEFEND YOUR TURF AND SUPPORT THE AIR

Capture cities with your Infantry; you'll need to maximize daily earnings to feed the war machine. Save your cash until you have enough funds to produce another Fighter to reinforce the secondary front. Use a Bomber to eliminate enemy Infantry in the mountains north of your base to keep it safe from capture. It is important that you retain this production facility. Mind the Black Arc's bomb zone, along with enemy Fighter and AA units near the Black Crystal.

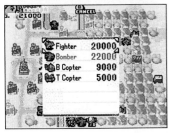

3 STAGE AN ASSAULT TEAM NEAR THE PASS

Continue capturing real estate and manufacturing units while the battle rages overhead. Build an assault team consisting of extra Infantry, a few Tanks or Md. Tanks and an APC for supply runs, along with indirect-attack units such as Artillery or Rockets. Stage your assault force near the mountain pass, where they'll be sheltered from falling bombs. Send your remaining Infantry eastward along the northern and southern borders. This should prevent the Black Hole Army from capturing bases while you tip the scales in your favor.

4 WEAKEN YOUR ENEMY

Slip through the mountain pass once the Black Arc is destroyed. Produce additional units if necessary. You'll face light resistance from Black Hole AA guns and Recon units, but they'll be cannon fodder for your Md. Tanks and aerial units. Send in Infantry to guard each property in the area from attack. Divide the Black Hole ground forces and prepare to conquer what's left of the dwindling army.

⭐ EVIL ENHANCEMENT: BLACK CRYSTAL

Each day, the Black Crystal reinforces any Black Hole units within two spaces of it. This can be a difficult obstacle to overcome, especially when it's surrounded by powerful units. Be sure to move in carefully and with enough firepower to conquer the zone quickly.

⭐ TWICE AS NICE: TAG BATTLE AND CO SWAP

Once you've secured victory on the secondary front, the CO leading that fight will join you on the main front. This gives you the ability to swap COs and Tag Battle when your CO's power is full. When you choose Tag Battle, remember to swap COs before ending your turn.

5 DESTROY THE BLACK CRYSTAL

Your primary objective is to destroy the Black Crystal, so stay focused on your mission as enemy forces scatter. A Neotank or a pair of Md. Tanks will make short work of Black Hole's resource-draining crystal. Ignore your enemy's remaining units—their Artillery and AA guns will likely retreat to a distant corner of the battlefield once your heavy hitters move into the neighborhood.

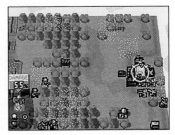

BLACK BOATS AHOY!

A large energy source—perhaps belonging to the Black Hole Army—has been detected in Red Rock Desert. Go investigate.

MISSION TERMS

Capture enemy HQ or destroy all enemy units to win. Black Hole HQ will be relatively unguarded once the battle heats up. An Infantry-laden APC with Tank backup should prove an ample strike force. Just remember to take out the Artillery and grab the hidden plans first.

Don't lose your Lander! Without your amphibious craft, you'll be unable to reach enemy HQ, and you'll suffer defeat.

VS.

JAKE   MAX

KINDLE

AREA PROPERTIES:

	●	●	●	○	Ⓐ	Ⓝ	✳
✈ AIRPORTS	-	-	-	-	-	-	-
🏠 BASES	-	-	-	-	-	-	-
🏙 CITIES	2	-	-	-	2	3	6
📡 COM TOWERS	-	-	-	-	-	-	-
⬜ MISSILE SILOS	-	-	-	-	-	-	-
⚓ SEAPORTS	-	-	-	-	-	-	-

BONUS POINTS: 0

OBJECT	#	PTS	TOTAL
🔲 BLACK CANNONS	-	-	-
▢ BLACK CRYSTALS	-	-	-
▣ BLACK OBELISKS	-	-	-
▤ MINICANNONS	-	-	-
▥ OOZIUMS	-	-	-
▦ PIPE JOINTS	-	-	-

✳ BLACK HOLE INTEL

You outnumber Black Hole forces in the area, so your enemy won't last long. Although the Black Hole attacks will cause damage, you shouldn't have a problem winning this fight.

⭐ MARCHING ORDERS

Efficiency is the key to earning an S rating here. Plan your moves carefully and maximize your attacks to speed the battle to an early finish.

MISSION TIMELINE

START ▪

Days 1-3
LOAD UP AND SET SAIL
Load Infantry and an armored escort into your Lander and head out.

Days 1-3 2
"YOU SANK MY BATTLESHIP!"
Deploy your Subs and sink Kindle's floating menace.

Days 3-7 3
HEAD EAST AND DIG IN
Move eastward, fighting all the way.

CO Power ★
Unleash Jake's or Max's CO Power when it's full.

Days 4-9 4
ADVANCE EAST AND RETRIEVE THE MAP
Press on and find the map that leads you to the secret Black Hole lab.

Days 7-11 5
CLEAR THE ISLAND AND CAPTURE HQ
Prepare the island for the troop landing and march to victory.

VICTORY ▪

DISPOSABLE HEROES: THE DELETE COMMAND

Mission 10 is the first to introduce the Delete command. You can remove one of your units from the field of battle by selecting Delete from the Options menu. Use this power wisely.

BLACK BOATS AHOY!

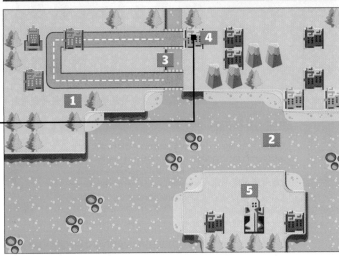

You'll find the map to the Black Hole research lab in this city.

1 LOAD UP AND SET SAIL

Position your Lander on the shoals outside your home area. Load a Tank and an Infantry or Mech unit into it, then set sail for Black Hole HQ over the course of several days. During your journey, mind the presence of Kindle's sea power. If you wander too close to her Battleship or Black Boats, you'll be sunk. Check your enemy's firing range before venturing into unsafe waters.

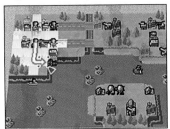

2 "YOU SANK MY BATTLESHIP!"

Float your Sub eastward toward the enemy Battleship, which is now on its last legs. Nearby Black Boats will move in to repair it, but it's a slow process. Dive your sub beneath the water's surface and lay low, thus avoiding the Battleship's wrath. On the third day, close the gap and sink Kindle's mighty seafaring weapon. By removing her strongest naval vessel from play, you'll make it easier for your ground forces to press eastward.

3 HEAD EAST AND DIG IN

Move each land unit on the mainland east toward the dual bridges, while minding the Black Hole Artillery unit's firing range as you go. Once you can snuggle up next to the big gun, blast it. Continue your eastward campaign and neutralize any enemy resistance you encounter. Your enemy's presence is fairly light, so you shouldn't have much difficulty beating down the forces and driving them to a hasty retreat.

4 ADVANCE EAST AND RETRIEVE THE MAP

Once it's safe to move your Infantry through the streets, capture all cities in the vicinity until you discover the location of the map to the Black Hole lab. Remember to find the document before you assault enemy HQ. Press onward to the east and shatter what's left of Kindle's smoldering forces—doing so will boost your power rating at the end of the conflict.

Commander Rachel! We've secured a map to a research lab in one of the cities.

CO TAG BATTLE STRATEGY

★★★★☆☆☆

If you execute your maneuvers efficiently, this could be a quick fight. You still may have the opportunity to use one of your CO's powers. Max's Max Force skill raises the firepower of any non-Infantry direct-combat unit, whereas Jake's Beat Down extends vehicle firing range.

★★★★★☆☆

5 CLEAR THE ISLAND AND CAPTURE HQ

Once you've landed on the shores of Black Hole HQ, your only threat is the lone Artillery unit guarding the island. Move your Tank outside of the cannon's firing range when you unload, then stage your assault. After the heavy unit is reduced to scrap, you'll be clear to capture the base. Following your success, you'll undertake bonus mission 11 (see page 44). If you're successful in it, you'll possess the technology to build your own Black Boats.

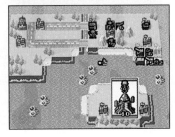

THE LONG MARCH

Plans in hand, you chase the Black Hole Army to its hidden laboratory. The enemy is cornered, and ready for a fight.

MISSION TERMS

Capture the lab or destroy all enemy units to win. This is another conflict that'll take careful planning and firm resolve to overcome. Your indirect-fire units—Artillery and Rockets—will be your best defense against the aggressive Black Hole forces, who by now are hell-bent on protecting their Black Boat technology.

JAKE   SASHA

VS.

RACHEL   COLIN

JUGGER   KOAL

AREA PROPERTIES:

		●	●	●	●	A	N	✦
🛩	AIRPORTS	-	-	-	-	-	2	-
🏠	BASES	-	2	-	-	2	2	-
🏙	CITIES	4	1	-	-	5	10	2
📡	COM TOWERS	-	-	-	-	-	-	-
▨	MISSILE SILOS	-	-	-	-	-	-	-
⚓	SEAPORTS	-	1	-	-	1	-	-

BONUS POINTS: 0

OBJECT	#	PTS	TOTAL
🔲 BLACK CANNONS	-	-	-
🔲 BLACK CRYSTALS	-	-	-
🔲 BLACK OBELISKS	-	-	-
🔲 MINICANNONS	-	-	-
🔲 OOZIUMS	-	-	-
🔲 PIPE JOINTS	-	-	-

RACHEL

BLACK HOLE INTEL

You'll deal with all manner of Black Hole units in this fight. To make matters worse, the Fog of War will obscure your long-range vision, so you'll need to probe carefully.

MARCHING ORDERS

You'll fight much of this battle on the high seas. Remember to keep your vessels away from powerful indirect-fire units on land.

MISSION TIMELINE

START

Days 1-4
SCOUT AHEAD AND SHELL THE ENEMY ①
The Fog of War will hinder your vision. Scout ahead and find your enemies.

Days 3-6
PRESS EAST AND HOLD YOUR GROUND ②
The Black Hole Army has some strong units. Bulk up your forces.

CO Power ★
By now, you should be charged up and ready to rock.

Days 3-9
BEGIN THE NAVAL ASSAULT ③
Claiming the bases and securing the bridges will strengthen your position.

Days 3-9
ADVANCE AND PREPARE FOR A RAID ④
Move stealthily under the cover of fog and advance toward enemy HQ.

CO Power ★

Days 5-8
SECURE THE SEAS AND GAIN THE EDGE ⑤
Sneak a few units through the southern region to ensure your victory.

Days 9-12
CAPTURE THE LAB, FIND THE PLANS ⑥
Capture the lab before you lay waste to the last enemy unit.

VICTORY

1 SCOUT AHEAD AND SHELL THE ENEMY

The Black Hole forces are concentrated on the southern peninsula, between Orange Star HQ and Blue Moon HQ. Attack visible enemies with your Artillery and Rocket units. Truck your Recon unit, presently stationed at the city in the east, to the forest in the south to improve visibility. Fire your Rocket on the Sub in the harbor. Back at Orange Star HQ, load your Mech into the APC and drive northeast toward the factories. Send a scout ahead of them, along with a Tank unit for support. March an Infantry unit behind the pack to capture the numerous properties. Over the next few days, continue the assault with Orange Star's indirect weapons. Keep moving them east and don't let up. Be wary of two enemy Artillery units hiding in the fog.

THE LONG MARCH

Ignore these cities; most of the action will take place in the southern region.

Pound the Black Hole Army hard with indirect fire while its units are concentrated on this peninsula.

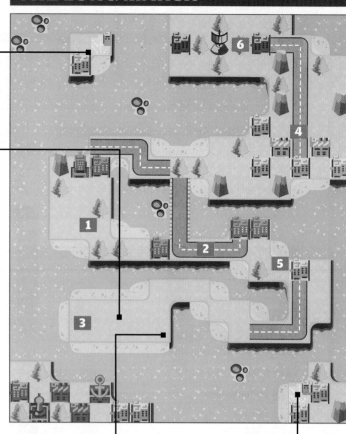

Protect your navy from enemy Artillery hidden under the Fog of War on the peninsula.

Capture this airport and crank out some air units to attack nearby pockets of Black Hole resistance.

3 BEGIN THE NAVAL ASSAULT

Blue Moon's navy is an excellent indirect assault force. Hit the Neotanks and Md. Tanks with all you've got. Load Infantry aboard the Lander and boat eastward to the airport. You'll gain the upper hand after you secure the airstrip. Keep a respectable distance from the peninsula, as enemy Artillery will be looking for you. Avoid the Black Hole Cruiser patrolling the waters. Submerse your Sub to conceal it from attackers.

2 PRESS EAST AND HOLD YOUR GROUND

Move your Artillery and Rocket units east to defend against Black Hole forces. Stand your ground and use the cities and woods for cover when possible. If a unit takes damage, retreat to an occupied city and let it heal. Resume the assault once you regroup. Concentrate your fire on the enemy's strongest or most numerous weapons. Once you've weakened them, they'll retreat.

4 ADVANCE AND PREPARE FOR A RAID

While the battle rages in the south, advance your assault force to the cluster of buildings. You'll likely engage enemy Mech and Tank units, but should have little problem disposing of them. Remember to stick to the cover of trees and cities hidden under the Fog of War. Secure the properties in this area while slowly advancing northward to the lab . . . and victory.

CO POWER STRATEGY

If you've been saving up your CO Power for a Tag Battle, now is a great time to utilize it. Push the enemy back and fortify your defenses before the final push to the lab. With Jake's ability to extend indirect-fire range along with Rachel's strong attacks, you should be able to hit the Black Hole Army hard and fast.

5 SECURE THE SEAS AND GAIN THE EDGE

Continue attacking with your Battleships and other naval units, focusing on the enemy Cruiser and Sub first. Track down the Black Boats next, since destroying them will eliminate Black Hole's ability to repair damaged units. Grab the airport to gain the ability to manufacture air units. Build an Infantry unit and capture real estate near Blue Moon HQ to boost daily income. If any naval vessels take severe damage, return them to the seaport for repairs. You can build additional marine units at the seaport to bolster your fleet or replace lost ships. Keep your watercraft a distance from the peninsula, out of Artillery firing range.

6 CAPTURE THE LAB, FIND THE PLANS

Advance toward the lab carefully, while keeping an eye open for the Artillery unit hiding under the trees nearby. Lead the way with your Recon unit to boost visibility. Move a Tank up to the Artillery and blast away. When you've cleared the area, send in your Infantry to capture the lab and secure the plans.

LIGHTNING STRIKES

Yellow Comet COs have arrived. It's time to test your skills and show them you're worthy of their trust and loyalty.

MISSION TERMS

Capture enemy HQ or destroy all opposing units to win.
Featuring combat on two fronts, this is the most complex battle yet. You can let your CO call the shots on the secondary front, but we recommend that you turn off the Auto CO function and take control yourself. Winning on the secondary front will allow you to combine forces and tag-team the main front. The sooner you can acheive this, the better.

  **VS.**

JAKE   RACHEL   GRIMM   SENSEI

AREA PROPERTIES:

		◯	N	◯
✈	AIRPORTS	-	2	-
🏭	BASES	2	1	2
🏙	CITIES	7	14	1
📡	COM TOWERS	-	-	-
⬚	MISSILE SILOS	-	6	-
⚓	SEAPORTS	-	-	-

BONUS POINTS: 0

OBJECT	#	PTS	TOTAL
🔲 BLACK CANNONS	-	-	-
▯ BLACK CRYSTALS	-	-	-
🔺 BLACK OBELISKS	-	-	-
🔳 MINICANNONS	-	-	-
🔲 OOZIUMS	-	-	-
🔳 PIPE JOINTS	-	-	-

GRIMM

YELLOW COMET INTEL

Just because they're your friends, don't assume Yellow Comet forces will go easy on you. They'll manufacture reinforcements, so it's imperative that you claim their bases.

★ MARCHING ORDERS

Get your hands dirty and fight both battles at once. While the Auto CO feature is fine and dandy, your brain is your best weapon. So turn off the autopilot and get to work!

MISSION TIMELINE

START

Days 1-4
CONTROL THE SECONDARY FRONT
Call the shots on the secondary front and steer the battle.
1

Days 1-5
FORTIFY DEFENSES
Keep your Infantry moving and fortify your defenses.
2

Days 4-8
CLAIM THE ISLAND; TAKE THE MAIN FRONT
Capture of the island base is essential for a speedy victory.
3

CO Power ★
Save your CO Power and use it during Tag Battle.

Days 10-15
FINISH THE JOB
Take the last few days to tag-team your way to an easy win.
4

VICTORY

LIGHTNING STRIKES

1 CONTROL THE SECONDARY FRONT

Turn off the Auto CO option on the Intel menu. Move your AA gun to HQ and transport it to the secondary front, since the Battle Copters there are your biggest concern. Build only two Infantry units on the first day, saving funds to create another AA battery on day two, which you'll send to the other front to boost your defenses in the southwest. When the copters swoop in to attack, hit them hard.

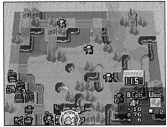

SECONDARY FRONT

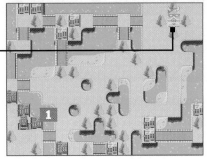

Lure enemy copters toward the AA guns you have guarding the secondary front's HQ.

Prevent enemy Infantry units from capturing this airport and activating the nearby Missile Silo.

MAIN FRONT

Capture the airport and other properties quickly. Turn the missiles against the Yellow Comet forces.

3 CLAIM THE ISLAND; TAKE THE MAIN FRONT

Capture of the island base should be your immediate priority. Once it's secured, you can manufacture units and strike the enemy hard and fast. Activate the nearby Missile Silos and fire upon enemy Infantry heading toward the northeast airport. Once the area is clear, send in an assault team and take it over. On the secondary front, position your units within your stronghold while shooting down any invading copters in range. Protect your Infantry and APCs. Once the skies are clear, drive the loaded APC toward HQ and either eliminate the remaining Mechs in the city or capture it to win the secondary front.

2 FORTIFY DEFENSES

Send Mech and Infantry units to the neutral properties in the north. It is imperative that you capture and secure the area and beat your opponents to the Missile Silo. Capture the neutral city east of HQ, then construct an Artillery unit and place it there. From this vantage point, you'll be able to pound your enemy's newly minted units as they emerge from the base. Stage some Infantry in the surrounding woods as backup.

CO TAG BATTLE STRATEGY

★★★★★★

Don't use your CO Power until Rachel joins you on the main front. This will give you an extra round of attacks and the advantage of Rachel's Covering Fire move, which launches three missiles from Orange Star HQ at your enemies.

★★★★★

★ DEATH FROM ABOVE: MISSILE SILOS

Missile Silos are effective against hordes of enemies. They can dish out damage across the battlefield, weakening the opposition forces before they get moving. Just be careful not to blast your nearby units with splash damage.

4 FINISH THE JOB

With two COs on the job, you'll make short work of the remaining Yellow Comet forces. Continue pounding new enemy units as they emerge from production, and sweep forces in from the north to surround what's left of your foes. You can either storm HQ or hunt down stragglers to seal your victory. Either way, you shouldn't have a problem securing a win from here.

FROZEN FORTRESS

Your pursuit of Black Hole forces takes you to a winter wonderland. Unfortunately, there's no time for snowboarding.

MISSION TERMS

Capture HQ or destroy all the enemies to win. While the icy landscape looks great on a Christmas card, it's torture on your units. Snowy weather impedes movement and indirect attack range, while increasing fuel consumption. Choosing the right COs for the job can compensate greatly for the weather. Build APCs to supply your field units with fuel and ammunition.

RACHEL   JAKE

SASHA   SENSEI

VS.

KINDLE   JUGGER

AREA PROPERTIES:

		●	●	●	●	A	N	✕
✈	AIRPORTS	-	-	-	-	-	1	-
🏠	BASES	3	2	-	-	5	6	-
🏢	CITIES	-	1	-	-	1	12	2
✴	COM TOWERS	-	-	-	-	-	-	3
▨	MISSILE SILOS	-	-	-	-	-	-	-
🚢	SEAPORTS	-	-	-	-	-	-	-

BONUS POINTS: 0

OBJECT	#	PTS	TOTAL
🔲 BLACK CANNONS	-	-	-
🔲 BLACK CRYSTALS	-	-	-
🔲 BLACK OBELISKS	-	-	-
🔲 MINICANNONS	-	-	-
🔲 OOZIUMS	-	-	-
🔲 PIPE JOINTS	-	-	-

BLACK HOLE INTEL

Black Hole's Com Towers boost their attack power. Their forces will move to capture properties near HQ, then begin producing heavy weaponry to aggressively advance on your turf.

MARCHING ORDERS

Holding the airport and southern base will give you a tactical advantage, but don't go crazy producing more units than necessary. Claim the Com Towers to boost your attacks.

MISSION TIMELINE

START

Days 1-6 — 1
START SMALL AND KEEP IT CLOSE
Crank out some Mechs and Infantry units.

Days 3-7 — 2
CAPTURE COM TOWERS
Earn a firepower boost with improved communication between forces.

Days 3-7 — 3
TAKE TO THE SKIES
Capture the airport and gain aerial superiority.

CO Power ★
Your powers should be charged up by now.

Days 4-9 — 4
ADVANCE INTO THE SOUTHWEST
Cover your in-transit troops with Tank support.

Days 6-13 — 5
FIND THE COM TOWER PLANS
Learn the secrets of the Com Towers and build some for yourself.

Days 10-16 — 6
SURROUND AND CONQUER THE ENEMY

VICTORY

1 START SMALL AND KEEP IT CLOSE

Build Infantry units the first couple of days, because you'll need to capture numerous properties on the battlefield to boost daily income. Crank out a combination of at least six Infantry and Mech units for Orange Star and five for Blue Moon. When you're done staffing your ground forces, make a pair of Tanks and an APC to supply them. Be sure to load ground units into the APCs before rolling out. You can cross the water only at the shallow shoals to the north and west, so plan your routes accordingly. Capture the nearby cities and factories with your Blue Moon forces, then manufacture two Artillery units to guard the airport. Send a ground force to capture the real estate in the northeast.

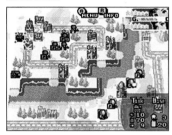

2 CAPTURE COM TOWERS

Push your Orange Star forces toward the Com Towers. You'll face little resistance from Black Hole troops as you convert each neutral city, because only one unit was stationed here to begin with. Capture the Com Towers and steal the firepower advantage from your enemy. Unfortunately, the captured Com Towers will not benefit your Blue Moon brethren.

We've captured a com tower! Now our troops will hit even harder! ♡

3 TAKE TO THE SKIES

Capture the airport with your Blue Moon forces. Securing this location gives you a tactical advantage, as it's in close proximity to Black Hole HQ. Fighting in this region will be fierce, and largely confined to a small area. As soon as you start building aircraft, your foe will begin producing AA guns to counter. Keep a couple of Tanks or Artillery nearby to take them out.

4 ADVANCE INTO THE SOUTHWEST

Have a Tank escort an Infantry-loaded APC with a tank to the south, and start your land grab. Capture the base first. Enemy units will move in and try to thwart your run—use armored backup to quell the insurgency. Once the area is yours, you're a stone's throw from Black Hole HQ. Before you storm the city's gate's, however, you should find the Com Tower plans.

5 FIND THE COM TOWER PLANS

The Com Towers are valuable assets, and you'll want the capability to build your own. The plans you seek are in the northeast. Send several Infantry-loaded APCs from either force to this area and scour the cities before you claim victory. Not only will you reap the rewards of manufacturing your own Com Towers, but you'll also unlock the hidden mission, Lash's Test.

Lady Sasha! We've found a map to a Black Hole research laboratory! ♡

FROZEN FORTRESS

Station a Rocket here. You'll be within striking range of any units produced at a nearby enemy base.

Park Tanks at these cities to guard your newly manufactured airport and to keep enemy at bay from your HQ.

CO POWER STRATEGY

Sasha's War Bonds power provides extra funds that will aid in unit production, and Rachel's Covering Fire will dish out pain to your enemies. Jake's power will boost the range of your mobile forces, while Sensei can call in multiple backup units.

6 SURROUND AND CONQUER THE ENEMY

Now that you've surrounded Black Hole HQ and its surrounding factories, victory is imminent. Combine your scattered forces and concentrate your efforts on the remainder of the opposing army. Provided you've already acquired the Com Tower plans, you're cleared for the final push. Capture the Black Hole HQ or sweep up the last bits of your foe's ailing presence.

★ CHATTER MAKES YOU BADDER: COM TOWERS

Communication is vital when coordinating complex military maneuvers. Having correct intel and sharing it among troops boosts morale and, ultimately, your firepower. The more towers you control, the greater the effect.

LASH'S TEST

Distracted by a video game, Lash drops the Black Bomb remote. Harness its destructive power and find the plans.

MISSION TERMS

Capture the lab or destroy all enemy units to win. You've got the power of the evil Black Bombs on your side this round. However, you'll need to free the dangerous explosives before you can hurl them at your nemesis. Remember to capture the Black Hole HQ before annihilating all of Lash's forces, or you'll forfeit possession of the Black Bomb's technology.

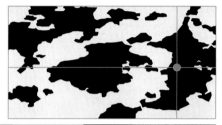

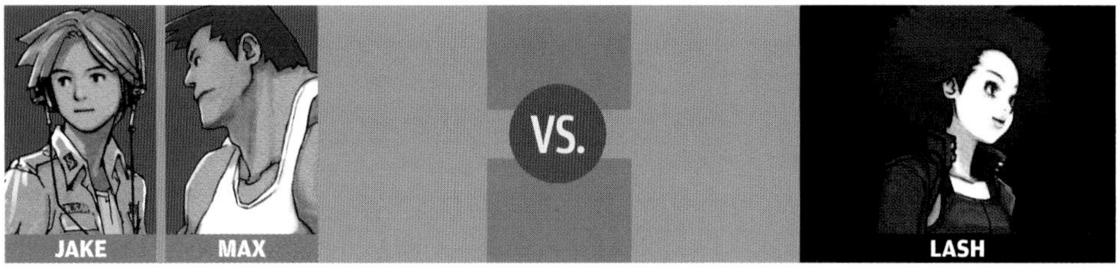

JAKE   MAX   **VS.**   LASH

AREA PROPERTIES:

	●	●	●	●	A	N	�֎
✈ AIRPORTS	-	-	-	-	-	1	-
⌂ BASES	-	-	-	-	-	-	-
�🏙 CITIES	7	-	-	-	7	4	2
� COM TOWERS	-	-	-	-	-	2	-
◪ MISSILE SILOS	-	-	-	-	-	-	-
⬓ SEAPORTS	-	-	-	-	-	-	-

BONUS POINTS: 0

OBJECT	#	PTS	TOTAL
▣ BLACK CANNONS	-	-	-
▣ BLACK CRYSTALS	-	-	-
▣ BLACK OBELISKS	-	-	-
▣ MINICANNONS	-	-	-
▣ OOZIUMS	-	-	-
▣ PIPE JOINTS	4	5	20

✶ BLACK HOLE INTEL

The Black Hole Army has brought along some big guns. They'll advance to the south and west in an attempt to steal your airport and cities.

★ MARCHING ORDERS

Hold the enemy at bay outside your northernmost city. This choke point will delay the enemy invasion. With six Black Bombs at your disposal, you have the upper hand.

MISSION TIMELINE

START ■

Days 1-4
FREE THE BLACK BOMBS   1
Blast the pipe joints and free the captive Black Bombs.

Days 3-7
RETURN TO SENDER   2
Give the Black Hole Army a taste of its own medicine.

Days 3-10
WHO WANTS SECONDS?   3
It's time to unload a few more Black Bombs on Lash's forces.

CO Power   ★
Use Jake's Beat Down CO Power, or save up for a Tag Battle.

Days 9-14
CAPTURE THE LAB, FIND THE BLUEPRINTS   4
Capture the enemy HQ and retrieve the Black Bomb plans.

VICTORY ■

1 FREE THE BLACK BOMBS

Before you can wield the immense destructive power of the mighty Black Bombs, you'll first have to free them from their "cages." Fly your Battle Copter from HQ north and begin blasting away at the pipe joint (near point 3 on the map). Load a Mech into your APC and head west. It'll take you a few days to reach and capture the Com Towers in the southwest, but the added firepower boost you'll earn will make it worthwhile. Fan out your other units to the northwest; you'll have to channel most of them through the choke point near your northern-most city (marked 2 on the map). Destroy the pipe joints that are keeping the western pair of Black Bombs from you. While you needn't eliminate all three of the joints, you'll earn bonus points for each one you do destroy.

3 WHO WANTS SECONDS?

By the time you arrive, the Black Bombs at this location should be free, but running low on fuel. Fly a pair to your APCs in the field and gas 'em up. Afterward, lob them at an enemy cluster of your choice. Remember that the bombs cut a wide swath of destruction, so do yourself a favor and target enemies that aren't next to your own forces. You should have plenty of targets to choose from in the northwest.

CO POWER STRATEGY

If you can save your CO power for a Tag Battle, you can really boost your army's reach. Jake's firing-range boost and Max's firepower increase will help you destroy enemies that would normally be just out of reach and tougher to take down.

LASH'S TEST

> Grab these Com Towers early to gain a firepower boost.

> Once breached, this section of pipe makes a great shortcut to the neutral airport.

2 RETURN TO SENDER

Station your Neotank and Md. Tank at the choke point (see the screenshot below) for several days. By blocking this narrow path, you'll prevent the Black Hole forces from advancing while you work on freeing the Bombs. Once you've broken the pipe, unleash the evil weapons on their former owners to the north (far away from your own forces). Send some troops to the airport and claim it.

★ MASS DESTRUCTION: THE BLACK BOMBS

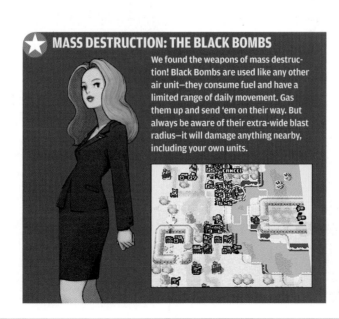

We found the weapons of mass destruction! Black Bombs are used like any other air unit—they consume fuel and have a limited range of daily movement. Gas them up and send 'em on their way. But always be aware of their extra-wide blast radius—it will damage anything nearby, including your own units.

4 CAPTURE THE LAB, FIND THE BLUEPRINTS

Once you've cut the Black Hole Army down to size, it's time to load up an APC with some Infantry and head for the enemy HQ. Check the firing range of each enemy unit before moving your own, and avoid rolling into a "last stand" scenario. Regardless of how you end the conflict, the plans will be yours for the taking, so capture the lab or eliminate the enemy forces. It's up to you.

> Hey! We found a blueprint for the black bomb! ♡

MISSION 15

VERDANT HILLS

It's time to test your battle tactics against two of Green Earth's finest COs, but are you prepared for the Mega Tank?

MISSION TERMS

Capture the HQ or destroy all enemy units within 15 days to win. You have just over two weeks to seal the deal on Green Earth. Though it's a friendly battle meant to test your mettle, you'll have to work extra-hard to supplant your opponents' heavy reserve of powerful units, which includes the Mega Tank. Use your own indirect-fire units strategically to get the upper hand for a swift victory.

MAX   JAKE

VS.

GRIMM   RACHEL

JAVIER   JESS

AREA PROPERTIES:

	●	●	●	●	Ⓐ	Ⓝ	✕
✈ AIRPORTS	-	-	-	-	-	1	-
🏠 BASES	2	-	-	-	2	1	-
🏙 CITIES	2	2	-	-	4	8	-
📡 COM TOWERS	-	-	2	-	-	3	-
🚀 MISSILE SILOS	-	-	-	-	-	-	-
⚓ SEAPORTS	-	-	-	-	-	-	-

BONUS POINTS: 0

OBJECT	#	PTS	TOTAL
🔲 BLACK CANNONS	-	-	-
🔲 BLACK CRYSTALS	-	-	-
🔲 BLACK OBELISKS	-	-	-
🔲 MINICANNONS	-	-	-
🔲 OOZIUMS	-	-	-
🔲 PIPE JOINTS	-	-	-

JAVIER

● GREEN EARTH INTEL

Your Green Earth friends are packing some serious heat, so it's imperative that you inflict significant damage to their heavy units early in the game.

★ MARCHING ORDERS

The Fog of War will impair your vision, so post Recon or Infantry units on high to improve your view. Utilize your indirect-fire units effectively to thin your opponents' ranks.

MISSION TIMELINE

START

Days 1-3
1
STALK YOUR PREY FROM THE SHADOWS
Conceal your units in the forest and wait for Green Earth to approach.

Days 1-5
2
HIT 'EM HARD
Concentrate your firepower on the Green Earth units stuck in the hills.

CO Power ★
Save it up for a Tag Battle later in the mission.

Days 3-6
3
CAPTURE THE COM TOWERS
Grab what you can to boost your firepower.

Days 3-6
4
CLEAR THE AREA
Forge a safe path to Green Earth HQ.

CO Power ★
Unleash a Tag Battle on Green Earth.

Days 4-8
5
CAPTURE GREEN EARTH HQ
Claim your foes' headquarters for a quick win.

VICTORY

1 STALK YOUR PREY FROM THE SHADOWS

Orange Star's mission is to contain the Green Earth forces for as long as possible inside the ring of mountains in the center of the battlefield. Manufacture and place some hardy units in the forests leading into the mountain range. Place an Infantry or Recon unit nearby to expose enemy locations. Crank out additional Infantry and split them up to capture the neutral real estate on both sides of your HQ, then station some Artillery nearby for defense.

2 HIT 'EM HARD

While Orange Star is blocking the northern pass, Blue Moon's job is to expose and attack Green Earth's forces penned up inside the ring of mountains. Advance your Infantry and Recon units to lift the fog that's concealing your enemies' numbers. Hit them hard and fast with every indirect-fire unit in range. It is crucial that you weaken or destroy many of Green Earth's armored units early on, so it'll be easier to take them down. Keep a lone Mech protected from enemy view. Once the opposition vacates its HQ, you'll be able to load your capturing force into an APC and sneak it behind enemy lines for a speedy victory.

3 CAPTURE THE COM TOWERS

Using your spare Blue Moon Infantry, capture Green Earth's Com Towers on both sides of the map and steal the firepower advantage from under their noses. Monitor enemy movement inside the mountain ring; eventually the units will head north to escape the confines of the mountains. Barrage the enemy forces with long-range attacks, moving your Artillery and Rockets in step to keep up the assault. Your units will consume more fuel than normal due to the harsh weather conditions, so take every opportunity to resupply your forces. Likewise, keep an eye on the ammunition situation, as your indirect-fire units will likely be running low on shells.

4 CLEAR THE AREA

After you've fragmented your opponents' army, it's time to move in and clear a path to their headquarters. Station a Recon patrol in the trees surrounding the hills and pinpoint the remaining Artillery and Tanks. The goal here is to pave a path for your loaded APC to safely reach Green Earth HQ. Take your time and keep shelling the opposition until the coast is reasonably clear.

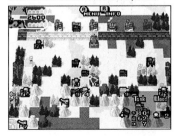

VERDANT HILLS

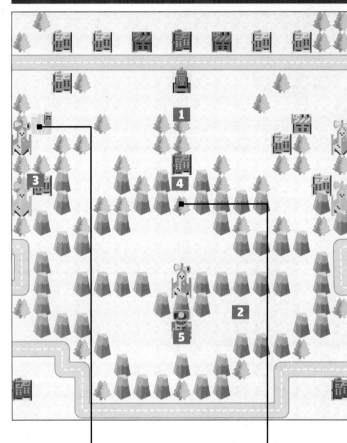

You might not have time to capture every neutral property on the map. Focus on capturing Green Earth's HQ.

Block the Green Earth advancement at this choke point and give yourself some time to build up strong forces.

CO POWER STRATEGY

Unless you find yourself in a tight spot early on, it's best to save up your CO Powers for a one-two punch later in the fight. As you make your push down through the mountain range, initiate a Tag Battle to keep Green Earth on the run.

5 CAPTURE GREEN EARTH HQ

Once your forces have crushed or flushed out all immediate threats surrounding Green Earth headquarters, it's time to slip in for the final assault. Remember to station some protective units nearby in case your capture team draws enemy fire. If you lose your men before they claim HQ, you'll have to truck in replacements to finish the job. Continue hammering away at the enemy forces in the interim.

SNOW HUNTERS

Hawke has assembled a new Black Hole Army. Now it's time to square off against more Piperunners than before.

MISSION TERMS

Your mission will be completed when you destroy all three minicannons, but it won't easy. The Black Hole Army has entrenched several Piperunners here. You'll have to keep Hawke's forces at bay in the east and south while you hack away at the Piperunner track, all while clearing passage for a Mech landing team to conquer the base in the southeast. You see, there are secret plans stashed nearby. . . .

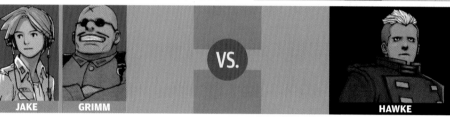

JAKE   GRIMM   VS.   HAWKE

AREA PROPERTIES:

	●	●	●	●	A	N	✖
✈ AIRPORTS	-	-	-	-	-	-	-
🏠 BASES	-	-	-	-	-	2	-
🏙 CITIES	4	-	-	-	4	2	4
📡 COM TOWERS	-	-	-	-	-	2	-
🚀 MISSILE SILOS	-	-	-	-	-	1	-
⚓ SEAPORTS	-	-	-	-	-	1	-

BONUS POINTS: 70

OBJECT	#	PTS	TOTAL
🔲 BLACK CANNONS	-	-	-
🔲 BLACK CRYSTALS	-	-	-
🔲 BLACK OBELISKS	-	-	-
🔲 MINICANNONS	3	10	30
🔲 OOZIUMS	-	-	-
🔲 PIPE JOINTS	8	5	40

◤ BLACK HOLE INTEL

Like his name suggests, Hawke strikes hard and fast. He's stocked to the gills with superior firepower, and he has every intention of using it. He'll stockpile CO Power at each turn, so look out.

★ MARCHING ORDERS

Have your cake and eat it, too. You can recover the secret plans and still earn an S rating by pressing toward the southeast island while preventing Hawke from regrouping in the west.

MISSION TIMELINE

START ■

Day 1
PREPARE FOR BATTLE 【1】
Load up your transports and coordinate troop positions.

Day 2
CLEAR THE SKIES, BUST SOME PIPES 【2】

Day 3
LAUNCH THE MISSILE BEFORE HAWKE DOES 【3】

CO Power ★
Unleash your CO Power, then switch to your other officer.

Day 4
ATTACK TWO MINICANNONS 【4】

Day 5
RETRIEVE THE SECRET PLANS 【5】
You'll unlock bonus content.

Days 6-8
FINISH THE JOB 【6】
Destroy the last Minicannon *after* you grab the secret plans, not before.

VICTORY ■

SNOW HUNTERS

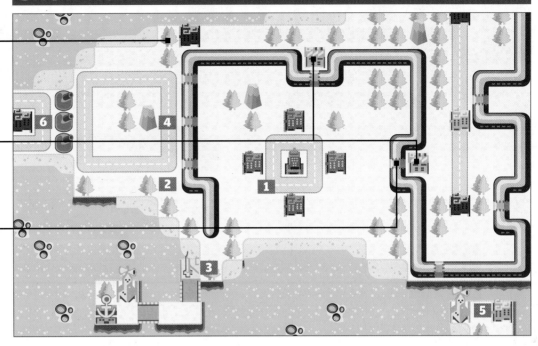

It is critical that you destroy two of Hawke's Minicannons before his forces reach this point, otherwise they will invade your home turf.

Prevent the enemy forces from capturing neutral factories; otherwise they will ramp up production and spit out reinforcements.

You can shatter the pipeline here and funnel some troops through the gap to capture this base, while simultaneously distracting Hawke's forces.

1 PREPARE FOR BATTLE

Relocate a pair of Artillery units near the pipe to the southeast, while taking care to stay outside of enemy firing range. Position your Rockets near your cities (see screenshot below), then load your Infantry into the APC and drive southwest toward the missile silo. Have an AA gun follow to provide protection. Send your remaining units to the west in preparation for your assault on the pipes and Minicannons. Lastly, load a Mech into your Lander. Once you've knocked out or diverted Hawke's forces in the east, you can send a strike force to the island in the southeast and snatch the secret plans from under Hawke's beak.

2 CLEAR THE SKIES, BUST SOME PIPES

With enemy aircraft advancing from the west, you'll want to shoot them down with your Missiles. Next, tear into the Piperunner joint in the southeast corner with your Artillery. Continue shelling enemy forces in the vicinity. Break the pipe joint to the west in preparation for your assault on the Minicannons.

3 LAUNCH THE MISSILE BEFORE HAWKE DOES

By the third day, your Infantry should be within reach of the Missile Silo. Activate the device and target the biggest, strongest cluster of Black Hole forces (they'll likely be concentrated in the northeast). Finish off the pipe joint in the southeast with your Artillery, then mop up the remainder of Hawke's aerial units. It is possible to lock the Piperunners between two busted pipe joints, so if you have units within firing range of other joints, blast away. Prevent the Black Hole Infantry from capturing neutral factories with Rocket fire.

CO POWER STRATEGY

★★★★★

If you've been using Jake this round, his Beat Down CO Power should be charged up. Use it to increase the firing range of his indirect-fire units. The added distance will help you eliminate distant targets such as Piperunners and Artillery, while keeping your own forces out of harm's way.

4 ATTACK TWO MINICANNONS

Now that the Piperunners are crippled (if not destroyed), it's time to hammer on two of the three Minicannons with your Md. Tank and regular Tank units. Capture nearby Com Towers to boost your firepower. Remember, don't eliminate the third Minicannon until you get the plans first.

5 RETRIEVE THE SECRET PLANS

While you continue your assault on the Minicannons in the west, beach your Lander on the southeast island and unload your Mech landing party. You'll find the elusive plans in the city east of the Com Tower. Up north, keep an eye on any remnant Black Hole forces moving westward to protect the Minicannons. Station available Rocket or Tank units nearby in case they get too close. Once the Piperunners are locked (or destroyed), stop targeting the pipe joints or you'll open your HQ up for an attack.

6 FINISH THE JOB

Hawke has most likely pounded you with his CO power by now, while healing his own units in the process. Regardless, your military strength should be sufficient to finish off the last Minicannon (after you've recovered the plans). Protect your HQ from invading forces and waste the remaining Minicannon to finish a job well done.

SPIRAL GARDEN

Secret plans in hand, you descend upon Kindle's secret Piperunner lab for a showdown against the egomaniac.

MISSION TERMS

Capture 15 properties to win. Quickly navigate the snowy plains and claim that real estate! You start the round with six of your own, and have nine more to go before victory.
You can also win by capturing the lab or destroying all enemy units. There are alternate victory conditions, but be warned: it'll take you much longer to wipe out Kindle's army, since she'll be constantly producing units. You decide.

JAKE JESS VS. KINDLE

AREA PROPERTIES:

	●	●	●	●	A	N	✶
AIRPORTS	-	-	-	-	-	1	-
BASES	2	-	-	-	2	2	2
CITIES	3	-	-	-	3	11	-
COM TOWERS	-	-	-	-	-	-	-
MISSILE SILOS	-	-	-	-	-	2	-
SEAPORTS	-	-	-	-	-	-	-

BONUS POINTS: 90

OBJECT	#	PTS	TOTAL
BLACK CANNONS	-	-	-
BLACK CRYSTALS	-	-	-
BLACK OBELISKS	-	-	-
MINICANNONS	-	-	-
OOZIUMS	-	-	-
PIPE JOINTS	18	5	90

BLACK HOLE INTEL

Kindle will constrict the narrow paths near her lab with units. When used, her CO Powers will damage any of your units currently stationed on a base.

MARCHING ORDERS

Counter-produce units at your factories that can easily neutralize anything your enemy manufactures. Tote plenty of Rocket and Artillery units with you as you progress through the Piperunner maze.

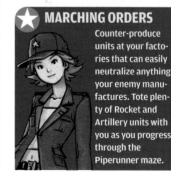

JUGGER

MISSION TIMELINE

START

Days 1-3
NAVIGATE THE PIPE MAZE — 1

Day 4
BUST MORE PIPE JOINTS — 2

Days 5-7
HARNESS THE MISSILE SILOS — 3

CO Power ★
Use it, or save it for a Tag Battle near the end.

Days 8-9
KEEP ON CHUGGIN' — 4
Make sure you reach this point before the enemy does.

Days 10-12
THE WALL OF DOOM — 5
Destroy the last minicannon *after* you grab the secret plans, not before.

CO Power ★
Initiate a Tag Battle if you've got the power.

Days 13-15
THERE GOES THE NEIGHBORHOOD — 6

VICTORY

1 NAVIGATE THE PIPE MAZE

Though you can win this battle in a variety of ways, we're going to detail how to emerge victorious through conquering 15 bases. Position your Artillery and Tanks within firing range of the pipe joints near your HQ and hammer away at the closest pair. Capture the neutral bases in your corner, then fan your troops out west, grabbing all properties in your path. The process will take you a few days. Manufacture Infantry (or Mechs), AA guns and an APC, and prepare to greet Kindle's approaching forces.

SPIRAL GARDEN

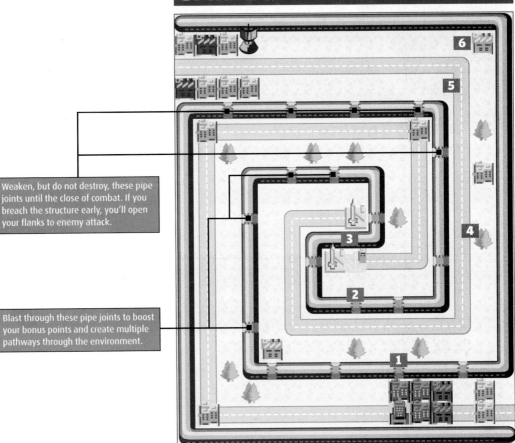

Weaken, but do not destroy, these pipe joints until the close of combat. If you breach the structure early, you'll open your flanks to enemy attack.

Blast through these pipe joints to boost your bonus points and create multiple pathways through the environment.

2 BUST MORE PIPE JOINTS

Use two Tanks and an Anti-air unit to destroy the enemy Battle Copter and Tank unit once they reach your position in the west. Keep the Piperunners at bay with suppressive fire from your Tank escort as you shuttle your loaded APC through. Hack away at the pipe joints (see map item #2) to reach the airport and the Missile Silo before the enemy does.

3 HARNESS THE MISSILE SILOS

Once you've broken through the second row of pipes (see tip #2), your Infantry should be near the Missile Silos if you've kept them moving. Fire on nearby Piperunners with your escorting Md. Tank or Artillery unit. Capture the airport with your ground troops. Keep your Artillery on standby and fire on any Md. Tanks that threaten your ground forces. Conquer the Missile Silos and launch them at your enemy if necessary. After you've secured the immediate area, continue your campaign to the north and capture each neutral and enemy property in the region.

4 KEEP ON CHUGGIN'

If you haven't already done so, eliminate the remaining Piperunners. Send two parallel teams consisting of various Tank units and Artillery up the eastern channels as depicted in the image below. You'll face a solid traffic jam of Kindle's forces, so use all available firepower to loosen things up. If you've got extra resources, continue weakening nearby pipe joints.

5 THE WALL OF DOOM

Send Mech or Infantry teams to capture any neutral cities, bases, or other real estate you may have missed along the way. It's time for the final push into Kindle's turf, so make sure your rolling invasion force is supplied, healthy and up to the task. Position your Artillery on the left flank (on the western side of the pipe) so that it can fire on any incoming enemy reinforcements. Park your closest Infantry or Mech atop the base in the northeast to prevent it from manufacturing additional units before you capture it.

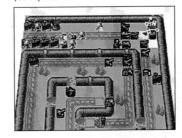

CO POWER STRATEGY

★★★★★★★

If you've stockpiled your CO Power, it's time to unleash a tag team of pain upon Kindle's struggling army. Between Jake's firing range increase and Jess's supply replenishment and movement boost, you should have little trouble putting the final nail in the coffin.

★★★★★★★

6 THERE GOES THE NEIGHBORHOOD

Raise your flag on the 15th property and crack open a cold one in celebration. This town belongs to you!

MISSION 18
OMENS AND SIGNS

Enemy HQ lies somewhere in Red Rock Desert, but you'll have to cross over dangerous waters to get there.

MISSION TERMS

Destroy the four Minicannons on the main front to win.
A floating fortress on the secondary front guards your four primary targets. Send air units skyward and let your CO call the shots upstairs.

If you lose the battle on the secondary front, the battle won't end. However, if you win, you can use both COs to finish the battle on the main front!

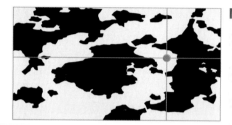

 VS.

SASHA   SENSEI   **JUGGER   KOAL**

AREA PROPERTIES:

	●	●	●	●	A	N	✴
✈ AIRPORTS	-	-	-	-	-	-	-
🏠 BASES	1	-	-	-	1	1	-
🏙 CITIES	2	-	-	-	2	5	9
📡 COM TOWERS	-	-	-	-	-	3	-
⚔ MISSILE SILOS	-	-	-	-	-	-	-
⚓ SEAPORTS	1	-	-	-	1	-	-

BONUS POINTS: 75

OBJECT	#	PTS	TOTAL
🔵 BLACK CANNONS	-	-	-
⬛ BLACK CRYSTALS	-	-	-
🔺 BLACK OBELISKS	-	-	-
🟢 MINICANNONS	4	10	40
⚪ OOZIUMS	-	-	-
🔶 PIPE JOINTS	7	5	35

✴ BLACK HOLE INTEL

Black Hole's Minicannons are heavily guarded by a massive floating fortress on the secondary front. Don't bother attacking them until you remove the threat from above.

⭐ MARCHING ORDERS

You have two new units at your disposal. The Carrier can secure, refuel and relaunch air units, and also use indirect-fire against aircraft. The Stealth Fighter can conceal its presence.

MISSION TIMELINE

START ■

Day 1
REINFORCE THE
SECONDARY FRONT   **1**

Day 1
ORGANIZE YOUR
FORCES   **2**

Day 2
FALL BACK AND
REGROUP   **3**

Day 3
REASSESS THE
SITUATION UPSTAIRS   **4**

Days 3-4
LAUNCH STEALTH
FIGHTERS   **5**

CO Power   ★

Days 5-8
HEAD EAST   **6**

CO Power   ★
With the sky
fortress out of the
way, it's time for
some tag-team
mayhem.

Days 9-12
DESTROY THE
MINICANNONS   **7**

VICTORY ■

OMENS AND SIGNS

1 REINFORCE THE SECONDARY FRONT

Lucky for you, your CO will fight the secondary front automatically this time. Make your CO selections, then start sending Fighters to the secondary front. When you select an air unit, move it to the desired location on the lower screen, then select "Send" from the menu to order it away. Remember to keep your jets out of Minicannon range—you'll need them at full strength if you want to make short work of the Black Arc flying fortress.

2 ORGANIZE YOUR FORCES

Don't bother attacking the Minicannons on the main front until the Black Arc is destroyed. Stay out of Minicannon range and lure enemy units to your zone instead. First, capture all neutral properties in your home zone with your available Infantry and Mech units. Position your APCs near your troops, since you'll want to load them in when they're done capturing bases and Com Towers. Move your air and sea units to the east, just before the line of shoals. You'll attract Black Hole's attention but will be out of range of Rocket fire. Fly your Bomber south and attack the pipeline in the southeast. Fire Rockets at the Cruisers locking your Carriers in the harbor. You can also take down enemy air units with indirect attacks from your Carriers.

3 FALL BACK AND REGROUP

Once the Black Hole forces take the bait and advance upon your remaining air squadron, fall back and regroup closer to HQ. At the same time, bomb away at the pipe joints in the south with your Bomber. Punish the Cruisers in the harbor with Rocket fire from the west (see the image above).

4 REASSESS THE SITUATION UPSTAIRS

Take note of progress on the secondary front. If your air force is taking a beating, send up an additional Fighter or two for support.

SECONDARY FRONT

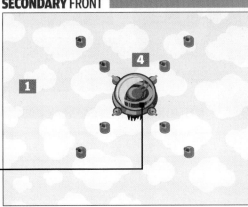

Always keep an eye on the skies and send up as much help as possible (after the air battle on the main front is finished).

MAIN FRONT

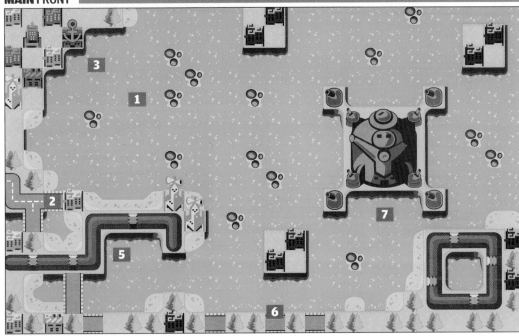

5 LAUNCH STEALTH FIGHTERS

Assault the Black Hole forces that cross the reef line. Submerse your Sub and go after the enemy Battleship patrolling the waters near the Minicannons. Open up the southern pipe with Rocket and Bomber fire, and continue to hammer on the Cruisers. Pull all Carriers out from the harbor and release the Stealth Fighters.

6 HEAD EAST

Cloak your released Stealth Fighter and fly east, eliminating any enemy forces you encounter. Protect the Carriers with your Bomber and Rocket units so you can launch your remaining planes. Launch Missiles from the Carriers at any targets that fall within their massive reach. Keep the Carriers nearby so you can land and refill as necessary.

7 DESTROY THE MINICANNONS

By now, you should have won the battle on the secondary front. Switch COs or execute your CO Power if you wish. Destroy the four Minicannons to end the drawn-out fight. Keep an eye on your Stealth Fighters—refuel them if necessary and keep them out of enemy Missile range. If you want the final bonus point, finish off the pipelines.

INTO THE WOODS

You push your way into Red Rock Desert, much to Lord Von Bolt's chagrin. Slice through the fog and defeat the enemy.

MISSION TERMS

Capture Black Hole HQ or destroy all enemy units to win. The Fog of War has rolled across the battlefield again, hiding victory from plain sight. You'll need to trust your instincts and head for high ground in the mountains to get a better look at the situation as you creep into unknown territory. Stay alert! Black Hole's newest, fiercest weapon—the Oozium—is lurking in the wild. . . .

JAKE | JESS

RACHEL | GRIMM

VS.

KINDLE | LASH

AREA PROPERTIES:

	●	●	●	○	A	N	✖
✈ AIRPORTS	-	-	-	-	-	1	-
⌂ BASES	-	-	-	-	-	-	-
🏙 CITIES	3	3	-	-	6	11	4
📡 COM TOWERS	-	-	-	-	-	1	1
⊘ MISSILE SILOS	-	-	-	-	-	3	-
🚢 SEAPORTS	-	-	-	-	-	-	-

BONUS POINTS: 80

OBJECT	#	PTS	TOTAL
BLACK CANNONS	-	-	-
BLACK CRYSTALS	-	-	-
BLACK OBELISKS	-	-	-
MINICANNONS	-	-	-
OOZIUMS	2	40	80
PIPE JOINTS	-	-	-

GRIMM

BLACK HOLE INTEL

Beware the might of the mysterious Oozium. If left unchecked, this strange new weapon will destroy your units one by one.

MARCHING ORDERS

You'll need to protect your weaker units by surrounding them with some heavy firepower as you creep through the murky fog. Stay together and forge into the unknown!

MISSION TIMELINE

START

Day 1
FORM A COLUMN AND MOVE OUT `1`

Day 2
PROCEED SLOWLY AND CAUTIOUSLY `2`

Days 3-4
LEAPFROG YOUR UNITS `3`

Days 3-4
DESTROY THE BATTLE COPTERS `4`

CO Power ★
Use your CO power now, or save it up for a Tag Battle later.

Days 5-7
BREAK ON THROUGH TO THE OTHER SIDE `5`

CO Power ★
If you've saved your CO Power, give the Black Hole Army a one-two punch.

Day 8
THE HOME STRETCH `6`

VICTORY

INTO THE WOODS

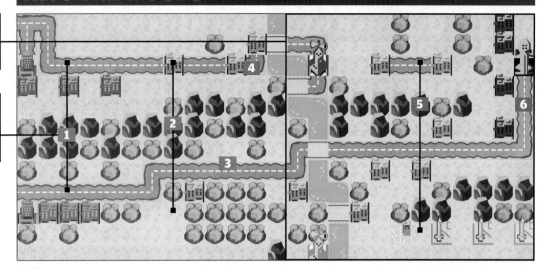

The entire eastern sector of the map will be blanketed in fog, so you won't know the position of enemy units until you're practically on top of them.

You'll move two separate platoons during this battle: one belonging to Orange Star and the other to Blue Moon. The tips on this page will give strategy for both.

1 FORM A COLUMN AND MOVE OUT

Move your Orange Star forces east as pictured below, keeping resilient units (like Tanks) up front to protect the weaker AA guns and APCs behind. Post an Infantry or Mech unit atop a mountain to increase your field of vision. Don't enter the woods just yet–keep to the road for now. Move the Blue Moon units in parallel with Orange Star, placing the powerful units to the rear while sending a Recon unit to the far east for maximum visibility. March the central Mech east, and load the remainder of your ground forces into the nearby APCs. Roll your tank eastward as well. Reposition the AA gun in the mountains as protection against enemy Battle Copters. Nudge your Artillery along with the pack.

3 LEAPFROG YOUR UNITS

Send an Orange Star Tank ahead of the pack to open up visibility. This should uncover most of the enemy units in your vicinity. Leapfrog a Tank embedded in your column to advance it to the front. Continue shuffling your units to the east while still avoiding the wooded areas. Black Hole's Oozium should be exposed by now, so stay out of its range. It is a direct-fire unit and can move only one space per turn, but its power is devastating.

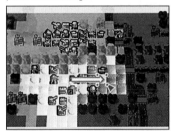

4 DESTROY THE BATTLE COPTERS

Quickly destroy the two Black Hole Battle Copters you've exposed in the north. If you don't remove the choppers speedily, your foe will activate a Tag Battle and dole out serious damage. Utilize your long-range Artillery to soften up any exposed Tanks or ground forces you see in the distance. Fire your AA guns at nearby aerial targets. Send a Mech to a mountaintop if you need to increase your field of vision. Use Rockets to finish off any remaining enemies.

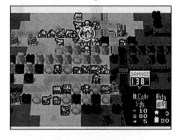

5 BREAK ON THROUGH TO THE OTHER SIDE

At this point, you should have engaged (and beaten) most of the Black Hole units you've lured to your position. It's time to cross the river into unknown terrain with your Orange Star forces. Place an Infantry unit on higher ground to negate the Fog of War in your immediate zone. Surround and assault the Oozium in one turn. Heavier Tanks, AA guns and Recon units work well, but you'll need to hit the slimy thing three or four times before it'll go away. Capture the Com Tower and airport. On the Blue Moon front, you'll encounter two Md. Tanks and a Neotank. Press east with Recon and Mech units in front and Artillery and AA guns in the rear. Keep your Rockets safe until Orange Star can launch the Missile Silos to help you take down Black Hole's heavily armored units.

2 PROCEED SLOWLY AND CAUTIOUSLY

Continue pressing the Orange Star cluster east in small steps. Your goal is to expose the enemy, not engage it. If you encounter a stray unit, feel free to blast it from afar, but do not give chase. Your intention here is to lure the Black Hole Army's Oozium out of hiding; stick to the road and don't venture off into the wooded areas. Move your Blue Moon units in a similar fashion and creep steadily to the east. Park your Recon where it landed during your last turn, and unload your troops. Form an Infantry barrier around your Artillery and AA guns to protect them from direct attacks.

★ NEW BLACK HOLE WEAPON: OOZIUM

Ooziums are creepy looking, but they're also impervious to your Rockets, Missiles and CO Powers. Though they move at a snail's pace and can attack only adjacent units, they are hardy and deadly. Surround them with heavy Tank units, AA guns or Recon units, and attack. They should go down in three or four hits.

Whoa! What's up with that jiggly, slimy thang? ♡

6 THE HOME STRETCH

Continue capturing real estate in the south with the Orange Star forces. Keep utilizing the Missile Silos to help destroy the remaining Black Hole Md. Tanks and Neotanks. If necessary, send some Orange Star forces to Blue Moon's aid to finish mopping up. If you're having trouble, build some Bombers and send 'em out into the field for backup.

MUCK AMOK!

Lord Von Bolt has ordered Lash and Hawke exterminated. Aid in their rescue, then pump them for information.

MISSION TERMS

Capture HQ or destroy all enemy units to win. The desert has grown even more inhospitable. Heavy sandstorms have reduced your indirect-fire range by one. To make matters worse, a horde of Ooziums has followed Hawke and Lash to your location. You'll need to put your hatred aside and bail your enemies out. When it's all over, you'll have extra help in the fight against the Black Hole Army.

MAX   HAWKE

VS.

GRIMM   LASH

KOAL

AREA PROPERTIES:

	●	●	●	●	A	N	✖
✖ AIRPORTS	-	-	-	-	-	-	-
▣ BASES	-	-	-	-	-	-	-
⬛ CITIES	3	-	-	-	3	-	2
✖ COM TOWERS	-	-	-	-	-	4	-
✖ MISSILE SILOS	-	-	-	-	-	-	-
⬛ SEAPORTS	-	-	-	-	-	-	-

BONUS POINTS: 700

OBJECT	#	PTS	TOTAL
⬛ BLACK CANNONS	-	-	-
⬛ BLACK CRYSTALS	-	-	-
⬛ BLACK OBELISKS	-	-	-
⬛ MINICANNONS	1	10	10
⬛ OOZIUMS	17	40	680
⬛ PIPE JOINTS	2	5	10

KOAL

BLACK HOLE INTEL

You are inundated with Black Hole Ooziums. They will attempt to group together and attack your forces. While fighting them off, avoid damage from the Minicannon in the north.

MARCHING ORDERS

Plan your movement carefully and keep your forces out of Oozium direct-fire range. Grab the Com Towers to boost your attacks and let 'em have it!

MISSION TIMELINE

START

Day 1
1
THE RETURN OF THE OOZIUMS

Day 2
2
SET THE BAIT

Day 3
3
CAPTURE THE EASTERN COM TOWERS

Days 4-6
4
BREAK UP THE OOZIUM CLUSTER

CO Power ★
Conserve your CO Power for a Tag Battle later on.

Days 7-9
5
CAPTURE THE NORTHERN COM TOWERS

CO Power ★
Initiate a Tag Battle.

Days 10-12
6
BUST THROUGH THE PIPELINES

Days 13-15
7
GRAB THE ENEMY HQ

VICTORY

1 THE RETURN OF THE OOZIUMS

In the previous mission, you had your first taste of the bitter Oozium. Now, you're up against 17 of them. Your primary goal is to keep Hawke and Lash alive, which will be tough considering they have only an APC and a Rocket between them. Ooziums can only move one space per turn, and cannot attack on diagonals—use these limitations to your advantage. Keep Hawke and Lash on the move and use their Rocket whenever possible. Load one Mech into your APC, and another into the Transport Copter. Head toward the Com Towers in the east, but don't unload either transport until day two. Move your Md. Tank, Recon unit, Battle Copter and Rockets north as a group. Reposition the remainder of your forces to the east as shown in the screenshot below.

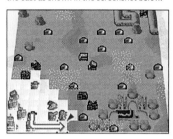

MUCK AMOK!

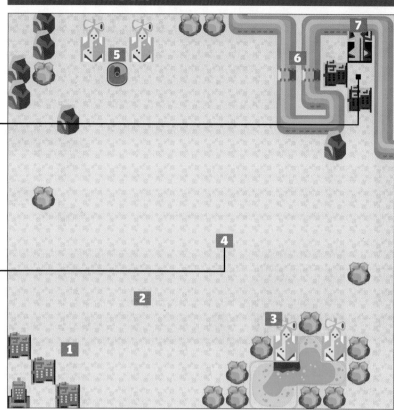

Lure the Oozium guarding Black Hole HQ out into the open, then sneak a Mech inside and capture the HQ for a quick win. (You'll sacrifice bonus points, however.)

Don't allow Ooziums to surround you. Always plan an escape route when venturing near them.

2 SET THE BAIT

You'll need to coax the Ooziums out of their cluster to destroy them. Split up your team to lure the Ooziums to each of your individual units. Eventually you'll drive your enemies apart, leaving yourself an opening to attack. You'll need to drive in and hit one Oozium hard with shots from multiple forces, while keeping out of direct fire from your enemy's backup nearby. If you expose a unit to attack, you can kiss it goodbye.

3 CAPTURE THE EAST-ERN COM TOWERS

Keep Ooziums away from the Com Towers in the south long enough to drop your Mech team in for capture. Once you've claimed the towers, load up for a hasty retreat.

4 BREAK UP THE OOZIUM CLUSTER

Ooziums will gather around this sector. If you can get them to separate, you can make a dash to enemy HQ for a quick win. Alternatively, you can single out each one and pick them off one at a time. Distract the Ooziums and lead them south, and away from the Com Tower and Minicannon. By the time you get a capture team on-site, you should face little resistance.

5 CAPTURE THE NORTH-ERN COM TOWERS

Drop your APC and Transport Copter troops off at the northern Com Tower area. Your CO Power should be at maximum strength—initiate a Tag Battle and make short work of the Minicannon while you're up there. Grab the remaining Com Towers.

CO POWER STRATEGY

★★★☆★★★

With two power-houses like Max and Grimm, you've got ample firepower. Once your Tag Battle power is charged up, hit the Oozium with everything you've got. You should be able to eliminate twice as many of the slippery foes as you normally would.

★★★☆★★★

6 BUST THROUGH THE PIPELINES

Once you've claimed the northern Com Towers for your own, blast at the pipeline with your Md. Tank. Remove the Missiles guarding enemy HQ. You can collect bonus points by destroying the remaining Ooziums. If the northeast area is clear, reunite your Md. Tank with the rest of your squad and keep hammerin'. Victory is just around the corner. . . .

7 GRAB THE ENEMY HQ

With the Oozium force now in ruins, transport a Mech to enemy HQ and claim it for your own.

HEALING TOUCH

With the guidance of your ex-Black Hole comrades, you soon arrive at the Tower of Rebirth. Destroy the Black Crystals.

MISSION TERMS

Shatter all six Black Crystals to win. Good Luck! Though the mission sounds easy enough, you'll need to maximize each turn to get the jump on Black Hole. You'll have to whittle down the enemy numbers each day, while blasting each cursed Black Crystal into bits. Each crystal will heal all adjacent units by two points per turn, so get crackin'!

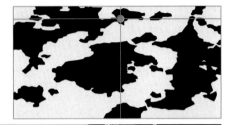

JAKE   HAWKE

JESS   LASH

VS.

KINDLE   JUGGER

AREA PROPERTIES:

	●	●	●	●	Ⓐ	Ⓝ	✖
🛫 AIRPORTS	-	-	-	-	-	1	-
🏭 BASES	-	-	-	-	-	1	-
🏙 CITIES	2	2	-	-	4	1	5
📡 COM TOWERS	-	-	-	-	-	-	6
⚔ MISSILE SILOS	-	-	-	-	-	5	-
⚓ SEAPORTS	-	-	-	-	-	-	-

BONUS POINTS: 150

OBJECT	#	PTS	TOTAL
🔲 BLACK CANNONS	-	-	-
◻ BLACK CRYSTALS	6	20	120
◼ BLACK OBELISKS	-	-	-
🔳 MINICANNONS	-	-	-
◻ OOZIUMS	-	-	-
🔲 PIPE JOINTS	6	5	30

BLACK HOLE INTEL

The Black Hole Army greatly outnumbers your forces, but its units are weak currently. They will huddle under the glow of the Black Crystal and regain two points per day.

MARCHING ORDERS

Hit the enemies while they're healing, and make haste to the silos. Maximize your movements and eliminate as many Black Hole units as you can daily, while also targeting the Black Crystals.

MISSION TIMELINE

START

Day 1
ORANGE STAR TACTICS
1
Make your way to the southwestern Black Crystal and take it out on Day 1.

Day 1
BLUE MOON TACTICS
2
Make your way to the southeastern Black Crystal and destroy on Day 1.

Day 2
LAUNCH THE MISSILES
3

Day 2
JOIN FORCES
4
Consolidate your forces and concentrate your attacks as a team.

Days 3-4
KEEP ON FIGHTING
5

CO Power ★
You should have stored up enough CO Power for a Tag Battle.

Days 5-7
SHATTER THE LAST CRYSTALS
6

VICTORY

1 ORANGE STAR TACTICS

Though the Black Hole forces are in shambles, they are slowly recuperating each day. The Black Crystal is their healing source, so you'll need to plow through the weaker units surrounding each crystal, then neutralize the crystal itself. Turn your Rockets on the closest enemy Infantry to open up a pathway, then drive your Mega Tank through and waste the first crystal. March an Infantry unit north and begin capturing the closest Com Tower. Take out the enemy Fighter with your AA gun, then reposition the rest of your units and eliminate as many enemies as you can. Before you know it, you'll have wasted a handful of Black Hole units in a single turn.

HEALING TOUCH

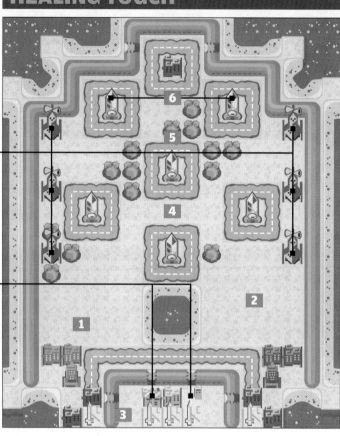

Immediately begin capturing the Com Towers with your Mech units. You'll boost your firepower and make short work of the opposition.

You'll find some extra help in the form of an airport and base in the south, but you'll have to bust through the pipeline to reach them.

2 BLUE MOON TACTICS

Once you've repositioned the Orange Star forces, it's time to work with Blue Moon. Load a Mech into the Transport Copter and drop your troops near the enemy AA gun in the south. Next, drive your APC south and trap the Missile battery to keep it from moving. Send your Mechs in to clear a path to the second crystal, then fly your Bomber in to finish the job. Use your AA gun to remove the closest enemy copter. Pilot your Stealth Fighter to the center crystal, then hide. Destroy the Artillery from afar and continue the assault. Target anything in range and blast away with your aerial and ground units. Send your Missiles north.

3 LAUNCH THE MISSILES

Activate the Missile Silo in the southwest and lob hot doom upon a crystal and its surrounding Black Hole forces.

4 JOIN FORCES

You probably suffered some losses after Black Hole's turn, but you've still got the advantage. Use Orange Star's units to do in nearby forces. Try to weaken, if not destroy, the central crystal. Your enemy will surround each crystal, making it difficult to get in and hack away. Neutralize any units that stand in the way of a clean shot. During Blue Moon's turn, finish off the black behemoth and sweep your forces to the middle of the battlefield. Take note of enemy positions; the forces will grow stronger each day.

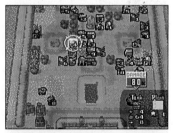

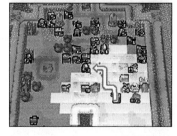

5 KEEP ON FIGHTING

Pound away at the pipeline with Orange Star forces and flood your troops inside. Once you breach the compound, launch missiles at the Black Crystal of your choice. Not only will this weaken your primary target, but it'll soften the units surrounding it. Make your move on the upper-middle crystal next, and wipe it from the map. Continue to eliminate nearby Black Hole forces, and keep capturing the Com Towers in the east. Use your APC to refuel or resupply any units in need. Your foe has been storing up plenty of CO Power, so hunker down and prepare for two consecutive rounds of hurt. You may need to restock your air or ground units, so manufacture reinforcements if you need 'em.

6 SHATTER THE LAST CRYSTALS

Launch another missile from the lower Missile Silos, then reposition the remainder of the Orange Star army near the northwest crystal. Piperunners patrol the perimeter, so you might want to take them out first. Check their firing range before committing to a unit movement, or you may find yourself a target. Move the Blue Moon forces to the crystal in the northeast. Blast away at it. Since your forces are likely in tatters by now, it may take you a few days to eliminate it. Manufacture any reinforcements as necessary, and remember to refuel and resupply the troops you have left in the field. Stay focused, and soon the win will come.

MISSION 22

CRYSTAL CALAMITY

The Black Obelisk lies buried beneath the desert, guarded by a technological nightmare 22,000 miles above the planet....

MISSION TERMS

Shatter the Black Obelisk to win. Before you can annihilate the vampire crystal, you'll need to remove its guardian high above the planet. **The Black Onyx satellite will fire in 50 minutes**, so get moving! There are nine Missile Silos equipped with anti-satellite munitions. Launch all nine missiles and destroy the Black Onyx, then take out the Black Cannon guarding your target.

| JAKE | RACHEL | HAWKE | VS. | KINDLE | KOAL |
| GRIMM | JAVIER | SENSEI | | | |

AREA PROPERTIES:

	●	●	●	○	Ⓐ	Ⓝ	✖
✈ AIRPORTS	1	-	2	-	3	2	2
🏠 BASES	2	1	1	-	4	2	3
🏙 CITIES	2	3	3	-	8	10	-
📡 COM TOWERS	-	-	-	-	-	2	-
⬛ MISSILE SILOS	-	-	-	-	-	9	-
⚓ SEAPORTS	-	1	-	-	1	1	-

BONUS POINTS: 145

OBJECT	#	PTS	TOTAL
🔲 BLACK CANNONS	1	30	30
🔳 BLACK CRYSTALS	-	-	-
🔲 BLACK OBELISKS	1	30	30
🔲 MINICANNONS	-	-	-
🔲 OOZIUMS	2	40	80
🔲 PIPE JOINTS	1	5	5

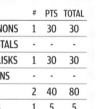

BLACK HOLE INTEL

The Black Hole Army is determined to protect its baby, the Black Obelisk. Its forces will try to beat you to the Missile Silos. Do not let them, or you'll fail the mission.

MARCHING ORDERS

Each team plays a distinct role. Have Orange Star hold the line and attack the Black Obelisk while Blue Moon blasts at the Black Cannon. Green Earth's job is to distract the enemy.

MISSION TIMELINE

START

Days 1-12
ORANGE STAR TACTICS
1
Reach the silos before your enemy does, or you'll lose the battle.

Days 1-12
BLUE MOON TACTICS
2

Days 1-12
GREEN EARTH TACTICS
3
Secure the enemy's southern airport and base.

CO Power ★
By now all COs will be ready to use their powers. Unleash them wisely.

Days 10-12
CRUSH THE CANNON
4
You must destroy the Black Cannon before you can attack the Black Obelisk.

Days 13-15
SHATTER THE BLACK OBELISK
5

VICTORY

THE BLACK OBELISK, BLACK ONYX & BLACK CANNON

Before you can obliterate the Black Obelisk, you'll need to destroy the Black Onyx satellite. Launch all nine missiles from the Missile Silos before your enemy can reach them. You must hit the satellite before it fully charges; otherwise you'll sustain heavy damage. Additionally, there is a Black Cannon guarding the obelisk. It has an enormous firing range, so you'll need to destroy it, too.

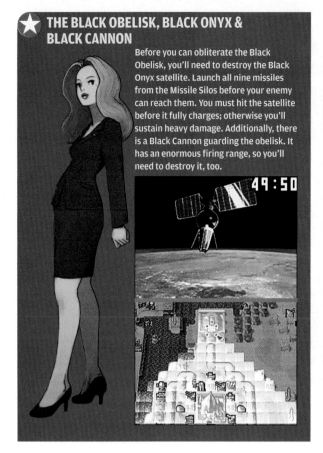

CRYSTAL CALAMITY

1 ORANGE STAR TACTICS

You'll need to beef up your forces, so immediately crank out a pair of Infantry units and start capturing the nearby cities. Once the immediate area is yours, you'll spread west collecting more properties, and ultimately activate all three Missile Silos. Build up your force each day—you'll need some heavy firepower to stave off the incoming Black Hole Oozium, Megatank and Battle Copters.

2 BLUE MOON TACTICS

Throughout this mission, you'll send the Blue Moon force south to pick up neutral real estate and Com Towers, and fire the missiles into space. Capture the port in the northeast, then start building Artillery and Tanks to trap and destroy the advancing enemy Md. Tank. Build a Lander to float an Infantry unit to the Missile Silo on the island. Eventually you'll station Rockets there to attack the Black Cannon.

3 GREEN EARTH TACTICS

Reposition your AA guns and Missiles to the south to eliminate any Battle Copters you encounter. Fire up the war machine and start cranking out Infantry, Tanks and AA guns to prevent the enemy from advancing on your turf. You'll need to send Infantry to the south to claim the airport ASAP, capture neutral properties and launch the three missiles at the Black Onyx.

4 CRUSH THE CANNON

The Black Onyx is no longer, so now it's time to lay into the Black Cannon guarding the life-draining crystal to the south. Load a Blue Moon Rocket unit onto a Lander and unload it on the small island west of the Black Cannon. You can also send Green Earth Artillery or Rockets to hit the cannon from the east.

5 SHATTER THE BLACK OBELISK

With the Black Cannon out of commission, it's time to bash the Black Obelisk. Have all available units converge at the center of the map and start blasting away. Lob Rocket and Artillery fire over the pipes to hit your target. There will be remnants of the Black Hole Army floating around, trying to protect their wicked creation. Blast 'em if they get in your way.

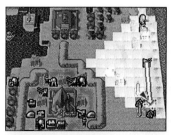

DARK AMBITION

The Black Hole Army retaliates with fury, decimating Omega Land. Regroup your forces and drive out the invaders.

MISSION TERMS

Capture the HQ or destroy all enemy units to win. You'll face Kindle and a mysterious evil clone of Olaf from Macro Land. To win, you'll need to breach enemy pipelines and storm the opposition's HQ, or eliminate all of their units . To make matters worse, a massive snow storm is raging, curbing your movement. Find and deactivate the Black Hole device that controls the blizzard, and press on to victory.

   VS.

| | SAMI | JAKE | RACHEL | | | KINDLE | OLAF CLONE |
| SONJA | EAGLE | HAWKE | | | | | |

AREA PROPERTIES: ● ● ● ● Ⓐ Ⓝ ✴

						A	N	✴
🗙	AIRPORTS	-	-	-	-	-	-	-
🏠	BASES	-	-	-	-	-	-	-
🏙	CITIES	1	1	1	-	3	-	7
📡	COM TOWERS	-	-	-	-	-	2	-
🚀	MISSILE SILOS	-	-	-	-	-	3	-
⚓	SEAPORTS	-	-	-	-	-	-	-

BONUS POINTS: 55

OBJECT	#	PTS	TOTAL
🔲 BLACK CANNONS	-	-	-
🔳 BLACK CRYSTALS	-	-	-
🔲 BLACK OBELISKS	-	-	-
🔲 MINICANNONS	4	10	40
🔲 OOZIUMS	-	-	-
🔲 PIPE JOINTS	3	5	15

✴ BLACK HOLE INTEL

The Black Hole Army is in a foul mood, and it's extra-aggressive this time. Don't be surprised if its forces break through the pipes and head straight for you.

★ MARCHING ORDERS

Capture the two closest Black Hole properties and quell the raging snowstorm. Move your Infantry units to the silos to prepare for launch.

MISSION TIMELINE

START ■

Days 1-3
ORANGE STAR TACTICS — 1

Days 1-3
BLUE MOON TACTICS — 2

Days 1-3
GREEN EARTH TACTICS — 3

Days 4-5
PREPARE FOR MISSILE LAUNCH — 4

CO Power ★
Fire when ready (don't save up for a Tag Battle).

Days 5-7
YA FEEL LUCKY, PUNK? — 5

CO Power ★
You have multiple options—think before you act.

Days 8-10
BREACH THE BLACK HOLE STRONGHOLD — 6

Days 11-12
CRUSH YOUR ENEMIES — 7

VICTORY ■

1 ORANGE STAR TACTICS

Load an Orange Star Infantry unit into each APC on standby then send one to the northern neutral city, and the other to the south. You'll find a device in either location that, when destroyed, will stop the foul weather (and lift your movement penalty). Once both cities are yours, load up your men and retreat to the west. Capture the Com Towers and activate the Missile Silos to weaken your enemies.

2 BLUE MOON TACTICS

Take a few days to reposition your Blue Moon forces to the east. Fly your air units to the front (and hide the Stealth Fighter before engaging in combat). Keep your Artillery in the rear and place an APC nearby to supply your units when necessary. Move your Aircraft Carrier east and prepare for the Black Hole assault.

3 GREEN EARTH TACTICS

Move your Green Earth units west, keeping your heavier Neotank and Megatank units on the front line and your AA guns and Artillery in the rear. The enemy Battle Copters will likely come at you first, so be prepared to knock them out of the sky. The fight is going to heat up quickly, so think fast and get ready for serious action.

4 PREPARE FOR MISSILE LAUNCH

Now that you've captured the eastern cities, retreat to the west and activate the Missile Silos. Pick your targets strategically to maximize damage to the enemy, but don't hurt your own forces in the process.

DARK AMBITION

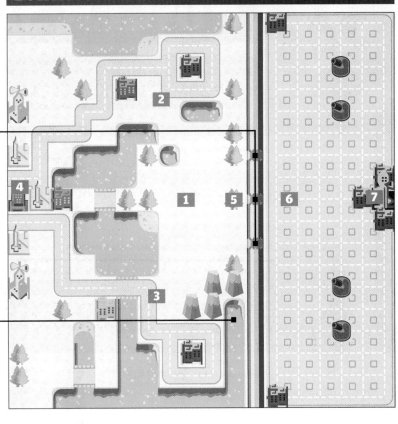

The Black Hole Army will be in a rush to break through the pipeline and attack you directly. Let 'em come to you.

Anchor the Green Earth Battleship here to assist your army. Lob a few shots at the Minicannons while you're at it.

5 YA FEEL LUCKY, PUNK?

You could throw caution to the wind and break the pipe joints first to net yourself some bonus points. It'll take some clever planning and teamwork, though. Stage your Blue Moon forces in the following formation: Fly a hidden Stealth Fighter up to the northernmost pipe joint and fire away. Line up your Rockets and Artillery to pound the enemy with indirect fire on the next turn. Swing the Blue Moon Bomber to the center pipe joint and pound it. During Green Earth's turn, tuck a Neotank into the gap—it'll be just out of enemy Minicannon range. Target the southern pipe joint with an Md. Tank and break the last section. As before, position your indirect-fire units behind to assault any enemy forces that creep through. Toss missiles from your Battleship at any target in range. Concentrate on Black Hole mobile forces first, then on the Minicannons.

6 BREACH THE BLACK HOLE STRONGHOLD

Your enemy will likely have used one or more CO Powers by now. If you've plugged up the gaps in the pipeline, you should be adequately protected from an all-out blitz. If you haven't already launched both missiles from the Missile Silos, do it now to weaken the clusters of Black Hole forces. When you're ready to breach the enemy stronghold, proceed with caution, and always check enemy firing range before moving your units.

7 CRUSH YOUR ENEMIES

Load your Orange Star infantry into the APCs and start heading toward enemy HQ. Clear out any remaining Black Hole forces to ensure the safe arrival of your capture teams. Chip away at the Minicannon defenses before you approach—once you park a unit inside their firing cone, it won't last long. Decide if you've got the strength to eliminate the remainder of the Black Hole forces, or if it would be easier to capture the enemy headquarters. Combine weaker units to increase their strength and firepower. Finally, don't forget to soften up enemy defenses with your seafaring vessels.

PINCER STRIKE

Despite Kindle's continued losses, she's extraordinarily confident in her abilities. Lord Von Bolt, on the other hand, isn't.

MISSION TERMS

Capture the HQ or destroy all enemy units to win. It's a veritable clone party on the battlefield, as Lord Von Bolt has sent in yet another cheap imitation to help lead his troops. Rains have muddied the land and are slowing your units. On top of that, the weather forecast calls for some fog, so be patient and expect a drawn-out fight. Use the landscape to your advantage and edge closer to ultimate victory.

| EAGLE | MAX |
| JAVIER | GRIT |

VS.

| JUGGER | DRAKE CLONE |

AREA PROPERTIES:

		●	●	●	●	A	N	✖
✈	AIRPORTS	-	-	-	-	-	1	-
🏠	BASES	2	-	-	-	2	3	1
🏙	CITIES	2	8	-	-	10	9	3
📡	COM TOWERS	-	-	-	-	-	2	-
⬜	MISSILE SILOS	-	-	-	-	-	2	-
⚓	SEAPORTS	1	-	-	-	1	1	-

BONUS POINTS: 0

OBJECT	#	PTS	TOTAL
BLACK CANNONS	-	-	-
BLACK CRYSTALS	-	-	-
BLACK OBELISKS	-	-	-
MINICANNONS	-	-	-
OOZIUMS	-	-	-
PIPE JOINTS	-	-	-

BLACK HOLE INTEL

Take a good look at the Black Hole forces while you can. In a few days, the Fog of War will roll in and conceal them. Expect a tense battle against some strong units.

MARCHING ORDERS

Send Recon units ahead and station Infantry on the mountain tops to cut through the fog. If you assemble your COs and stick to the battle plans, you should emerge as the winner.

MISSION TIMELINE

START

Day 1
ORANGE STAR TACTICS   1

Days 1-3
BLUE MOON TACTICS   2
Keep Max on the front line until the end of the third day, then switch to Grit.

Day 2
PIERCE THROUGH THE FOG   3

Days 3-4
CLEAR THE FOREST   4

Days 5-8
TROUBLE ON THE SEAS   5

Days 5-8
BLUE MOON ATTACKS!   6

CO Power   ★
You may need to use your CO Power at this point if you're struggling.

Days 9-12
COMBINE YOUR FORCES   7

CO Power   ★
Initiate a Tag Battle if you can.

Day 12-15
CHOOSE THE ENDING   8

VICTORY

1 ORANGE STAR TACTICS

Time is of the essence, so it is of utmost importance that you manage your units intelligently. Sail the Battleship to the northeast cove. Load the western Battle Copter into the Cruiser, then pull out of port and park near the Battleship. Unload the Battle Copter. Reposition the rest of your naval and aerial units as shown in the screenshot below. Create two Infantry units and park the APC next to the eastern base. Move the Recon unit, Tank and Megatank to the neutral base to the northeast of your HQ (see image below). Use available Infantry to begin capturing the base.

PINCER STRIKE

You have only three days before the Fog of War rolls in. Prepare your forces and take note of the Black Hole Army's unit positions.

Get the upper hand and reach the Missile Silos before your nemeses do. Launching these munitions will weaken your foes.

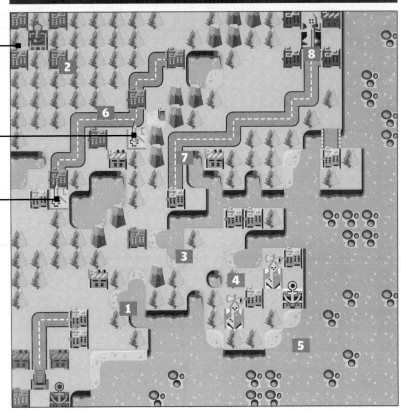

2 BLUE MOON TACTICS

Use Max as your Blue Moon CO for the first two days, then at the end of Day 3 switch to Grit and harness his increased range. Reposition your units out of enemy Rocket range, and move your Rockets to your city in the south (see the screenshot below). Keep your units stationary until the fourth day, when you'll attack the enemy from afar (see Blue Moon Attacks!).

3 PIERCE THROUGH THE FOG

By now, the fog will have rolled in. To increase visibility, dive with your Sub and maneuver north into the little alcove near your Battleship. Unleash an attack from your Battleship and damage the enemy's Missiles, then finish the job with your Battle Copters. Create more Infantry and capture all real estate as you fan out from your HQ. Load an Infantry unit into the Lander; you'll use it deliver a capture team to the east. Reposition your Mega Tank and Recon unit in the mountain on the southern shore.

4 CLEAR THE FOREST

By the third day, the enemy Battleship will be closing in. Your job is to clear the woods and get out of there before it arrives. Deposit your Infantry from the Lander and start capturing real estate to the east. Return the Lander to your Base and continue this process of transporting and depositing Infantry to the east. Flush out and attack the enemy Tank, Artillery and Infantry with your Battle Copters, Mega Tank and Battleship.

5 TROUBLE ON THE SEAS

Using your Sub and Cruiser, protect your Battleship from harm and neutralize any enemy units that wander into your range. Your Sub will likely be discovered by incoming forces, though.

6 BLUE MOON ATTACKS!

At the end of the third day, switch to CO Grit and fire your Missiles at the Black Hole units in range. Your foes will hold their ground, but will likely not advance. After you've eliminated three or more enemy units, fan out your units to the southeast but take care to stay out of the woods and out of enemy Battleship firing range. Remove the existing enemy Artillery and AA guns with your forces.

7 COMBINE YOUR FORCES

After more than a week in the field, Blue Moon should be regrouping with Orange Star around the center of the map. Continue pressing eastward and northward while capturing the airport and other properties along the way. Activate the Missile Silo and weaken the enemy cluster of choice. Send a Recon unit to the front, with a Neotank or Megatank behind, followed by Rockets and Artillery. You should have plenty of firepower available to hit the Black Hole units as you discover them.

8 CHOOSE THE ENDING

In about two weeks, you should be close to victory. Assess the situation and decide how you want to end the battle. If you've got the time, eliminate the remainder of the Black Hole Army, or grab the HQ.

RING OF FIRE

You have just 18 days to destroy all the Black Hole units at the foot of the Twin Crown volcanoes.

MISSION TERMS

Destroy all enemy units within 18 days to win. You'll square off against Koal and a clone of Commander Kanbei this round. After 18 days, the volcanoes will erupt, consuming your units. Victory must be well-timed. The battle takes place on two fronts, and it's up to you to decide how to fight. Either tweak the AI to fight the secondary battle for you, or take the helm and call the shots yourself.

GRIT   **MAX**   **VS.**   **KOAL**   **KANBEI CLONE**

AREA PROPERTIES:

	●	●	●	●	A	N	✖
 AIRPORTS	-	-	-	-	-	1	-
BASES	-	-	-	-	-	2	-
CITIES	4	-	-	-	4	11	4
COM TOWERS	-	-	-	-	-	2	-
MISSILE SILOS	-	-	-	-	-	2	-
SEAPORTS	-	-	-	-	-	-	-

BONUS POINTS: 40

OBJECT	#	PTS	TOTAL
BLACK CANNONS	-	-	-
BLACK CRYSTALS	-	-	-
BLACK OBELISKS	-	-	-
MINICANNONS	-	-	-
OOZIUMS	1	40	40
PIPE JOINTS	-	-	-

✖ BLACK HOLE INTEL

Tread lightly around the twin volcanoes. Black Hole units will likely make a run to claim the neutral bases before attacking you. Keep your eyes on both fronts.

★ MARCHING ORDERS

Let Max fight defensively on the secondary front. Grit's long-range abilities make him an asset on the main front. Utilize your Rockets and Artillery to waste enemies each day.

MISSION TIMELINE

START ■

Days 1-4   1
TO FIGHT OR NOT TO FIGHT?
It'll take four days or more to win on the secondary front.

Days 1-4   2
MAIN-FRONT TACTICS

Whenever Possible   3
ATTACK CENTRAL BLACK HOLE UNITS

CO Power ★
Activate your CO Powers to dish out the pain to the Black Hole Army.

Days 5-8   4
CAPTURE THE BASE

Days 5-8   5
TAKE THE AIRPORT

CO Power ★
If you were victorious on the secondary front, you can now use your Tag Battle powers.

Days 9-12   6
THE FINAL SWEEP
Though you have 18 days, you'll likely win in less than two weeks.

VICTORY ■

1 TO FIGHT OR NOT TO FIGHT?

With Max as your secondary-front CO, decide if you want him to fight for you automatically (Auto CO) or if you want to take control. If you choose Auto CO, adjust the AI to Defense mode and let the battle play out. Send two AA guns and a Missile to the secondary front. You'll want to capture the closest Com Towers and push east to the mountain range. Once you attract the attention of advancing Black Hole forces, withdraw your Infantry and send in your AA guns to take down Black Hole Battle Copters. Deploy some Mechs to the mountains to assist your Battle Copters in wrecking the enemy's Neotank.

RING OF FIRE

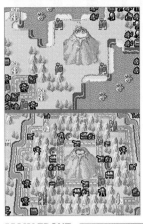

SECONDARY FRONT

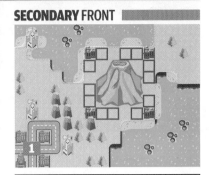

Beware of the fallout from the volcano on the secondary front. The red squares denote the danger zones.

MAIN FRONT

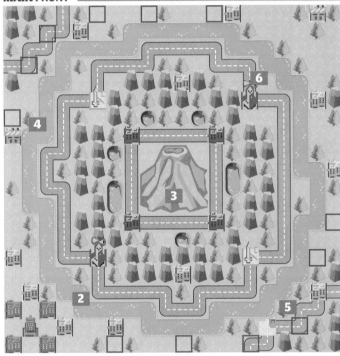

2 MAIN-FRONT TACTICS

Load Infantry into an APC and push east while avoiding the volcano fallout (see the Main Front map). Using your Mechs, capture the two closest cities. Over the next few days, continue capturing neutral properties with your ground units. Make sure you also grab the base to the north of your HQ. Keep Artillery and Rockets on standby to protect your on-foot teams. Attack any Black Hole forces within range with your indirect-fire units. Continue spreading out and capturing neutral real estate. You'll want the firepower boost that the Com Towers bestow, so be sure to grab them, as well.

4 CAPTURE THE BASE

Station your Rockets and Artillery along the river in anticipation of enemy forces. The Black Hole Army won't be happy when you claim this base for your own, so be sure to shell approaching Tanks to keep your troops safe. Once you've got the ability to manufacture units at the base, build what you need and proceed east. Activate the Missile Silo and capture nearby neutral ground. Remember to check enemy firing range before moving.

5 TAKE THE AIRPORT

Continue protecting your capture team with Artillery and Rockets on standby. When you grab the airport in the southeast, you'll have to contend with the approaching Black Hole units. Next, send your men to the Missile Silo and target a cluster of enemy units. If you need additional firepower, don't forget to utilize your Battle Copter and long-range units across the river.

3 ATTACK CENTRAL BLACK HOLE UNITS

Although the Artillery and Black Boats surrounding the lower volcano are landlocked, they still pose a threat. When the opportunity arises, eliminate the Black Boats first.

Avoid placing any units on the spots marked with a red box. After the first day, each volcano will erupt daily and seriously damage anything in these zones.

6 THE FINAL SWEEP

By now, your second CO should have joined you on the main front. If you haven't already done so, direct your firepower to the center and wipe out any remaining units at the foot of the volcano. Claim the remaining neutral properties on the central island to give nearby units a place to get supplies. Destroy the remainder of the Black Hole Army still puttering

SURROUNDED!

Your search for another Black Obelisk is cut short. You have only 24 days to stop the launch of Black Armageddon!

MISSION TERMS

Capture the four Com Towers within 24 days to win.
Kindle's back with a few surprises. First off, she's pointing Black Hole's ultimate weapon—Black Armageddon—at each city on the continent. Second, she's brought along a clone of Commander Andy from Cosmo Land to fight. Time is against you, so you'll need to think ahead to capture all four Com Towers, or it's curtains for the allied forces!

 JAKE   EAGLE

 VS.

JAVIER   SAMI

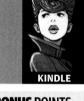

KINDLE   ANDY CLONE

AREA PROPERTIES:

	●	●	●	○	Ⓐ	N	✖
✈ AIRPORTS	-	-	-	-	-	2	-
🏠 BASES	2	1	-	-	3	1	4
🏙 CITIES	3	5	-	-	8	17	4
📡 COM TOWERS	-	-	-	-	-	-	4
⬛ MISSILE SILOS	-	-	-	-	-	2	-
⚓ SEAPORTS	-	-	-	-	-	-	-

BONUS POINTS: 10

OBJECT	#	PTS	TOTAL
BLACK CANNONS	-	-	-
BLACK CRYSTALS	-	-	-
BLACK OBELISKS	-	-	-
MINICANNONS	-	-	-
OOZIUMS	-	-	-
PIPE JOINTS	2	5	10

SAMI

BLACK HOLE INTEL

Kindle and company will try to steamroll your army with their Md. Tanks. While you're distracted by the enemy's armored units, they'll make a run for the Missile Silos. Beat them there!

MARCHING ORDERS

Start clearing and capturing the southern and easterns regions first, then make your way to the northern and western zones.

MISSION TIMELINE

START

Days 1-4
ORANGE STAR TACTICS
1

Days 1-4
BLUE MOON TACTICS
2

Days 1-4
ORANGE STAR DEFENSE
3

Days 1-4
BLUE MOON DEFENSE
4

★ **CO Power**
Use your CO Powers separately this time around.

Days 5-7
LAUNCH THE MISSILES
5

★ **CO Power**
Hit the enemy with another round of individual CO Powers.

Days 7-9
SNAG THE LAST COM TOWER
6

VICTORY

1 ORANGE STAR TACTICS

Orange Star will be tasked with capturing the Com Towers in the northwest and southeast. Begin by loading Infantry into your APC and relocating it outside of enemy firing range. Move your heavier units toward the Com Tower in a bid to flush the enemy out of hiding. Once they make a move on your force, quickly neutralize the Tank, AA gun and Rockets guarding the Com Tower. When you've got the funds, create additional Infantry units and capture the neutral and enemy real estate in the immediate area. Capture the base.

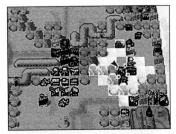

2 BLUE MOON TACTICS

Similar to Orange Star's marching orders, Blue Moon's job is to grab the Com Towers in the southwest and northeast. Load a Mech into your APC and reposition it outside of enemy range. Advance your AA guns up the line and confront the enemy Battle Copters. After a day or two, the coast should be clear for a capture team. Send reserve Rockets and Artillery northward to guard your bases. Snatch any cities and bases nearby to boost your daily intake so you'll have the funds to crank out reinforcements. If necessary, park a unit on top of the Black Hole base to prevent it from manufacturing any units in the interim.

SURROUNDED!

Bust through the pipeline if you want to assist Blue Moon in capturing the northeastern Com Tower.

Blast through this pipeline and assist Orange Star if they're having trouble reaching the silos.

3 ORANGE STAR DEFENSE

Capture the neutral cities in the center as you sweep the Orange Star forces northwest following your capture of the first Com Tower. You will likely be assaulted by Black Hole's Md. Tanks, so do your best to take them out. You could place some expendable Infantry out in the open as bait, then shell the heck out of the Tanks with Artillery as they approach if you're feeling especially cruel.

4 BLUE MOON DEFENSE

While you're waiting for the Blue Moon crew to arrive, pump out some Infantry or Mechs and capture the airport and neutral real estate in the area surrounding your northern base. If Black Hole resistance makes things hairy, consider requesting help from nearby Orange Star forces. You may get a shot at capturing the Com Tower early, but be wary of new units springing forth from the nearby enemy base.

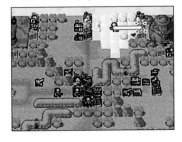

CO POWER STRATEGY

★★★★★★★★★★

Keep Eagle in charge of the Blue Moon forces for the first few days. The Black Hole Army will try to hit you with its Tag Battle first, so beat them to the punch with Eagle's Lightning Strike.

CO POWER STRATEGY

★★★★☆☆☆

Jake should lead the Orange Star war effort and charge his CO Powers over the first days of battle. Your enemy will try to strike hard and fast with a Tag Battle, but you can get in the first shot, provided you've substantially filled Jake's CO Power meter.

5 LAUNCH THE MISSILES

Send some Tanks, Rockets or Artillery to escort one or more Infantry or Mech units to the two Missile Silos in the west. The Black Hole Army will undoubtedly send its own troops in a bid to beat you to the punch. Waste them from afar with your indirect-fire units. Once your boys reach the launch controls to the towers, light 'em up—you're almost done! Target any immediate threats or clusters of powerful Black Hole armored units and pave the way for victory. Blast through the pipeline and send in Blue Moon troops if needed.

6 SNAG THE LAST COM TOWER

The last Com Tower sits in the northwest. Combine, supply or reinforce your remaining units and descend upon your final objective. Snag your prize and soak in the celebration music.

FOR THE FUTURE!

The search for the true Black Obelisk leads you to the bottom of the Crimson Sea, where you must confront Lord Von Bolt.

MISSION TERMS

Destroy the Black Obelisk to win. Finally, the huffing head in a fishbowl steps out from the shadows for a showdown at the bottom of the sea. Lord Von Bolt reveals his plan to leech the planet's life source to sustain his worthless hide for eternity, but the allied forces won't stand idly by. In order to sabotage his rickety operation, you'll need to command your forces with finesse and conviction.

JAKE | RACHEL | HAWKE | VS. | VON BOLT
MAX | SASHA | EAGLE

AREA PROPERTIES:

	●	●	●	●	Ⓐ	N	✖
✖ AIRPORTS	-	-	1	-	1	1	1
🏢 BASES	2	1	1	-	4	4	3
🏙 CITIES	7	6	6	-	19	8	8
COM TOWERS	-	-	-	-	-	-	3
MISSILE SILOS	-	-	-	-	-	-	-
SEAPORTS	-	1	-	-	1	1	1

BONUS POINTS: 195

OBJECT	#	PTS	TOTAL
BLACK CANNONS	-	-	-
BLACK CRYSTALS	3	20	60
BLACK OBELISKS	1	30	30
MINICANNONS	4	10	40
OOZIUMS	-	-	-
PIPE JOINTS	13	5	65

MISSION TIMELINE

START

Days 1-3
ORANGE STAR TACTICS — 1
It's up to Orange Star to capture the Com Towers.

Days 1-3
BLUE MOON TACTICS — 2
Blue Moon's job is to take control of the western waterfront.

Days 1-3
GREEN EARTH TACTICS — 2
Green Earth must take control of the eastern waterfront.

Days 4-6
ASSIST YOUR FELLOW FORCES — 4

CO Power ★
Sasha's power can reduce the enemy's CO Power.

Days 7-9
DESTROY THE BLACK CRYSTALS — 5

CO Power ★
Engage in a Tag Battle if you've got the strength.

Days 10-12
BLAST THROUGH THE PIPELINE — 6

Days 13-15
DESTROY THE TRUE BLACK OBELISK — 7

VICTORY

BLACK HOLE INTEL

For a wheezing derelict on life support, Von Bolt is one tough customer. Beware his Ex Machina CO Power—it knocks three points off affected units and paralyzes them for a turn.

★ MARCHING ORDERS

While Orange Star creeps up the center, have the other forces flank the perimeter. Von Bolt may target Orange Star with his CO Power, so get Blue Moon and Green Earth troops through the pipeline ASAP to help out.

1 ORANGE STAR TACTICS

Start this mission with Jake as the Orange Star CO. Your goals over the first few days of the conflict are to capture the outlying Com Towers first, then the middle one. You'll want to advance your indirect-fire forces up the center of the map while staying out of range of Von Bolt's Minicannons. The Mega Tanks should lead the way, with the smaller ones behind as depicted in the image below. Since you possess a pair of bases, beef up your roster of Artillery, Tanks and Rockets each day—the action will soon heat up. Create and load a Mech unit into the waiting APC to aid your capture team. Within a day or two, Von Bolt will strike hard. Before this happens, switch to Max as the Orange Star CO. Until the first row of Minicannons is destroyed, do not venture past the Com Tower line, or you'll risk obliteration. It will be the job of Blue Moon and Green Earth to weaken the shoreline defenses, so don't fret. Just keep your units healthy and supplied in the days leading up to the first attack.

2 BLUE MOON TACTICS

Blue Moon's role here is to go on the offensive. Over the course of the first two days, manufacture a Lander at your port and an Artillery unit at your factory. You'll soon load an Infantry or Mech unit inside it and set sail for the base in the north. Using your available ground forces, capture the cities in your vicinity. Move your Artillery in step with your Infantry to protect it from attack. Sail your Battleship within striking range of the Minicannon and unleash a devastating attack. Your Sub and Cruiser should also travel northward (refer to the screenshot below) to take out enemy naval units. Capture properties when it's safe.

3 GREEN EARTH TACTICS

Green Earth's tactics will mirror Blue Moon's somewhat, though you'll be using air power in place of a naval force. Create a Transport Copter and load it with an Infantry unit. Send your Battle Copter and Bomber north to attack the closest Minicannon. Your local ground troops should capture nearby real estate to boost your daily income. Once the first Minicannon is exterminated, fly your capture team to the northern base and grab it. Fly your Stealth and Fighter units in tandem as support, but take care to shelter them from enemy fire. Always check the enemy's firing range before positioning any of your units in the vicinity.

4 ASSIST YOUR FELLOW FORCES

By now, Von Bolt has unleashed his crippling CO Power (most likely hitting the Orange Star group in the center). In addition, those annoying Black Crystals are busy healing his units. With one of your armies severely wounded and paralyzed, you'll have to send in reinforcements from the other two groups. Blast through the pipe joints and send in available units to protect your wounded brethren. Replace destroyed Tanks and Artillery and send them up the line. Lob indirect fire from any naval vessels you have within range to thin the enemy ranks.

5 DESTROY THE BLACK CRYSTALS

Blue Moon and Green Earth must destroy the Black Crystals; otherwise their healing properties will prolong an already drawn-out and difficult conflict. Also dedicate some firepower to the remaining Minicannons.

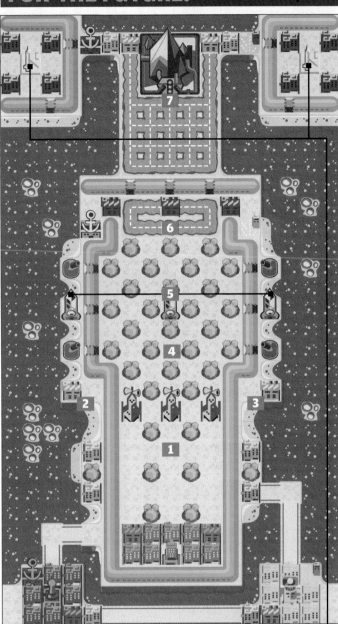

FOR THE FUTURE!

Launch the missiles as soon as you get the chance, but be warned: they are heavily guarded by Black Hole units and surrounded by a pipe ring.

6 BLAST THROUGH THE PIPELINE

You're almost there—the Black Obelisk sits behind a pipe wall, continuously sucking energy from the planet like an overgrown tick. It's time to smash through its last remaining defenses and squeeze it out of existence! Reposition your Orange Star forces up the line and hack away at the joints. Send your flanking forces up the sides and assist in the effort. Attack any Black Hole vessels or units that intervene. You should be able to bust through in a couple of days. Once you're inside, beat on the enemy units without mercy.

7 DESTROY THE TRUE BLACK OBELISK

Continue attacking and conquering neutral property with your Infantry. You may want to send some troops inside the compounds in the northeast and northwest to activate the Missile Silos for additional firepower. Hammer on the cancerous crystal until it shatters into a million pieces, thereby sabotaging Von Bolt's plans for immortality.

MEANS TO AN END

It's time for the final showdown against Von Bolt and his pasty girlfriend. Get ready to fight the Grand Bolt Oozium!

MISSION TERMS

Shatter the three Black Crystals on the top screen and defeat Von Bolt on the touch screen within 24 days to win. There's a lot to keep track of during this final fight, but it's easier than it looks. The secondary front will be commanded by the CO of your choice (we recommend Hawke) while you'll be responsible for warding off the onslaught of Ooziums and capturing real estate below.

JAKE   HAWKE

VS.

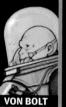 

VON BOLT   KINDLE

AREA PROPERTIES:

		●	●	●	●	Ⓐ	N	✖
🛫	AIRPORTS	2	-	-	-	2	2	-
🏢	BASES	2	-	-	-	2	20	2
🏙	CITIES	4	-	-	-	4	2	-
📡	COM TOWERS	-	-	-	-	-	4	-
◪	MISSILE SILOS	-	-	-	-	-	-	-
⚓	SEAPORTS	-	-	-	-	-	-	-

BONUS POINTS: 650

OBJECT	#	PTS	TOTAL
🔲 BLACK CANNONS	-	-	-
◻ BLACK CRYSTALS	-	-	-
▢ BLACK OBELISKS	-	-	-
▣ MINICANNONS	-	-	-
◯ OOZIUMS	16	40	640
▦ PIPE JOINTS	2	5	10

BLACK HOLE INTEL

In a last-ditch effort at self-preservation, Von Bolt will let loose the Grand Bolt—a gigantic über-Oozium with limitless reserves. He'll fight aggressively up top and defensively below.

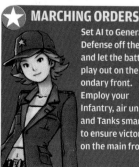

★ MARCHING ORDERS

Set AI to General or Defense off the bat and let the battle play out on the secondary front. Employ your Infantry, air units and Tanks smartly to ensure victory on the main front.

MISSION TIMELINE

START

Days 1-4
BULK UP YOUR MILITARY ①

Days 5-8
THE SOUTH SHALL FALL AGAIN ②
Move your forces to the south and begin capturing real estate while you crush the local resistance.

CO Power ★
Initiate Jake's CO Powers to decimate the enemy forces.

Days 9-12
FEND OFF THE NORTHERN FORCES ③

Days 13-16
MOP UP SOME OOZIUMS ④

CO Power ★
Consider using your CO Powers independently rather than in a Tag Battle.

Days 17-20
GOODBYE, CRUEL WORLD ⑤

VICTORY

1 BULK UP YOUR MILITARY

You've made it to the final battle (we swear, no more surprises). You'll have to contend with the ooziest of Ooziums, the Grand Bolt, on the main front as the action rages on the upper screen. Pump out a quartet of Infantry on the first day, then let Hawke fight the secondary front on the AI setting of your choice (see your Marching Orders on the preceding page). Begin capturing both Com Towers on your next turn and send your other men to grab the neutral bases and cities nearby. The whole process of converting this area to Orange Star property should take a few days, but it'll be worth it. Build and send forth a pair of Battle Copters to the south in preparation for your assault. You might be tempted to send additional units to the secondary front, but in all likelihood you shouldn't have to—Hawke is quite capable of destroying the Black Crystals on his own.

2 THE SOUTH SHALL FALL AGAIN

Crank out several Transport Copters and AA guns in preparation for the southern assault. Load your Infantry into the choppers and begin the invasion. Send your antiair support in tow in case the stray Ooziums slithers in for an attack. Immediately target Von Bolt's Infantry units and wipe them out before they get a chance to capture all the neutral territories. You'll want to minimize the Black Hole Army's income and prevent it from manufacturing any powerful units at the bases near the Grand Bolt. Once the opposing ground troops are gone, convert each city, base and Com Tower in the south to Orange Star colors. Continue building Recon units and AA guns to assist in warding off the slimy Oozium threats that are rolling about the countryside. If you attack one, be sure to hit it with three or four units simultaneously to avoid a needless sacrifice.

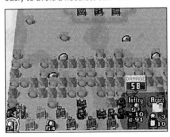

MEANS TO AN END

SECONDARY FRONT

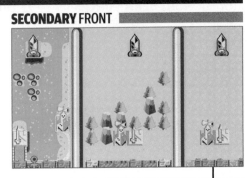

Let your CO on the secondary front fight the battle. Hawke is an able leader, so you shouldn't need to send him reinforcements.

MAIN FRONT

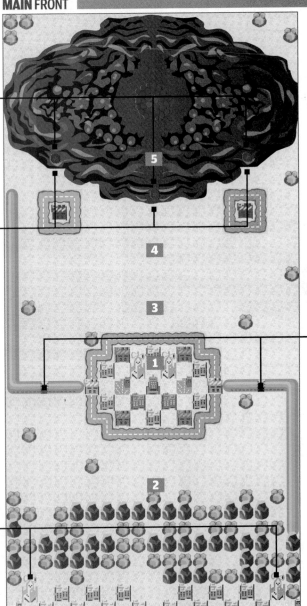

Don't bother attacking the Grand Bolt until the secondary front's three Black Crystals protecting it have been destroyed.

The Grand Bolt will squirt out three Ooziums every six days. By the 18th day, it'll give up its last offspring.

If you decide to manufacture Piperunners, you'll need these joints intact to maximize their effective fighting range.

Make it your priority to wipe out Von Bolt's Infantry units as fast as possible, or they'll capture the southern real estate.

STRATEGY CONTINUED ON THE NEXT PAGE

3 FEND OFF THE NORTHERN FORCES

Continue capturing the last of the southern bases and cities, effectively cutting off Von Bolt's revenue. Once you own every last inch of real estate, swing around and rejoin the Orange Star forces by HQ. Bolster your army with new units, preferably with Md. Tanks or Neotanks along with AA guns if you can spare the cash. While you've been occupied in the south, Black Hole forces have been advancing from the north in the form of Infantry, Recon, Anti-air and Ooziums. Regroup and meet them head-on. Refer to the screenshot below when you're ready to fight. Systematically destroy each enemy with the appropriate firepower.

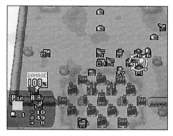

4 MOP UP SOME OOZIUMS

Hawke should be close to victory on the secondary front. In the meantime, you'll have to contend with six or more Ooziums in your immediate area. Your war coffers should be overflowing, so spend your capital on the beefiest units you can afford. Envelop and destroy each Oozium with three or four AA guns or your most powerful tanks. Remember that Ooziums can move one space per day, and can attack only directly. Plan your movements accordingly and avoid needlessly losing your units to their crushing attacks. Once the final Black Crystal is shattered, the Grand Bolt will be vulnerable.

5 GOODBYE, CRUEL WORLD

With the Black Crystals now out of the way, it's time to say goodbye to the Grand Bolt. Continue pushing your forces north, capturing any real estate you encounter. By the 18th day, the giant pile of goo will have birthed its last trio of Ooziums. Stay away from the three red eyes on this day, as anything directly in front will be destroyed. Send your heavy hitters to the front line and blast away at each red eye. The rest of your forces should concentrate on cleaning up the remaining Black Hole forces in the field. After you administer a good shelling, it'll give up the ghost. It's payback time, Von Bolt!

WHO WILL DO THE FINAL HONORS?

It all comes down to this: Von Bolt's Black Hole empire is a shattered mess, yet he remains defiant in the face of defeat. He'll prattle on endlessly like the sociopath he is, until you are tasked with making the final difficult decision. Do you show Lord Von Bolt the mercy he has denied to so many across Omega Land? Or do you let your rage take over and put him out of his misery yourself? Your fellow COs will leave it up to you, so think long and hard to determine the fate of the evil dictator. If you replay the game in Hard Campaign mode, you can make a different choice.

BUT THAT'S NOT ALL!

You won! In addition to the satisfaction of having saved the world, your victory earns you the right to visit Hachi to purchase new COs, maps, the Hard Campaign, the sound room, the gallery and much more. The more you play, the more you can buy and unlock in the Battle Maps shop.

FUNDS	1950
Sound Room	2000
Gallery	2000
Oozium	1000
Kindle	4000
Rachel	150
Andy	150

Hey, if you're coming in, come in... And shut the door! Were you born in a barn?!

CAMPAIGN

THE BATTLE RAGES ON

So, you've beaten the game, saved Omega Land from the withered clutches of Von Bolt and restored peace to the world. Congratulations are in order for a job well done. But don't sprain your arm patting yourself on the back, hotshot—there's still an entire game's worth of fighting to do. That is, if you've got the guts to tackle the Hard Campaign. . . .

A TOUGHER BATTLE

If you're looking for punishment, you've come to the right place. Learn about the wickedly tough Hard Campaign and its nuances here.

DIFFERENT BY DESIGN

Though you'll be fighting on the same battlefields as you did in the Normal Campaign, each mission's design has been tailored to test your mettle. Some changes are subtle, but you'll soon realize it'll take careful planning (and additional days) to triumph.

A NEW APPROACH

Though the Hard Campaign missions share the same names and locations as their Normal Campaign cousins, you'll need to alter your approach to win. Terrain features and the numbers and positions of available real estate have changed. Examine each new environment and consider ways to use it to your advantage for both offensive and defensive tactics.

FEWER OPTIONS

There will be some significant changes to the maps from the start, and you won't be able to harness the stronger firepower of Md. Tanks, Neotanks, Rockets and Missiles right away. That means you'll be at an immediate disadvantage, so you'll need to overcome the situation with superior strategy.

BIGGER THREATS

You'll face a greater number of stronger enemies this time around. Don't be surprised when your opponent whips out Neotanks and Black Bombs much earlier in the campaign.

MORE POINTS

Finally, some good news: with the increased difficulty of the Hard Campaign, you'll have the opportunity to amass some serious bonus points. Make it a priority to score big each round.

THE SKILLS TO SUCCEED

It's even more important this time around that you pick the right CO to command each mission. Examine the situation at hand and compare each officer's strengths and abilities before jumping headfirst into war. Feel free to experiment and staff each army any way you see fit—you might discover a winning combination. If you run into trouble, try using our suggested COs.

STRATEGY BRIEFING

Did you think the Normal Campaign was tough? You ain't seen nothin' yet! But we're not sending you into combat unarmed. Take this knowledge to heart and bring it with you—what you learn today might save your hide tomorrow.

- **KNOW YOUR ENEMY, USE THE ENVIRONMENT**
  Every CO has a particular strength and weakness. Exploit your enemy's shortcomings and use the battlefield to your advantage.

- **CHOOSE COs ACCORDING TO BATTLEFIELD CONDITIONS**
  Choose the right CO for the job. Check your units and those of your opponent, as well as the battlefield conditions when making your selections.

- **EQUIP EFFECTIVE SKILLS**
  Be sure to adjust your equipped skills to complement the units you'll use and go up against. Effective use of these skills will give you an edge.

- **PLAN OFFENSIVE AND DEFENSIVE MANEUVERS**
  Sometimes you'll need to think defensively before you can move in and take the fight to your enemy. Knowing when to stand your ground and fortify a defensive position while you prepare an assault elsewhere on the battlefield can mean the difference between a glorious victory and an agonizing defeat.

MISSION DETAILS

The following pages concentrate on the differences between the Normal and the Hard Campaign missions. Below you can learn what's changed, and how the changes will affect your overall strategy for each mission.

DIFFERENT, HARDER

For the Hard Campaign, we've made a few changes to the way we present strategy. The mission terms and the map for each mission are identical to those in the Normal Campaign, so we've omitted them from the following pages. We've expanded the mission timeline to account for the new strategies you'll likely employ when tackling these challenging levels.

THE CHOICE IS YOURS

The beauty of Advance Wars: Dual Strike is that there's more than one way to approach a situation. We've listed our recommended CO picks for each scenario, though we encourage you to experiment. If you have a favorite CO that you've invested lots of time and energy building up, by all means drop him into the fray and put him to the test.

INTEL REPORTS

The intel reports outline the basic differences you'll face in the Hard Campaign version of a particular mission. In addition, we've revised the CO Power strategy, changing the advice so that it's relevant to the new scenario. Remember that we've tailored the strategy to work with our CO choices, so your tactics may differ when you employ your own officers in battle.

MISSION **1**

JAKE'S TRIAL

SAMI   HAWKE   **VS.**   RACHEL

AREA PROPERTIES:

		N	
AIRPORTS	-	-	-
BASES	1	1	2
CITIES	3	8	1
COM TOWERS	-	-	-
MISSILE SILOS	-	-	-
SEAPORTS	-	-	-

BONUS POINTS: 0

OBJECT	#	PTS	TOTAL
BLACK CANNONS	-	-	-
BLACK CRYSTALS	-	-	-
BLACK OBELISKS	-	-	-
MINICANNONS	-	-	-
OOZIUMS	-	-	-
PIPE JOINTS	-	-	-

☾ BLUE MOON INTEL

Rachel will command her Blue Moon forces to capture properties aggressively. Not only will she start the mission with powerful units, but she'll crank out additional Tanks and Artillery as the battle rages.

★ MARCHING ORDERS

You'll need to build and effectively use your Artillery to shell your opponent at arm's length if you want to boost your Power and Technique scores. Use your cities to boost your defensive stats.

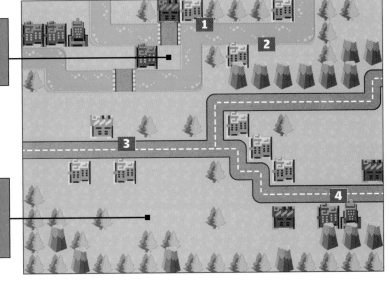

Place Artillery near the riverbanks and target enemies as they approach your home zone.

Once you convert the central base, park a loaded APC here for the final push toward Blue Moon HQ.

MISSION TIMELINE

START

Days 1-5
SECURE THE NEARBY PROPERTIES
Begin the mission with Sami and quickly grab real estate. Switch COs daily to build their CO Powers evenly.

Days 3-8
FIRE ARTILLERY ACROSS THE RIVER
Shell the Blue Moon forces from across the river to weaken their numbers while keeping your own squad intact.

Days 4-10
BUILD YOUR FORCES
Convert the central base and begin manufacturing Tanks and Artillery. Stage a loaded APC here to advance on enemy HQ.

CO Power ★
Save your powers for Tag Battle. Sami's Victory March will enable you to capture a base in one turn.

Days 8-12
CAPTURE BLUE MOON HQ
Activate Tag Battle and send your loaded APC to Blue Moon HQ. Switch to Sami and claim your victory.

VICTORY

CORNERED AND OUT-GUNNED

Blue Moon will begin the mission with three Md. Tanks in its arsenal, along with two bases compared to your single one. As a result, they'll pump out twice as many reinforcements, so your first priority should be to capture the neutral properties in the west. Immediately capture the neutral city south of your Mechs and stand your ground as the Md. Tanks advance. Park a pair of Artillery units nearby to whittle down enemy numbers.

CO POWER STRATEGY

By switching your COs daily, you'll increase both of their powers at an even pace. Toward the end of the conflict, you'll want to activate a Tag Battle and unload a Mech at Blue Moon's front door during Hawke's turn. When you switch to Sami, she'll be able to convert your opponent's stronghold to Orange Star colors in one move rather than the regular two-day cycle.

 JAKE HAWKE **VS.**   JUGGER

AREA PROPERTIES:

	●	●	●	●	A	N	✕
✈ AIRPORTS	-	-	-	-	-	-	-
🏠 BASES	-	-	-	-	-	-	-
🏙 CITIES	3	-	-	-	3	-	-
COM TOWERS	-	-	-	-	-	-	-
MISSILE SILOS	-	-	-	-	-	-	-
SEAPORTS	-	-	-	-	-	-	-

BONUS POINTS: 0

OBJECT	#	PTS	TOTAL
BLACK CANNONS	-	-	-
BLACK CRYSTALS	-	-	-
BLACK OBELISKS	-	-	-
MINICANNONS	-	-	-
OOZIUMS	-	-	-
PIPE JOINTS	-	-	-

✕ BLACK HOLE INTEL

Black Hole's forces have been beefed up with a pair of Neotanks in the north and south. They will advance toward your weakened front line in a bid to capture your headquarters.

★ MARCHING ORDERS

Fire your Artillery continuously at the units approaching from the east. Your sole Neotank in the southern sector should have little trouble annihilating the Black Hole cluster to the west.

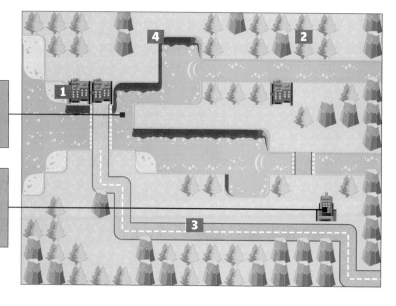

The water will insulate your Artillery from direct fire while keeping the bridge within reach.

Protect your HQ from the Black Hole forces in the west, or the battle could end quickly in your defeat.

MISSION TIMELINE

START

Day 1
MOVE YOUR INFANTRY TO SAFETY
Retreat your wounded Infantry to a nearby city to replenish its health.

Days 1–5
HIT THE TANKS WITH ARTILLERY
Soften up the enemy Md. Tanks and Neotanks from across the water with your Artillery.

Days 1–5
SECURE THE SOUTH WITH YOUR NEOTANK
Protect your HQ and destroy all enemy presence in the south with your Neotank.

★ CO Power
Boost your Artillery's firing range with Jake's Beat Down power.

Days 6–10
SEEK AND DESTROY
Continue pursuing the remaining Black Hole units until you've wiped them out.

VICTORY

BETTER PREPARED AGAINST A STRONG ENEMY

Your Infantry may be on its last legs, but you should be able to retreat to safety to replenish its numbers. Run along the waterline and take a load off at the nearest city. Use your Artillery on the strip of land to beat on the Black Hole units creeping westward. Even though you can't destroy them all at once, you should be able to thin their numbers significantly as they drive by. Patrol the grounds near you HQ using your lone Neotank, but don't stray too far from your building or you'll risk losing it to a capture party.

CO POWER STRATEGY

Use Jake exclusively for the first few days to charge up his CO Power. By the fourth day, you should be able to boost the firing range of your indirect-fire units to improve their reach across the river. The battle shouldn't last long enough for you to use a Tag Battle or Super CO Power, so there's no need to charge up Hawke's meter. You may want to switch COs if you desire Hawke's superior firepower, though.

MISSION 3

MAX ATTACKS

EAGLE HAWKE

VS.

LASH

AREA PROPERTIES:

	●	●	●	●	Ⓐ	Ⓝ	✕
✕ AIRPORTS	-	-	-	-	-		-
▣ BASES	-	-	-	-	-		-
▥ CITIES	3	-	-	-	3	1	1
▣ COM TOWERS	-	-	-	-	-		-
▨ MISSILE SILOS	-	-	-	-	-		-
▨ SEAPORTS	-	-	-	-	-	-	-

BONUS POINTS: 40

OBJECT	#	PTS	TOTAL
▣ BLACK CANNONS	-	-	-
▣ BLACK CRYSTALS	-	-	-
▣ BLACK OBELISKS	-	-	-
▣ MINICANNONS	4	10	40
▣ OOZIUMS	-	-	-
▣ PIPE JOINTS	-	-	-

✕ BLACK HOLE INTEL

Your enemy's forces are ample. Keep your units outside of Minicannon firing range. Beware the Black Bomb hovering in the southwest.

★ MARCHING ORDERS

Draw the Black Bomb north and detonate it away from your cluster of units. Likewise, if you can lure Black Hole units north, their HQ will be unguarded.

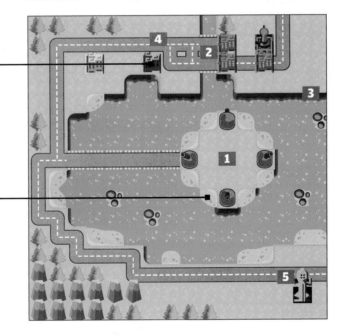

Capture this Black Hole city early on to give your army an extra place to heal and get supplies.

Lure the Black Bomb away from your concentration of Battle Copters to minimize inflicted damage.

FLY LIKE AN EAGLE

Send a few of your Battle Copters south to meet the Black Hole Md. Tanks and Neotanks head-on. Your strategy should be to weaken their numbers significantly before they reach your home zone in the north. Eliminate the northern Minicannon so you can move freely, then send the remainder of your air units to guard your home turf (and to lead the enemy away from its own headquarters).

CO POWER STRATEGY

Switch COs every few days to charge up both of their power meters. It's highly likely that you'll win this battle before you'll have the opportunity to use a Super CO Power or enact a Tag Battle, so employ Eagle's Lightning Drive and Hawke's Black Wave to bolster your unit stats on the ground and in the air, respectively.

MISSION TIMELINE

START

Days 1-4 [1]
FIRE ON THE NORTH MINICANNON
Remove the northernmost Minicannon to make the region safer. You can ignore the others if you prefer.

Days 1-5 [2]
SET UP A LINE OF DEFENSE
Move your Artillery, Rockets and Battle Copters near the bridge to meet the incoming threat.

Days 1-7 [3]
LOAD TROOPS AND WAIT UNTIL SAFE
Load troops into your Transport Copter and wait outside of Minicannon firing range until the southern coast is clear.

Days 4-10 [4]
REPEL THE ENEMY ASSAULT
Let the Black Hole Army come to you in the north. Hold your ground and destroy the enemy's heavier units first.

CO Power ★
Use your CO powers to give your ground and air units more attack power.

Days 8-12 [5]
DROP YOUR TROOPS
While the enemy forces are occupied in the north, slip your loaded Transport Copter behind enemy lines and grab the HQ.

VICTORY

RECLAIM THE SKIES

JAKE   ANDY

VS.

JUGGER

AREA PROPERTIES:

	●	●	●	○	Ⓐ	N	✖
✖ AIRPORTS	-	-	-	-	-	-	-
▣ BASES	-	-	-	-	-	-	-
▥ CITIES	4	-	-	-	4	-	6
▦ COM TOWERS	-	-	-	-	-	-	-
▨ MISSILE SILOS	-	-	-	-	-	-	-
▩ SEAPORTS	-	-	-	-	-	-	-

BONUS POINTS: 0

OBJECT	#	PTS	TOTAL
👁 BLACK CANNONS	-	-	-
▯ BLACK CRYSTALS	-	-	-
▲ BLACK OBELISKS	-	-	-
◑ MINICANNONS	-	-	-
▢ OOZIUMS	-	-	-
▤ PIPE JOINTS	-	-	-

✖ BLACK HOLE INTEL

You start the mission flanking Black Hole's forces. With few options to choose from, they'll circle their Bombers and Battle Copters around their small ground presence as protection.

★ MARCHING ORDERS

Employ your AA guns effectively to dismantle the Black Hole aerial squadron. Concentrate especially on the Bombers. Isolate your enemy's ground forces on the tiny island and keep them away from your properties.

Hold your Rockets back a smidge to protect them from an untimely direct attack.

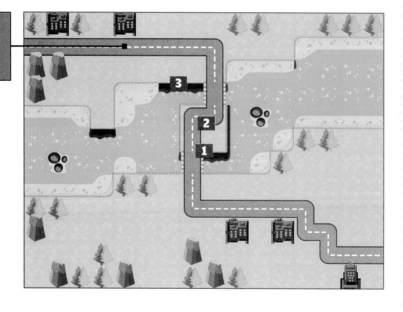

THE UNFRIENDLY SKIES

The skies are filled with Black Hole Battle Copters and Bombers, but you've got the situation covered with Anti-air guns and Missiles. Concentrate your attacks on the Bombers and Tanks first to get the heavy hitters out of the way. Target the Battle Copters only if they're the closest units in range. It won't take you long to crush the opposing army with plenty of time to spare on the counter.

CO POWER STRATEGY

With so much action going on, Jake and Andy will be ready to Tag Battle fairly quickly. Jake's Block Rock gives him more range on indirect attacks, making your Rockets deadlier at a greater distance. Andy's Hyper Upgrade will heal all units by 5 HP, increase mobility by one space and improve firepower for crippling attacks.

MISSION TIMELINE

START

Days 1-5
UNLEASH YOUR AA GUNS
Confront enemy air units with your Anti-air guns and Missiles.

Days 1-5
CONTAIN ENEMY GROUND TROOPS
Eliminate the Black Hole ground units while they're corralled on the island.

CO Power
Activate a Tag Battle when you're charged up.

Days 4-10
MAKE A CLEAN SWEEP
You should have little trouble destroying every enemy unit before the missile timer runs out.

VICTORY

MISSION 5

NEVERENDING WAR

  HAWKE   JAKE VS.   KOAL

AREA PROPERTIES:

	●	●	●	●	Ⓐ	N	✕
⊠ AIRPORTS	-	-	-	-	-	1	-
⌂ BASES	2	-	-	-	2	2	1
🏙 CITIES	3	-	-	-	3	10	6
⊡ COM TOWERS	-	-	-	-	-	-	-
▨ MISSILE SILOS	-	-	-	-	-	-	-
⊠ SEAPORTS	-	-	-	-	-	-	-

BONUS POINTS: 30

OBJECT	#	PTS	TOTAL
🔲 BLACK CANNONS	-	-	-
▣ BLACK CRYSTALS	-	-	-
🔲 BLACK OBELISKS	-	-	-
🔲 MINICANNONS	3	10	30
◉ OOZIUMS	-	-	-
⊞ PIPE JOINTS	-	-	-

BLACK HOLE INTEL

Two mountain ranges divide the battlefield. Koal's got three Minicannons and some heavy aerial firepower on hand. He'll start building Neo Tanks after the first few days of action.

★ MARCHING ORDERS

It is imperative that you secure as many cities and bases as you can. You'll fight offensively in the south, pressing onward to grab available real estate. In the north you'll employ your Artillery as a defense.

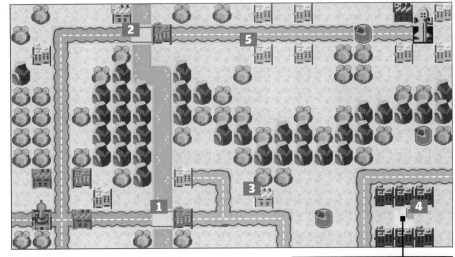

HEAVY DEFENSE IN THE NORTH, SNEAK EAST

Capture of the two neutral bases is your immediate priority. Load a Mech into your APC and grab the base in the north first. Block the advancing forces with your APC. Manufacture at least four Artillery units in the first week and position a tank close by to defend against the advancing Neotank and other Black Hole units. In the south, Lure Koal's Tank to its doom by parking yours on a city. Station Artillery just behind it—when the enemy rolls into town, he'll land smack dab into a trap. Pursue invading Mechs with your Tank. Don't let your foes expand their reach or increase their earnings by acquiring new properties. Build an AA gun or two to fend off incoming Battle Copters. As you advance east, stagger your Artillery with other units to keep them intact, even if it means sacrificing other units to lure your foes to an untimely end.

Once you've amassed enough Infantry, capture this region and claim the airport. Post several units here to guard against enemy invasion.

CO POWER STRATEGY

If you can hold out, charge up your CO Power for a Tag Battle. The combination of Hawke's and Jake's Super CO Powers will put you over the top: Hawke will suck HP from the enemy and add it to your forces, whereas Jake will extend the reach of his Artillery and other indirect-fire units. Don't hesitate to use your powers if the tide is turning against you early in the mission.

MISSION TIMELINE

START ■

Days 1-6 ▮1
SECURE THE SOUTH
Lure enemies to the bridge with your Tanks and Artillery. Once they come within range, hit 'em with all you've got.

Days 1-10 ▮2
DEFEND THE NORTH
Send a pair of Mechs north to secure this base. Station Artillery to fend off incoming Black Hole units.

Days 3-10 ▮3
EXPAND YOUR EMPIRE
Claim the base before your opponent does, then start cranking out Artillery and Tanks to quash Koal's presence in the south.

CO Power ★
Hawke's powers leech HP from the enemy and heal your own forces.

Days 7-15 ▮4
OWN THE NEIGHBORHOOD
Cut off Koal's funding and increase your own. Manufacture a Bomber to give your army a boost.

Days 8-23 ▮5
TIGHTEN THE NOOSE
Advance your northern army toward Black Hole HQ. Lure the enemies out of hiding and hit them from afar.

VICTORY ■

MISSION 6

THE OCEAN BLUE

HAWKE | **JAKE**

VS.

LASH

AREA PROPERTIES:

	●	●	●	◐	Ⓐ	Ⓝ	✖
🛫 AIRPORTS	-	-	-	-	-	-	-
🏠 BASES	-	-	-	-	-	-	-
🏙 CITIES	2	-	-	-	2	2	-
📡 COM TOWERS	-	-	-	-	-	-	-
🚀 MISSILE SILOS	-	-	-	-	-	-	-
⚓ SEAPORTS	-	-	-	-	-	-	-

BONUS POINTS: 0

OBJECT	#	PTS	TOTAL
🔲 BLACK CANNONS	-	-	-
🔳 BLACK CRYSTALS	-	-	-
🔲 BLACK OBELISKS	-	-	-
🔲 MINICANNONS	-	-	-
🔲 OOZIUMS	-	-	-
🔲 PIPE JOINTS	-	-	-

✖ BLACK HOLE INTEL

Lash has upped her arsenal to two Battleships, two Cruisers, a Sub and a Lander. Guarding her HQ is a Neo-tank, a Tank, Artillery, an AA gun and Infantry. You'll have to clear the area before you land troops there.

★ MARCHING ORDERS

You'll need to divide and conquer the Black Hole naval units by luring the Cruisers into open water and away from the Battleships. Your Sub and Battle Copters should have no problem eliminating the Battleships.

Refuel your ships as they pass through the channel with your APC.

Move your Rockets to the far side of the islet and keep it outside of enemy Battleship range.

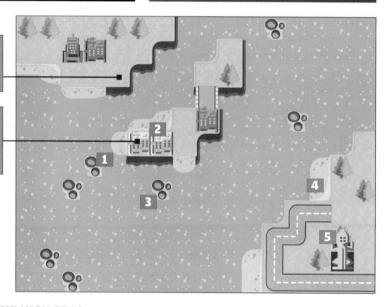

HYSTERIA ON THE HIGH SEAS

The battle at sea is a tough one; you'll need to move your units carefully to stay out of enemy attack range. Keep your navy strong to increase your chances of a smooth victory. Lure Lash's Cruisers away from her Battleships, then go on the offensive. Keep your Sub submerged for as long as possible to avoid taking damage. When the Black Hole Sub advances on your Battleship, sink it with shots from your Cruiser. Once the seas are finally safe, victory is only days away. The enemy has strong units stationed near its HQ, so pummel them mercilessly with your Battleship and Battle Copters before staging a land assault.

CO POWER STRATEGY

You're better off utilizing each CO's power when it's available rather than saving up for a Tag Battle. The added range from Jake's Beat Down will increase the range of your island-based Rocket attacks. Hawke's Black Wave and Black Storm reduce enemy HP and restore your own, giving you the advantage when the fighting gets rough. Since this mission is especially tough on the high seas, you'll need all the help you can get.

MISSION TIMELINE

START ■

Days 1-5
STAY ON THE MOVE 1
Reposition your land and sea forces outside of enemy firing range while you plan each attack.

Days 1-5
LOAD UP AND MOVE OUT 2
Prepare your landing force. Stage a rocket assault from the central island, but beware of fire from the Battleship.

Days 3-10
DIVIDE AND CONQUER 3
Bait the enemy Cruisers and lead them away from the Battleships. Sink them with your Battle Copters and Sub.

CO Power ★
Use your CO Powers when they're available to boost your HP and add range to Rockets and Artillery guns.

Days 8-16
REDUCE ENEMY FORCES 4
Once you've sunk Lash's fleet, move in for the final blow. Begin your systematic dismantling of the enemy forces near their HQ.

Days 15-20
DROP YOUR TROOPS 5
Clear the enemy shores with your Battleship and Battle Copters. Drop your ground team and capture the enemy headquarters.

VICTORY ■

FOG ROLLS IN

SONJA   HAWKE   VS.   KOAL

AREA PROPERTIES:

	●	●	●	●	Ⓐ	N	✖
✈ AIRPORTS	-	-	-	-	-	1	-
🏠 BASES	2	-	-	-	2	1	1
🏙 CITIES	2	-	-	-	2	8	2
✚ COM TOWERS	-	-	-	-	-	-	-
◪ MISSILE SILOS	-	-	-	-	-	-	-
⚓ SEAPORTS	-	-	-	-	-	-	-

BONUS POINTS: 0

OBJECT	#	PTS	TOTAL
🔲 BLACK CANNONS	-	-	-
🔲 BLACK CRYSTALS	-	-	-
🔲 BLACK OBELISKS	-	-	-
🔲 MINICANNONS	-	-	-
🔲 OOZIUMS	-	-	-
🔲 PIPE JOINTS	-	-	-

✖ BLACK HOLE INTEL

Black Hole has stationed naval units in the lakes scattered across the battlefield, though none of them pose a real threat. They'll move to capture the airport early, so beat them to the punch.

★ MARCHING ORDERS

Move your forces covertly through the trees and mountains. You'll get the upper hand in most battles using the element of surprise, plus provide protective cover to your troops in transit.

Prevent the enemy APC from restocking the Black Hole Battleship's shells.

Flank the foes in the south and crush their hopes of acquiring new land.

THE FOG CONCEALS A STRONG OPPONENT

The reefs hide some powerful vessels—and not just Landers as before. Use caution when moving units near bodies of water, and don't let the Battleship become a factor in the fight. Though it's in a weakened state, it can still dish out a fight, especially after it receives supplies from an APC. Don't be too concerned with destroying every enemy ship, or the units hiding in the shadows of the reefs and forests. Rather than seek out every Black Hole unit, your quickest path to victory will be through grabbing enemy headquarters when the opportunity presents itself.

CO POWER STRATEGY

Provided you can hold off until your CO Powers are fully charged, you'll maximize your attacks with a Tag Battle. Sonja's indirect-fire boost will allow you to reach Koal's units from a greater distance. If your units are in a weakened state, Hawke's powers are invaluable; they'll steal HP from the opposition and replenish the health of your own troops. If you're having a tough time early on, use the CO Powers as they become available to hold off Koal's Neotanks.

MISSION TIMELINE

START

Days 1-6
SECURE THE CENTER 1
Move in and secure the central properties. This will give you a point from which to launch your assault forces while you hold off enemy advancement.

Days 1-6
HEAD NORTH AND SECURE THE AIRPORT 2
Immediately send forces to the north to grab and hold the airport before you opponent does.

Days 3-10
HOLD OFF THE ENEMY 3
Now that the central zone is in your possession, begin building units for your impending assault on Black Hole HQ.

CO Power ★
Hawke's powers will sap health from Koal's forces and add them to your own.

Days 8-23
MOVE IN AND CRUSH THE ENEMY HQ 4
Invade the northeastern section and obliterate the remaining resistance. Gain control of Black Hole headquarters.

VICTORY

TAG BATTLE

 HAWKE JAKE VS.   JUGGER LASH

AREA PROPERTIES:

	●	●	●	●	A	N	✸
✈ AIRPORTS	-	-	-	-	-	1	-
🏠 BASES	2	-	-	-	2	4	1
🏙 CITIES	3	-	-	-	3	10	1
📡 COM TOWERS	-	-	-	-	-	-	-
🚀 MISSILE SILOS	-	-	-	-	-	-	-
⚓ SEAPORTS	-	-	-	-	-	-	-

BONUS POINTS: 0

OBJECT	#	PTS	TOTAL
BLACK CANNONS	-	-	-
BLACK CRYSTALS	-	-	-
BLACK OBELISKS	-	-	-
MINICANNONS	-	-	-
OOZIUMS	-	-	-
PIPE JOINTS	-	-	-

✳ BLACK HOLE INTEL

A well-placed Artillery gun guards the Piperunner, so you'll need to take it out before you capture the base there. You'll also face a pair of Battle Copters that you'll want to destroy when you can.

★ MARCHING ORDERS

Capture and convert the airport within the first week to gain the advantage here. Send a Battle Copter or Tank after the Artillery guarding the Piperunner in the center.

Build an additional AA gun to meet the Battle Copter flying in from the south.

Station a team of Mechs and Artillery here to protect the central bases from attack.

Send your Battle Copter to destroy the Black Hole Artillery parked near the pipe.

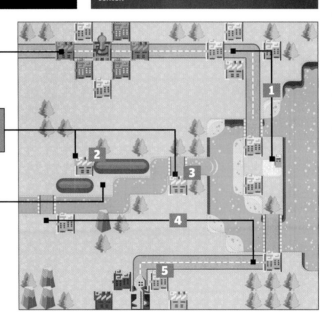

DOUBLE THE FUN

Your immediate priority is to capture the airport in the east. Load your APC and assemble your strike team; send along a Tank for some protection during the journey. Capture the neutral properties as you go. Keep your anti-air defenses strong, as you'll have a pair of Battle Copters to contend with shortly.

It is imperative that you defeat the Black Hole units patrolling the central area, so make sure your invasion force is of the right size and strength to neutralize the Piperunner and Artillery already there, as well as the advancing Infantry. Battle Copters make fine escorts.

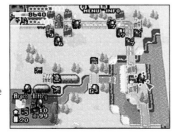

CO POWER STRATEGY

Save up your CO Powers for a Tag Battle. Hawke will weaken your opponent and strengthen your own units, which is useful considering that Jugger and Lash will likely strike you first and damage your army. You should be able to form a two-pronged attack fairly quickly. Keep a few Battle Copters and Tanks ready to move in for a quick and lethal attack.

MISSION TIMELINE

START ■

Days 1-6
CAPTURE THE NEIGHBORHOOD 1
Protect your loaded APC en route to the airport with an Anti-air unit to fend off enemy Battle Copters.

Days 4-6
TAKE OUT THE PIPERUNNER 2
Remove the Artillery and Piperunner units in the center of the map and grab the real estate nearby.

Days 4-8
STAVE OFF THE ENEMY 3
Prevent the Black Hole Army from capturing this base to hamper its ability to build reinforcements.

CO Power ★
Put the hurt on your foes and unleash a Tag Battle when you're ready.

Days 7-15
STAGE A TWO-PRONGED ATTACK 4
Descend on enemy HQ on two fronts, capturing land as you go. Build and deploy reinforcements if you need them.

Days 10-17
CONTAIN AND DESTROY THE ENEMY 5
Once you're within range of enemy HQ, you'll have to eliminate only what's left of their forces to win. Fire at will.

VICTORY ■

MISSION 9

VICTORY OR DEATH!

 EAGLE · HAWKE **VS.** KOAL · LASH

AREA PROPERTIES:

	●	●	●	●	A	N	X
✈ AIRPORTS	-	-	-	-	-	1	-
🏠 BASES	1	-	-	-	1	3	-
🏙 CITIES	4	-	-	-	4	12	-
📡 COM TOWERS	-	-	-	-	-	-	-
◪ MISSILE SILOS	-	-	-	-	-	-	-
🚢 SEAPORTS	-	-	-	-	-	-	-

BONUS POINTS: 20

OBJECT	#	PTS	TOTAL
🔲 BLACK CANNONS	-	-	-
🔲 BLACK CRYSTALS	1	20	20
🔲 BLACK OBELISKS	-	-	-
🔲 MINICANNONS	-	-	-
🔲 OOZIUMS	-	-	-
🔲 PIPE JOINTS	-	-	-

❌ BLACK HOLE INTEL

On the main front, the Black Hole Army has placed plenty of Mechs, a pair of Bombers and some Md. Tanks. High above, a Black Bomb hovers near the sky fortress.

★ MARCHING ORDERS

Eagle will fight admirably on the secondary front, while Hawke will keep things moving below. Bulk up your military might with plenty of AA guns to combat the wealth of enemy units you'll face.

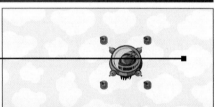

A Black Bomb floating around this area will likely damage some of your air forces.

If this base falls into enemy hands, take it back after Eagle has won the secondary front.

Claim these bases to curb the Black Hole Army's ability to produce additional firepower.

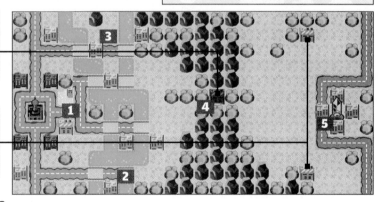

RULE THE SKIES

You'll prevent an unnecessary loss on the secondary front if you send up a Bomber to attack the sky fortress's guns after the Black Bomb and most other enemy air units have been destroyed. On the ground, your job is to press eastward, destroying enemies as you encounter them. Use your air units to purge ground forces from the battlefield. The Black Hole military is in an especially aggressive mood, as its air force and ground troops will push toward your home turf. Bulk up your Fighters and spit out a few extra AA guns to counter their presence, and retain as much property as you can.

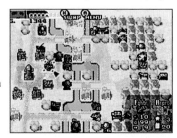

CO POWER STRATEGY

Save your CO powers for a Tag Battle after Eagle has won the secondary front. Eagle's Lightning Strike will allow all non-Infantry units to move twice without a firepower penalty. You can significantly diminish the Black Hole forces in one turn with this power. Hawke will drain two HP from enemy units and replenish your army's health. In three turns, you'll devastate anything in your path.

MISSION TIMELINE

START

Days 1-3
① CAPTURE THE BASE AND AIRPORT
With your central base temporarily incapacitated, you'll need these two properties to build units for the early skirmishes.

Days 1-5
② INTERCEPT ENEMY FORCES IN THE SOUTH
Escort your Infantry to secure the city between the rivers in the south.

Days 1-7
③ DESTROY ENEMIES IN THE NORTH
Move your Tank and Anti-air gun to face the enemies in the north. Hold them off until you can send in reinforcements to clear the region.

Days 4-10
④ SECURE THE CENTER BASE AND FORTIFY
Try to prevent the Black Hole Army from stealing your base here, otherwise reclaim it and start cranking out units.

★ CO Power
Conserve your CO Power and use it in a Tag Battle.

Days 8-12
⑤ DESTROY THE CRYSTAL
Once you've secured the mountain pass, build Tank reinforcements and obliterate the Black Crystal.

VICTORY

BLACK BOATS AHOY!

HAWKE   DRAKE   VS.   KINDLE

AREA PROPERTIES:

	●	●	●	○	Ⓐ	Ⓝ	✖
✈ AIRPORTS	-	-	-	-	-	-	-
🏭 BASES	-	-	-	-	-	-	-
🏙 CITIES	2	-	-	-	2	3	6
📡 COM TOWERS	-	-	-	-	-	-	-
🚀 MISSILE SILOS	-	-	-	-	-	-	-
🚢 SEAPORTS	-	-	-	-	-	-	-

BONUS POINTS: 0

OBJECT	#	PTS	TOTAL
🟦 BLACK CANNONS	-	-	-
⬛ BLACK CRYSTALS	-	-	-
🔺 BLACK OBELISKS	-	-	-
🟩 MINICANNONS	-	-	-
⬜ OOZIUMS	-	-	-
🟫 PIPE JOINTS	-	-	-

✖ BLACK HOLE INTEL

This battle contains one more weakened Battleship in the harbor than the Normal Campaign version does. There are plenty of Black Boats sailing nearby to repair them, though. You'll also face additional ground units.

★ MARCHING ORDERS

Focus on eliminating your enemy's naval forces early in the mission. If you leave the Black Boats operational, they will heal the Black Hole Battleships, which will spell trouble for your military.

MISSION TIMELINE

START

Days 1-3
LOAD 'EM UP AND MOVE 'EM OUT
Load Infantry into your Lander and ship them over to enemy HQ. Drop them off outside of Artillery firing range. Begin moving your other units eastward.

Days 1-4
ATTACK THE BLACK BOATS
Methodically destroy each of the Black Boats in the harbor using your Cruisers. Deploy your Sub and go after the Battleship, but submerge once you're in range.

Days 2-6
SECURE THE CITY AND FIND THE MAP
The action will boil over across the bridges. Conquer the city and find the hidden map.

CO Power
A Tag Battle will wound the Black Hole Army en masse.

Days 2-6
SINK THE ENEMY BATTLESHIPS
Attack the weakened Battleships with your Sub before they regain strength.

Days 4-10
CAPTURE ENEMY HEADQUARTERS
Send a loaded Lander with a Tank or Artillery escort to Black Hole HQ and claim it as your own.

VICTORY

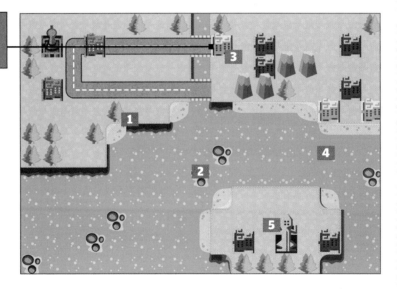

You'll find the secret map in this city, like before. Find it as you move eastward.

THE BLACK LAGOON

The Hard Campaign version of this mission isn't much different from the Normal one, though you'll have to wade through a whole mess of Black Boats to eventually destroy the enemy Battleships in the harbor. Keep your Sub under the surface and proceed when it's safe. Make sure you monitor its fuel situation; otherwise you'll send the crew to a premature, watery grave.

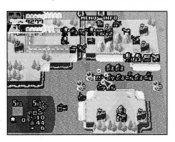

CO POWER STRATEGY

Both Hawke's and Drake's CO Powers dole out damage to the Black Hole Army as a whole. Hawke will hurt enemy forces while healing your own, but Drake will damage your opponents only with a mighty tsunami. Following his crushing water attack, the Fog of War will set in and cloud much of your vision. Hold off on using the Tag Team approach until the enemy is concentrated in the northeast; otherwise you'll lose sight of all of its units.

MISSION 11

THE LONG MARCH

 HAWKE JAKE SONJA DRAKE

VS.

 JUGGER KOAL

AREA PROPERTIES:

	●	●	●	●	A	N	✖
AIRPORTS	-	-	-	-	-	2	-
BASES	-	2	-	-	2	2	-
CITIES	4	1	-	-	5	10	2
COM TOWERS	-	-	-	-	-	-	-
MISSILE SILOS	-	-	-	-	-	-	-
SEAPORTS	-	1	-	-	1	-	-

BONUS POINTS: 0

OBJECT	#	PTS	TOTAL
BLACK CANNONS	-	-	-
BLACK CRYSTALS	-	-	-
BLACK OBELISKS	-	-	-
MINICANNONS	-	-	-
OOZIUMS	-	-	-
PIPE JOINTS	-	-	-

BLACK HOLE INTEL

There are more Black Boats patrolling the waters than in the Normal Campaign; that means more regenerative power in your opponent's hands. Stay alert and watch out for Battle Copters in the northeast.

MARCHING ORDERS

You'll have your hands full defending your HQ in the south from a Black Hole invasion. Move your forces outside of the enemy's indirect-fire range as you push toward the lab.

Enemy units guard the lab. Flush them out and destroy them before attempting to capture the building.

Start pumping out units after you capture the bases here.

Block the enemy from advancing past this point. You'll need to hit the forces with serious muscle to fend them off.

You must dodge incoming fire from Artillery and Rockets. Send in Blue Moon reinforcements when you can.

CONCENTRATED FIREPOWER

Black Hole has an incredibly strong army assembled on the peninsula. Fending off the forces will be tough, especially if they employ Tag Battle attacks fairly early and cripple your army. Hold them off as best as you can until you have captured the bases east of your HQ. Once you've secured these properties, you can go on the offensive, building heavy equipment to reinforce your wounded military. Your navy should move outside of the range of enemy indirect-fire units while it fires on their Infantry. Once you've cleared the peninsula, send in Blue Moon to bring up the rear.

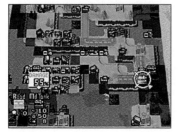

CO POWER STRATEGY

You've got four COs to play with—that translates into plenty of Super CO Powers to throw around. Sonja's improved vision really helps slice through the Fog of War, while Hawke and Drake both slam all the enemies on the field. It will take some time to charge the powers of each CO, but if you can hold out it will definitely pay off.

MISSION TIMELINE

START

Days 1-5 **1**
MOVE IN THE SHADOWS
Keep your units hidden out of range of indirect fire. Eliminate the enemy's Recon units and hamper their vision.

Days 1-5 **2**
STRIKE HARD WITH YOUR NAVY
Use your Battleships to wipe out your enemy's strongest weapons before they are used against you.

Days 1-8 **3**
CAPTURE BASES AND CITIES
Follow your Infantry with Missiles and AA guns—enemy Battle Copters are waiting in the northeast.

CO Power ★
Conserve your CO Power for Tag Battle double damage.

Days 4-8 **4**
CROSS THE SEA AND SECURE THE AIRPORT
Order Blue Moon to build a Lander and load it with Infantry. Send it across the water to speed your capture of neutral real estate.

Days 9-14 **5**
MOVE NORTH AND CAPTURE THE LAB
An enemy Tank and Artillery unit wait near the lab. Proceed with caution and ample firepower.

VICTORY

MISSION 12 LIGHTNING STRIKES

 HAWKE   JAKE

 VS.

GRIMM SENSEI

AREA PROPERTIES:

		●	[N]	○
🅧	AIRPORTS	-	2	-
🅜	BASES	2	1	2
🅣	CITIES	7	14	1
🅒	COM TOWERS	-	-	-
◪	MISSILE SILOS	-	6	-
🅢	SEAPORTS	-	-	-

BONUS POINTS: 0

OBJECT	#	PTS	TOTAL
🅒 BLACK CANNONS	-	-	-
🅓 BLACK CRYSTALS	-	-	-
🅝 BLACK OBELISKS	-	-	-
🅒 MINICANNONS	-	-	-
🅞 OOZIUMS	-	-	-
🅟 PIPE JOINTS	-	-	-

✔ YELLOW COMET INTEL

Yellow Comet has flown in extra Battle Copters to fight you this time. You'll need additional Anti-air guns on the main and secondary fronts to take them down before they wipe you out.

★ MARCHING ORDERS

Employ similar tactics to the ones used during the Normal Campaign mode. Control the secondary front and line up a strong defense with your AA units while you proceed with operations on the main battlefield.

Transport some Infantry to the secondary-front HQ after you eliminate the Battle Copter forces.

You'll need three Anti-air guns to repel the incoming Battle Copters.

Though it's far off, do your best to keep the enemy from capturing this airport.

Capture and secure this region as soon as possible and launch the missiles at your enemies.

The Black Hole Army will continuously throw units toward this area. Make sure you station an ample defense here.

DOUBLE TROUBLE ON DUAL FRONTS

Immediately take control of the second front. Hunker down and assume a defensive stance in the southwest. When the Battle Copters swoop in, hit them hard with your AA guns. Once the skies are cleared, you can load up an APC with some troops and knock on the enemy's front door. Hawke will rejoin Jake on the main front after his win, and his added CO Power will come in handy. Place some Artillery near the eastern base to shell new Black Hole units as they leave the base. Secure each airport as you head north and east. Activate every Missile Silo and target clusters of powerful, hardy foes to tip the scales in your favor.

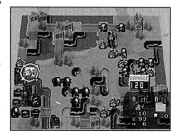

CO POWER STRATEGY

Though it's tempting to use your CO Powers immediately, save them up for a Tag Battle to hit Yellow Comet where it hurts. It'll be much easier to target and eliminate enemy forces this way. If you're having a hard time winning on the secondary front, go ahead and activate your powers early.

MISSION TIMELINE

START

Days 1-4 ①
SET UP A LINE OF DEFENSE/OFFENSE
Station some Infantry and Artillery or Anti-air units near the eastern city to beat back the opposition. Once you've built reinforcements, send some north as well.

Days 1-4 ②
CONTROL THE SECONDARY FRONT
Set up a strong defense on the secondary front and ward off the incoming Battle Copter armada.

Days 2-6 ③
LAUNCH THE MISSILES
Escort some Infantry or Mechs to the north and capture the airport. Activate the Missile Silos once you're there.

CO Power ★
Hold out for a Tag Battle if you can manage it.

Days 2-6 ④
SECURE THE ISLAND
Capture the base and launch the missiles at the Black Hole unit clusters of your choosing.

Days 4-10 ⑤
ADVANCE ON ENEMY HQ AND CAPTURE IT
Make the final push to Black Hole HQ and take it over.

VICTORY

MISSION

13

FROZEN FORTRESS

 OLAF   JESS   HAWKE   JAKE **VS.**   KINDLE JUGGER

AREA PROPERTIES:

	●	●	●	●	Ⓐ	N	✕
✕ AIRPORTS	-	-	-	-	-	1	-
▦ BASES	3	2	-	-	5	6	-
▥ CITIES	-	1	-	-	1	12	2
▣ COM TOWERS	-	-	-	-	-	-	3
◪ MISSILE SILOS	-	-	-	-	-	-	-
▧ SEAPORTS	-	-	-	-	-	-	-

BONUS POINTS: 0

OBJECT	#	PTS	TOTAL
◉ BLACK CANNONS	-	-	-
▯ BLACK CRYSTALS	-	-	-
▲ BLACK OBELISKS	-	-	-
▣ MINICANNONS	-	-	-
▢ OOZIUMS	-	-	-
▱ PIPE JOINTS	-	-	-

✕ BLACK HOLE INTEL

Two Battle Copters patrol the battlefield, and are accompanied by some Md. Tanks and Mechs. Needless to say, you're opponent is packing some mighty firepower.

★ MARCHING ORDERS

If you can stay outside of enemy Md. Tank attack range, you can avoid taking heavy casualties. Do your best to prevent the enemy from acquiring land.

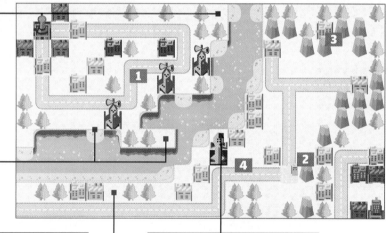

Place a Tank here to greet incoming Black Hole forces from the east.

Place Artillery and Rockets on these shores and shell units across the river.

Secure the southwestern corner if you've got the firepower to remove the Md. Tank waiting here.

Park an Anti-air unit on this spot to quickly eliminate any Black Hole Infantry attempting to capture this base.

ANOTHER COLD DAY IN THE FIELD....

The bad weather is back, slowing down your unit movement. Olaf likes to roll in the snow like a Siberian husky, so he's a natural pick for this kind of inclement weather. Build half a dozen Infantry units and quickly secure the Com Towers in the vicinity. In the southeast corner, instruct Blue Moon to fan out and capture the airport and surrounding properties. When you've got the cash, you can pump out reinforcements from there. Orange Star should manufacture some indirect-fire units, such as Rockets and Artillery, to soften the enemy's forces across the river. Once you've weakened or destroyed the bulk of the Black Hole Army, move in for the final play.

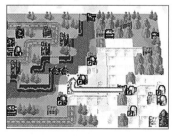

CO POWER STRATEGY

When you unleash Olaf's and Hawke's Powers, you'll injure all of your enemy's units at once (and consequently cause them to burn more fuel). Jake's increased firing range means you'll have something to balance out the movement penalty inflicted by the snow. Jess will refuel and resupply your units in addition to upping vehicular movement by two spaces.

MISSION TIMELINE

START

Days 1-8 1
SECURE PROPERTIES AND COM TOWERS

Build enough Infantry to to capture the Com Towers as quickly as possible. You'll need additional units stationed nearby to fend off incoming enemy reinforcements.

Days 1-8 2
CAPTURE THE AIRPORT

Order Blue Moon to capture each city and base near the airport. Entrench a pair of Artillery units to ward off advancing threats. Capture the airport once it's safe to move your men. Stay outside of enemy Md. Tank attack range.

Days 1-8 3
CAPTURE THE CITY TO FIND THE MAP

Sneak a Blue Moon Infantry unit into the northern city to find the map. Watch for the patrolling Md. Tank nearby and check its range before moving.

CO Power ★
You may want to use your CO Powers when they are ready.

Days 9-14 4
MOVE IN AND VANQUISH YOUR FOES

Once you've secured the map, continue hitting the enemy from both sides or capture the Black Hole HQ to win.

VICTORY ■

LASH'S TEST

RACHEL NELL VS. LASH

AREA PROPERTIES:

	●	●	●	●	A	N	✖
✈ AIRPORTS	-	-	-	-	1	-
🏠 BASES	-	-	-	-	-	-
🏙 CITIES	7	-	7	4	2
📡 COM TOWERS	-	-	-	2	-
⚔ MISSILE SILOS	-	-	-	-	-
⚓ SEAPORTS	-	-	-	-	-

BONUS POINTS: 20

OBJECT	#	PTS	TOTAL
🔲 BLACK CANNONS	-	-	-
🔲 BLACK CRYSTALS	-	-	-
🔲 BLACK OBELISKS	-	-	-
🔲 MINICANNONS	-	-	-
🔲 OOZIUMS	-	-	-
🔲 PIPE JOINTS	4	5	20

✖ BLACK HOLE INTEL

Lash has augmented her already large presence with a Battleship, Cruiser and Piperunner. She'll likely target your penned-up Black Bombs before going after your other units.

★ MARCHING ORDERS

Try to eliminate the Piperunner and Rockets in the west on the first day. Concentrate on freeing your Black Bombs in the east with your Battle Copter and Rockets. Constantly advance your forces toward enemy HQ.

MISSION TIMELINE

START ■

Day 1
DETONATE THE BLACK BOMBS

Set off both Black Bombs and clear the immediate area of Black Hole forces.

Days 1-4
GET MOVING

Send out your Infantry and Mechs. Capture the Com Towers and neutral properties as you march north.

Days 2-6
TARGET LASH'S NAVY

Free your Black Bombs in the east and target Lash's naval vessels. Finish the job with your Battle Copters.

Days 5-8
GUARD THE CHOKE POINT

The enemy intercepts your forces here. Set up your defenses and let 'em have it!

CO Power ★
Use CO Powers here, or save up for a Tag Battle.

Days 9-12
REPEL THE INVASION

Push back the Black Hole Army and continue pressing northward.

CO Power ★
Tag Battle your heart out.

Days 13-15
CHOOSE YOUR VICTORY

VICTORY ■

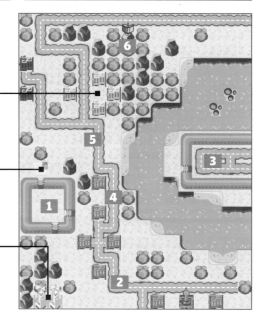

Don't bother capturing these neutral cities; your enemy will fight you vigorously for possession.

Make it your priority to nab this airport. Send in a capture team before your opponent does.

Snatch the Com Towers early in the mission to increase your firepower.

CORNERED ANIMALS WILL FIGHT

In this case, those cornered animals are your Black Bombs. With nowhere to go at the start of the mission, your best bet is to detonate the western bombs early; you'll quickly eliminate nearby enemy units. Set off an eastern bomb when enemy naval units are close. Fly a Battle Copter over to finish the job, then use it to break the pipe joint to free the remaining Black Bomb. Keep your troops on the move. Guard the choke point with Artillery and Rockets.

CO POWER STRATEGY

If you can save up your CO Powers for a Tag Battle, you can unleash a pair of ruinous attacks upon your foe. First use Nell's Lady Luck attack to drastically increase her chances of striking the enemy with massive firepower. Once you've seriously weakened Lash's units, use Rachel's Covering Fire to mop up the remnants by launching three Missiles from Orange Star HQ.

MISSION 15

VERDANT HILLS

KANBEI SASHA ADDER FLAK

VS.

JESS JAVIER

AREA PROPERTIES:

	●	●	Ⓐ	N	●
✖ AIRPORTS	-	-	-	1	-
⊞ BASES	2	-	2	1	-
⊟ CITIES	2	2	4	8	-
✖ COM TOWERS	-	-	-	3	2
◨ MISSILE SILOS	-	-	-	-	-
⬓ SEAPORTS	-	-	-	-	-

BONUS POINTS: 0

OBJECT	#	PTS	TOTAL
⬛ BLACK CANNONS	-	-	-
⬛ BLACK CRYSTALS	-	-	-
⬛ BLACK OBELISKS	-	-	-
⬛ MINICANNONS	-	-	-
⬛ OOZIUMS	-	-	-
⬛ PIPE JOINTS	-	-	-

❋ BLACK HOLE INTEL

The Black Hole Army is rolling deep with two Mega-tanks, two Neotanks and a sizeable troop presence. With so much firepower on hand, they'll come at you hard and fast.

★ MARCHING ORDERS

You're armed with additional Artillery, so put them to good use and arc your shots over the mountains at the Black Hole units while you can.

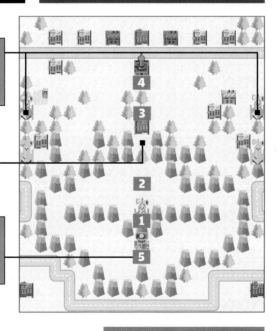

> Be sure to capture the Com Towers on both sides of the map to bulk up your attacks.

> Guard the choke point and slow the enemy troops as they invade your home area.

> Sneak an infantry or mech over mountains to capture enemy HQ and guard it from attack with your Artillery and Rockets.

LOCKED IN A CAGE (BUT NOT FOR LONG)

Looks can be deceiving, especially in a Fog of War battle. Though the Black Hole Army must funnel its units through a narrow opening in the mountain range, you'll have a tough time keeping it contained. Make sure you hammer the opposing forces mercilessly while they're grouped in the south. In the meantime, park some heavy Artillery and Rockets near the northern exit to slow their advance. The conflict should end in less than two weeks.

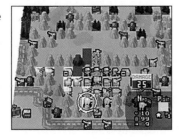

CO POWER STRATEGY

Adder and Flak perform a powerful Tag Battle. Use Adder first—his Sidewinder attack increases your unit movement by two spaces. Flak's Barbaric Blow drastically increases unit attack power, and changes the dispersion rate, which affects the amount of damage a target receives. Use Sasha first. Her power generates extra funds in proportion to damage inflicted upon the enemy. Kanbei's Samurai Spirit strengthens the offensive and defensive stats of all units.

MISSION TIMELINE

START ■

Day 1 1
STAGE YOUR MECHS AND ATTACK
Perch your Mechs in the mountains, then fire at the enemy with your Rockets and Artillery.

Day 2 2
BUILD YOUR ARMY
Continue on the offensive with Blue Moon's units while Orange Star produces Infantry to capture more real estate.

Days 3-5 3
GUARD THE CHOKE POINT
Have your Artillery and other forces waiting to meet the Black Hole threat at the valley.

CO Power ★
Use Adder and Flak in a Tag Battle.

Days 6-8 4
BRACE YOURSELF
Your enemy has escaped the central mountains. Brace yourself for Black Hole's powerful Tag Battle retaliation.

CO Power ★

Days 9-11 5
GRAB ENEMY HQ OR WIPE 'EM OUT

VICTORY ■

SNOW HUNTERS

KANBEI · DRAKE

VS.

HAWKE

AREA PROPERTIES:

	●	●	●	●	A	N	✖
✈ AIRPORTS	-	-	-	-	-	-	-
🏠 BASES	-	-	-	-	-	2	-
🏙 CITIES	4	-	-	-	4	2	4
📡 COM TOWERS	-	-	-	-	-	2	-
☢ MISSILE SILOS	-	-	-	-	-	1	-
⚓ SEAPORTS	-	-	-	-	-	1	-

BONUS POINTS: 70

OBJECT	#	PTS	TOTAL
🔲 BLACK CANNONS	-	-	-
🔲 BLACK CRYSTALS	-	-	-
🔲 BLACK OBELISKS	-	-	-
🔲 MINICANNONS	3	10	30
🔲 OOZIUMS	-	-	-
🔲 PIPE JOINTS	8	5	40

✖ BLACK HOLE INTEL

You'll notice some extra naval firepower—a Battleship, a Sub and two Cruisers—in the southwest, along with more Md. Tanks and Artillery. Expect Hawke to put up a strong fight.

★ MARCHING ORDERS

Though your own forces are more plentiful than last time, you're still at a slight disadvantage. Maintain a strong presence in the west and eliminate the Bomber and Battleship before they advance.

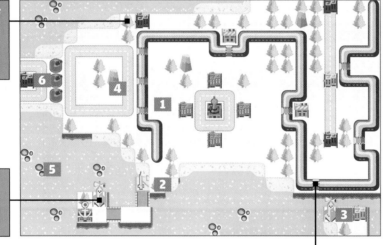

Station Rockets here to prevent the enemy from sending in reinforcements from the east.

Once you've launched the missile from the silo, grab the Com Tower and port.

Bust the pipe joint with your Battleship to limit the Piperunners' movement.

MISSION TIMELINE

START

Days 1-3
STRENGTHEN YOUR POSITION
Protect your Rockets at all times. Break one pipe joint to start, then gradually open more of them.

Day 3
REACH THE MISSILE SILO FIRST
Move your Infantry toward the silo and launch the missile before your opponent does.

Days 3-4
GRAB THE SECRET PLANS
Station your Battleship in the harbor and assault the pipeline and Piperunners until the coast is clear.

CO Power ★
Use Kanbei.

Days 4-6
ADVANCE ON THE ENEMY
Send in your AA guns and take out the Battle Copters and Bombers. Use Rockets, Artillery and Md. Tanks to clean up.

Days 7-9
SINK THE BATTLESHIP
Attack Hawke's Battleship with your Sub and/or Battle Copters, but beware enemy Cruisers.

CO Power ★

Days 10-12
DESTROY THE THREE MINICANNONS

VICTORY

THE CENTER OF ATTENTION

Position the majority of your forces along the western pipe. When you break through, send in your AA guns first, followed by Md. Tanks, Artillery and Rockets. Quickly launch the missile from the silo and claim the Com Tower and port. Constrict Piperunner movement by blasting at the southern pipe joint with your Battleship. Deploy some Artillery to assist the effort. If you've got the manpower, send in some Infantry through the eastern pipe and grab the neutral base. When the area is safe, send a loaded Lander to the island and grab the secret plans. Keep your Sub submerged to protect it while you close the gap between you and Hawke's navy.

CO POWER STRATEGY

Use Kanbei's CO Power, Samurai Spirit, to increase the offensive and defensive stats of your units. It'll come in handy around the fourth day, when you're pressing west and dealing with Hawke's forces. Drake's Typhoon is best used after Hawke enacts his CO Power, Black Storm. Your enemy will heal his units by two HP, but Drake will kick them back to their original health with a furious wave.

MISSION 17

SPIRAL GARDEN

JAKE   JESS

VS.

KINDLE

AREA PROPERTIES:

	●	●	●	●	Ⓐ	Ⓝ	✖
AIRPORTS	-	-	-	-	-	1	-
BASES	2	-	-	-	2	2	2
CITIES	3	-	-	-	3	11	-
COM TOWERS	-	-	-	-	-	-	-
MISSILE SILOS	-	-	-	-	-	2	-
SEAPORTS	-	-	-	-	-	-	-

BONUS POINTS: 90

OBJECT	#	PTS	TOTAL
BLACK CANNONS	-	-	-
BLACK CRYSTALS	-	-	-
BLACK OBELISKS	-	-	-
MINICANNONS	-	-	-
OOZIUMS	-	-	-
PIPE JOINTS	18	5	90

✖ BLACK HOLE INTEL

Kindle has increased her numbers with an extra Neotank, Piperunner and Infantry. Though it doesn't sound like much, you'll have a harder time advancing through the pipe maze.

★ MARCHING ORDERS

The battle conditions are the same this time around. Capture 15 cities or destroy all enemy units and claim the lab to win. You've lost an Artillery unit but gained some AA guns and a Tank in return.

> Don't destroy every pipe joint in these areas, or you'll let the enemy flood in and surround you.

> Claim the airport and launch the missile before Kindle gets her claws on it.

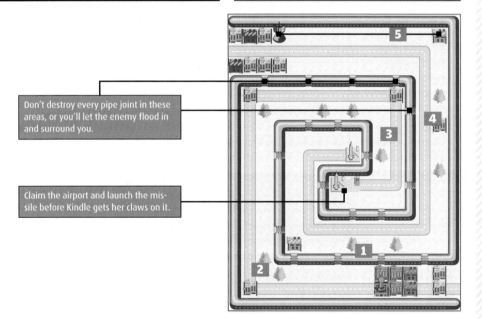

PIPES ARE FOR PLUMBERS

Continuously build up your forces, crafting enough Artillery and Md. Tanks to meet the approaching army. Begin shelling the pipe joints from the get-go.

Not only will you gain bonus points, but you'll limit Piperunner movement and reach the airport quickly. Capture each city you encounter, moving clockwise from your HQ. Use your indirect-fire units to hit the enemy from behind the cover of the spiraling pipes.

CO POWER STRATEGY

Save your CO Powers for a Tag Battle. The combination of both officers' skills will give you that extra oomph during the final days to break through your enemy's front line as you approach the last city (or descend upon the lab). Jake will hit Kindle from a greater distance with Block Rock, and Jess will add movement range to vehicular units, along with superior firepower.

MISSION TIMELINE

START ■

Days 1-3 [1]
BLAST THROUGH THE PIPE
Build at least two Artillery and a few Tanks to breach the southern pipe.

Days 4-6 [2]
STOP THE ENEMY ADVANCEMENT
Have a few Tanks, Anti-air units and Artillery units on standby to meet the advancing forces.

Days 7-9 [3]
THE OTHER SIDE OF THE PIPES
Once you've claimed the airport, station some Artillery here and shell Kindle's units on the other side of the pipe.

CO Power ★
Use it, or save it up for a Tag Battle.

Days 10-12 [4]
KEEP ON TRUCKIN'
Lead your assault with Md. Tanks, placing your Artillery in the rear for additional firepower.

CO Power ★
Deliver a Tag Battle surprise if you can.

Days 13-15 [5]
GRAB THE LAND OR DESTROY ALL UNITS

VICTORY ■

MISSION 18

OMENS AND SIGNS

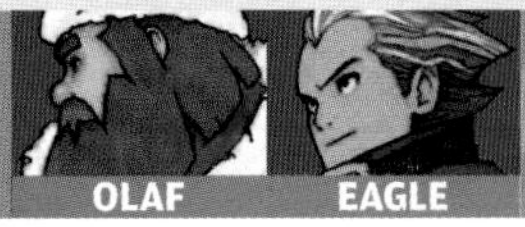
OLAF
EAGLE

VS.

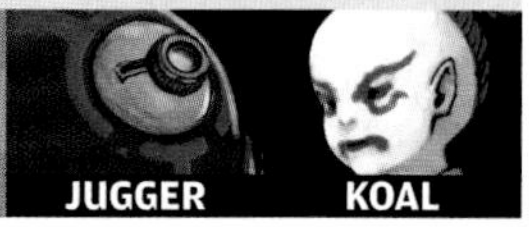
JUGGER
KOAL

AREA PROPERTIES:

	●	●	●	●	A	N	■
AIRPORTS	-	-	-	-	-	-	-
BASES	1	-	-	-	1	1	-
CITIES	2	-	-	-	2	5	9
COM TOWERS	-	-	-	-	-	3	-
MISSILE SILOS	-	-	-	-	-	-	-
SEAPORTS	1	-	-	-	1	-	-

BONUS POINTS: 75

OBJECT	#	PTS	TOTAL
BLACK CANNONS	-	-	-
BLACK CRYSTALS	-	-	-
BLACK OBELISKS	-	-	-
MINICANNONS	4	10	40
OOZIUMS	-	-	-
PIPE JOINTS	7	5	35

BLACK HOLE INTEL

The secondary front has been beefed up with additional Fighters, but on the ground you'll face more Missiles, various Tanks, a Bomber and a Sub.

MARCHING ORDERS

You've got more airpower, but you'll really need to be on the defensive on the main front since you've been given only an extra Tank in exchange for Infantry.

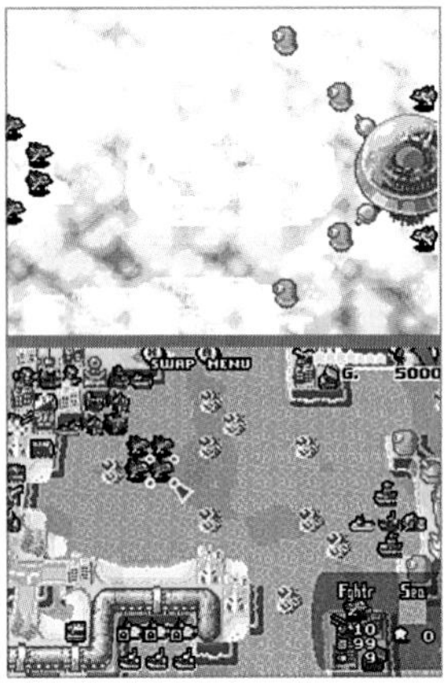

THEY DON'T CALL IT DUAL STRIKE FOR NOTHING!

Even though your CO will fight on the secondary front for you, you'll need to keep an eye on things. Send up reinforcements if necessary, and tweak the AI settings to your exact liking.

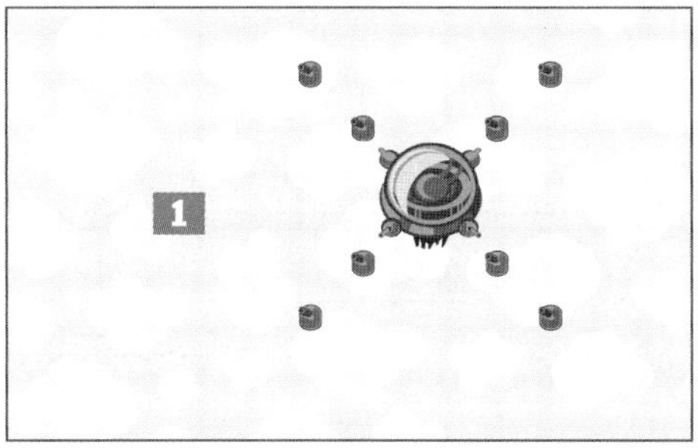
1

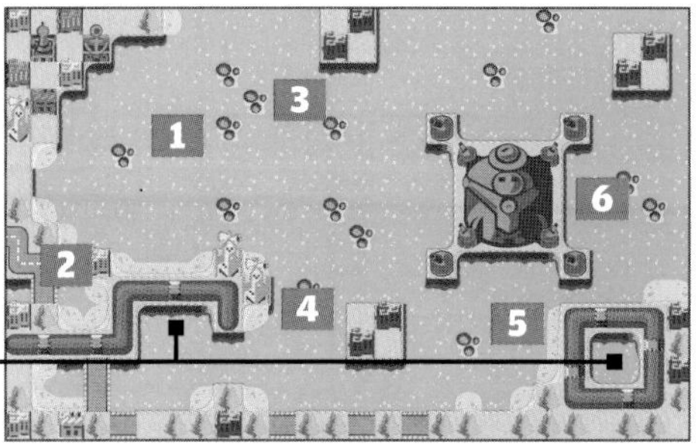
1
2
3
4
5
6

It is imperative that you protect your Carriers and launch the Stealths as quickly as possible.

BATTLE ABOVE AND BATTLE BELOW

You'll have a tough time winning the battle without first destroying the Black Arc floating high in the sky. Send up some air support and adjust the AI settings to match your preference. While Eagle fights the war up top, Olaf should send Rockets, Artillery and a Bomber to the aid of the Carriers in the harbor. Once you are able to release the Stealths, cloak them from attack. Keep the Carriers protected and healthy so your Stealth Fighters can refuel.

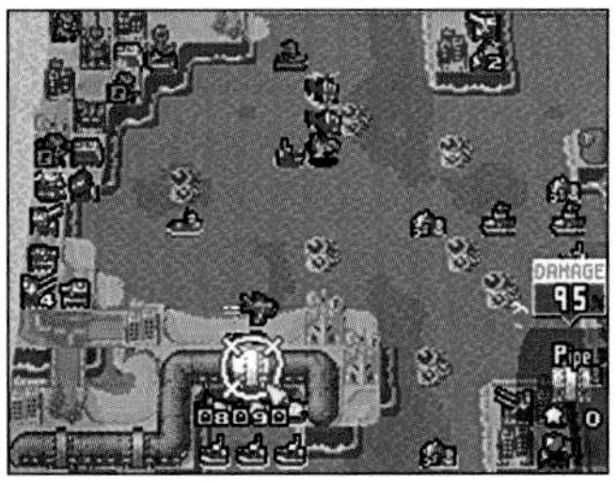

CO POWER STRATEGY

It only makes sense that someone with the name of Eagle would be the best CO to fight an air war for you. He'll fire off his CO Power when he feels like it, but once the secondary front is won, you'll be able to utilize his Lightning Strike to move twice during a turn. Olaf will conjure up a wicked snowstorm with Winter Fury, which will not only damage all enemy units by 2 HP, but slow them down and cause them to burn fuel at a faster clip.

MISSION TIMELINE

START

Day 1

1 SEND UP SOME AIR SUPPORT

Send at least two Fighters to the secondary front. Move your other units eastward like before.

Days 2-4

2 RELEASE THE STEALTHS

Move Artillery, Rockets and a Bomber to the south to assist the Carriers in the harbor.

★ CO Power

Let loose one of Olaf's powers.

Days 4-6

3 LURE THE ENEMY AND ATTACK

Once the Black Hole Army takes the bait, pull back then attack.

Days 7-9

4 SINK THE NAVY

Use your naval vessels and air power to sink the Black Hole navy.

★ CO Power

After you win on the secondary front, it's Tag Battle time.

Days 10-12

5 PRESS EASTWARD

Days 13-15

6 DESTROY THE ENEMY FORTRESS

VICTORY

MISSION 19

INTO THE WOODS

 RACHEL NELL   JAKE   SONJA

VS.

 KINDLE   LASH

AREA PROPERTIES:

	●	●	●	●	Ⓐ	N	✖
✖ AIRPORTS	-	-	-	-	-	1	-
BASES	-	-	-	-	-	-	-
🏙 CITIES	3	3	-	-	6	11	4
COM TOWERS	-	-	-	-	-	1	1
MISSILE SILOS	-	-	-	-	-	3	
SEAPORTS	-	-	-	-	-	-	-

BONUS POINTS: 160

OBJECT	#	PTS	TOTAL
🗲 BLACK CANNONS	-	-	-
BLACK CRYSTALS	-	-	-
BLACK OBELISKS	-	-	-
MINICANNONS	-	-	-
OOZIUMS	4	40	160
PIPE JOINTS	-	-	-

✖ BLACK HOLE INTEL

There's too much fog blanketing the battlefield for you to get an accurate assessment of the Black Hole Army's strength, though it's safe to assume they've got more Battle Copters, heavier Tanks and Ooziums with them.

★ MARCHING ORDERS

You've got extra units, but not enough. As the saying goes, you go to war with the army you've got, not the one you want. Use COs with greater vision range and stick to the high ground to find the enemy.

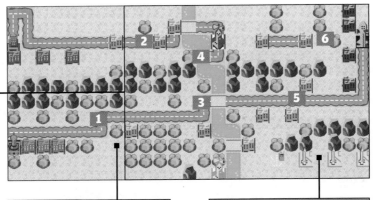

The Fog of War will obscure your view of the entire east. Advance slowly and pack some serious heat.

Avoid exploring the woods until you lure the two hiding Ooziums out into plain sight.

Claim the airport and Missile Silos before your enemy can. The extra firepower comes in handy.

HIDE AND SEEK

Since you won't be able to see your enemies until you're practically on top of them, you'll need to proceed with caution as you slowly advance east. Place ground troops on high to broaden your range of vision, and send Recon units to the front. Protect your Artillery and Anti-air units from attack, as you'll need their superior firepower to hit faraway Tanks and incoming Battle Copters, respectively. Don't enter the southern woods; instead lure enemy units out of hiding before engaging them. Like you did in the Normal Campaign, wait until your foes come to you.

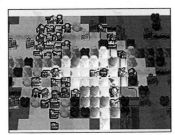

CO POWER STRATEGY

Save up your CO Power for a wicked one-two punch against your enemy. Nell and Rachel have an astounding Tag Battle attack—Covering Fire and Lady Luck will seriously weaken the Black Hole Army. Sonja's Counter Break will increase your vision and allow you to see into woods and reefs. Jake's Super CO Power, Block Rock, will prove useful in hitting the enemy from afar.

MISSION TIMELINE

START

Days 1-2
1 ORANGE STAR GOES ON THE OFFENSIVE

Days 1-2
2 BLUE MOON GOES ON THE DEFENSIVE
Hang back and creep to the east, uncovering enemies as you go.

Days 3-5
3 TAKE THE BRIDGE
Enemy Rockets and Artillery will be waiting, so move with caution.

CO Power ★
Save up your CO Power for a Tag Battle.

Days 3-5
4 THE BLUE BREAKS THROUGH
A Megatank and a Md. Tank wait by the bridge, so send in an APC and Infantry as a decoy.

Days 6-7
5 SQUASH THE OOZIUMS
You'll encounter a sizeable enemy force that includes some nasty Ooziums. Be prepared to fight.

CO Power ★
It's time for a Tag Battle!

Days 8-9
6 FINISH THE JOB

VICTORY

MUCK AMOK!

 KANBEI   MAX   SONJA   LASH

VS.

 KOAL

AREA PROPERTIES:

	●	●	●	●	Ⓐ	N	✳
✈ AIRPORTS	-	-	-	-	-	-	-
🏠 BASES	-	-	-	-	-	-	-
🏙 CITIES	3	-	-	-	3	-	2
📡 COM TOWERS	-	-	-	-	-	4	-
◪ MISSILE SILOS	-	-	-	-	-	-	-
⚓ SEAPORTS	-	-	-	-	-	-	-

BONUS POINTS: 900

OBJECT	#	PTS	TOTAL
🔲 BLACK CANNONS	-	-	-
🔲 BLACK CRYSTALS	-	-	-
🔲 BLACK OBELISKS	-	-	-
🔲 MINICANNONS	1	10	10
🔲 OOZIUMS	22	40	880
🔲 PIPE JOINTS	2	5	10

✳ BLACK HOLE INTEL

As if you didn't face enough Ooziums the last time, Black Hole has added five for a grand total of 22 of the nasty things. You'll also be greeted by an extra Tank and Anti-air gun.

★ MARCHING ORDERS

You'll have extra air support in the form of Battle Copters, along with extra Mechs and an APC to assist you in capturing the northern Com Towers. Be wary of Black Hole Artillery, as it will pursue your troops.

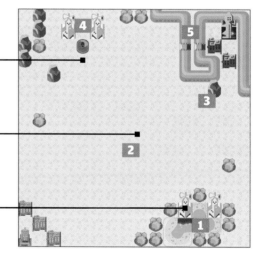

Avoid getting caught in the Minicannon's firing cone. Outflank it or wait until your Tag Battle to attack it.

Don't get your units caught within one space of multiple Ooziums. You must surround and attack them individually.

You'll need the firepower bonus that comes with possessing the Com Towers, so occupy them all.

MISSION TIMELINE

START

Days 1-6
1
CAPTURE THE COM TOWERS
Grab every Com Tower on the battlefield and boost your firepower.

CO Power ★
Use Kanbei and Max in a Tag Battle when they're ready.

Days 6-10
2
SPLIT UP THE OOZIUM CLUSTER
Draw the enemy toward your troops (keep your units one space apart), then surround and destroy each one.

Days 6-10
3
BUM-RUSH THE HEADQUARTERS
If you can lure the guardian Oozium away from HQ, fly a capture team in for a quick win, albeit with little bonuses.

Days 6-10
4
ELIMINATE THE MINICANNON
Check the Minicannon's firing range, then move in for the kill. Blast it to smithereens and capture the Com Towers.

CO Power ★

Days 10-15
5
BREAK THE PIPES AND CLAIM THE HQ

VICTORY

OOZIUMS AS FAR AS THE EYE CAN SEE

If your mother saw the condition of this battlefield, she'd probably say, "This place is a mess! I want you to clean it up right now!" Your job is to rid the area of as many Ooziums as you can on your way to capturing the Black Hole HQ. Start off the round by loading your Transport Copters and APCs with ground troops. Head east to capture the Com Towers there. Eventually, you'll reroute these fellas to the north to complete the same task. Move your other units in three small packs. When you lure an Oozium away from a cluster, surround and destroy it with your heaviest units.

CO POWER STRATEGY

Kanbei and Max possess some wicked skills. When you dish out a Tag Battle using this CO pair, you'll eliminate Ooziums at a faster pace using powered-up attacks. Save up your powers for this purpose—it may take a little while to get things going, but once their meters are charged up, you'll clear the battlefield at breakneck speed. Since Lash and Sonja have few units to work with, you can safely use their powers individually when they're available.

MISSION 21

HEALING TOUCH

   VS.

HAWKE ANDY EAGLE LASH KINDLE JUGGER

AREA PROPERTIES:

	●	●	●	●	A	N	✖
AIRPORTS	-	-	-	-	-	1	-
BASES	-	-	-	-	-	1	-
CITIES	2	2	-	-	4	1	5
COM TOWERS	-	-	-	-	-	-	6
MISSILE SILOS	-	-	-	-	-	5	-
SEAPORTS	-	-	-	-	-	-	-

BONUS POINTS: 150

OBJECT	#	PTS	TOTAL
BLACK CANNONS	-	-	-
BLACK CRYSTALS	6	20	120
BLACK OBELISKS	-	-	-
MINICANNONS	-	-	-
OOZIUMS	-	-	-
PIPE JOINTS	6	5	30

BLACK HOLE INTEL

The Black Hole Army has added a lone Md. Tank to its ranks, but every unit on the battlefield has twice the health it did before. With the Black Crystals boosting enemy HP daily, you're in for a tough fight.

MARCHING ORDERS

Orange Star has been graced with a Battle Copter, and Blue Moon now possesses a Fighter. The key to victory is to eliminate as many weak units as you can, then take out each crystal as quickly as possible.

Shatter these two pipe joints to earn bonus points before you destroy the final Black Crystal.

There are six Com Towers in the area. Make sure you send a capture team to each one to boost your firepower; otherwise the enemy will become more powerful as each unit regains HP.

Reach and activate the Missile Silos as soon as possible. The ones inside the pipe will take longer to reach, but are worth the extra effort.

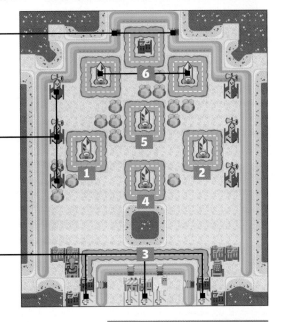

MISSION TIMELINE

START

Day 1 1
HIT THE FIRST CRYSTAL
Clear a path to the first crystal and take it out with your Megatank. Send troops to the silo.

Day 2 2
HIT THE SECOND CRYSTAL
Clear a path to the second crystal and take it out with your Bomber. Send troops to the silo.

Day 3 3
LAUNCH THE MISSILES

Day 3 4
BREAK UP THE ENEMY CLUSTERS
Black Hole units will congregate around the Black Crystals. Clear a path and send in a heavy hitter to destroy each one.

CO Power ★

Days 4-6 5
CONFRONT THE ADVANCING FORCES
The enemy will send out units to attack your armies. Fend them off. Consider joining forces to increase unit strength.

CO Power ★

Days 7-10 6
DESTROY THE LAST TWO CRYSTALS
Keep your eyes on the Piperunners. Blast them to ensure safe passage to the final pair of crystals, then do the deed.

VICTORY

MIRROR IMAGE

Each army's tactics will vaguely mirror that of the other. On the first day, Orange Star should send a loaded APC and Battle Copter to the south to activate the outside Missile Silo. The remainder of the Orange Star forces should head for the closest crystal and blow it apart. Blue Moon's job is similar: escort a capture team to the outside Missile Silo, then target the closest crystal and eliminate it. The faster you destroy the Black Crystals, the less they will be able to heal the existing Black Hole forces.

CO POWER STRATEGY

Andy and Hawke make an interesting pair. Both have the ability to heal your units, and Hawke's can damage enemy units at the same time. Since the Black Hole Army is already in a sorry state, the Tag Battle approach is quite effective. Eagle's Lightning Strike will add an extra turn to non-Infantry units, which is handy when you're pursuing retreating Black Hole targets. Lash's CO Power will double terrain effects, thus increasing your attack strength.

CRYSTAL CALAMITY

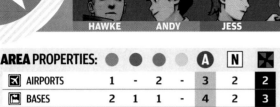

HAWKE | ANDY | JESS | JAVIER | HACHI | SENSEI | **VS.** | KINDLE | KOAL

AREA PROPERTIES:

	●	●	●	●	Ⓐ	N	✖
✈ AIRPORTS	1	-	2	-	3	2	2
🏠 BASES	2	1	1	-	4	2	3
🏙 CITIES	2	3	3	-	8	12	-
📡 COM TOWERS	-	-	-	-	-	2	-
🚀 MISSILE SILOS	-	-	-	-	-	9	-
⚓ SEAPORTS	-	1	-	-	1	1	-

BONUS POINTS: 225

OBJECT	#	PTS	TOTAL
🔲 BLACK CANNONS	1	30	30
🔳 BLACK CRYSTALS	-	-	-
🔲 BLACK OBELISKS	1	30	30
🔲 MINICANNONS	-	-	-
🔲 OOZIUMS	4	40	160
🔲 PIPE JOINTS	1	5	5

✖ BLACK HOLE INTEL

The enemy has swapped out some existing gear in favor of heavier air units. The same goes for ground and sea units, as you'll have to contend with heavier tanks, more Ooziums, some extra troops and a boat.

★ MARCHING ORDERS

It's a swap-o-rama on Crystal Calamity. Each of your teams has traded some of its smaller weaponry for more powerful forces, in addition to some extras to balance things out.

THE EVIL EYE HIGH IN THE SKY

Every 10 minutes, the Black Hole satellite will fire upon your forces and blast away massive amounts of their HP. Knock the Cold War remnant from space by hitting it with every available missile on the battlefield.

You must launch all nine missiles to destroy the satellite. After that, take out the Black Cannon. Then it's obelisk time!

TIME IS OF THE ESSENCE

Black Hole's menacing satellite will unleash massive destruction in a mere 50 minutes, so it's a race against the clock to take it out first. On top of that, every 10 minutes, the blasted thing will fire upon your units and dish out immense damage, taking eight HP from entire squadrons. You must launch all nine missiles into space to rid the world of this threat, and to do that you'll need to send your ground troops into the field quickly. The Black Hole Army will unleash its CO Powers and take an extra turn, which will make it harder for you to reach your destinations ahead of your foe. Lure heavier enemy units into range, then blast them with Artillery from afar. Clear the area, send your forces in and activate the silos one by one. Fire up the war machine and manufacture needed armaments when you can. Once the satellite is gone, remove the Black Cannon that guards the Black Obelisk.

CO POWER STRATEGY

Each pair of COs will have a unique effect on the battlefield, so save up your Tag Battle powers and unleash them when they're ready. Andy and Hawke will replenish Orange Star HP and damage your opponents. Jess and Javier will increase certain unit movements and bolster defenses, while tripling the effect of Com Towers. Hachi and Sensei will allow you to send out cheap reinforcements in droves.

MISSION TIMELINE

START

Days 1-10
CONTROL THE SOUTH — 1
Orange Star should launch all missiles in range and take control of the south. Don't advance until you reach tip number five.

CO Power ★
It's Tag Battle time.

Days 1-10
DOMINATE THE WEST — 2
Capture the Com Towers and base, and launch the missiles. Don't advance until the cannon is gone.

Days 1-10
LOCK DOWN THE EAST — 3
Build Infantry, Tanks and AA guns. Capture properties and launch the missiles. Don't advance until the cannon is destroyed.

CO Power ★
It's Tag Battle time.

Days 10-13
TAKE OUT THE BLACK CANNON — 4
Set up Rockets on the small island near Blue Moon's HQ and destroy the Black Cannon.

CO Power ★
One more time for Tag Battles.

Days 15-18
DESTROY THE BLACK OBELISK — 5

VICTORY

MISSION 23

DARK AMBITION

   VS.

SAMI | SONJA | EAGLE | ANDY | KANBEI | GRIMM | KINDLE | OLAF CLONE

AREA PROPERTIES:

	●	●	●	●	Ⓐ	N	✖
✈ AIRPORTS	-	-	-	-	-	-	-
🏠 BASES	-	-	-	-	-	-	-
🏙 CITIES	1	1	1	-	3	-	7
📡 COM TOWERS	-	-	-	-	-	2	-
⚔ MISSILE SILOS	-	-	-	-	-	3	-
⚓ SEAPORTS	-	-	-	-	-	-	-

BONUS POINTS: 55

OBJECT	#	PTS	TOTAL
🔵 BLACK CANNONS	-	-	-
🔵 BLACK CRYSTALS	-	-	-
🔵 BLACK OBELISKS	-	-	-
🔵 MINICANNONS	4	10	40
🔵 OOZIUMS	-	-	-
🔵 PIPE JOINTS	3	5	15

✖ BLACK HOLE INTEL

The enemy has added one Megatank, two Battle Copters, two Rockets, two Md. Tanks, a pair of Infantry and one Black Bomb. The Md. Tanks are on your side of the pipe and will attack your troops.

★ MARCHING ORDERS

All three of your armies have been outfitted with extra gear, including Rockets, Tanks and Anti-air units. It might not look like much, but every little bit will help you win the fight against the Black Hole threat.

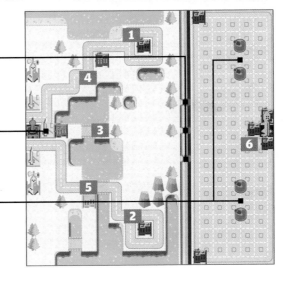

Allow your opponents to do the honors of breaking the pipe joints here. They'll bunch up near the choke points and filter through one at a time.

Activate the Missile Silos before the enemy invaders have a chance to do it.

Knock out these Minicannons to earn bonus points if you want to, but be quick about it.

MISSION TIMELINE

START ■

Days 1-3 ❶
CAPTURE YOUR FIRST CITY
Send a loaded APC to this location and capture this city. Search for the weather device inside.

Days 1-4 ❷
CAPTURE YOUR SECOND CITY
Send a loaded APC to this location and capture this land. Search inside for the weather device.

Days 2-4 ❸
ORANGE STAR FALLS BACK
Position indirect-fire units on the bridges to stem the influx of the Black Hole military.

CO Power ★
Use Sami's power.

Days 4-7 ❹
DESTROY THE INCOMING UNITS
Swing Green Earth behind Orange Star and support your brothers in arms.

CO Power ★
Use all CO Powers individually.

Days 4-8 ❺
BLUE MOON TACTICS
Like Orange Star did, command your units to fall back and target incoming Black Hole forces.

Days 9-12 ❻
WIPE OUT OR CAPTURE THE ENEMY

VICTORY ■

THREE TIMES THE ACTION

Begin the round by loading Mechs or Infantry into the available APCs and shipping them out to capture the forward cities. Inside one of them is a device that controls the weather. When you find it, you can stop the raging snowstorm and lift the movement penalty afflicting your armies. Once that's done, send your troops back west to capture the Com Towers and launch the missiles. Once the Black Hole Army breaks through the pipe joints in the east, they will send in most of their forces. Have your armies fall back and pick them off one at a time as they pour in. After you've weeded most of them out, make your move on their HQ.

CO POWER STRATEGY

Using your COs' powers individually in this round works effectively. Keep Sami in front for Orange Star operations, as she can capture properties faster, even when her units are damaged. Eagle should swoop in on the enemy and activate his CO Power to double his turn. Afterward, switch to Andy and use his healing power to repair any damage you take. Kanbei and Grimm can dish out—and take—a lot of punishment.

PINCER STRIKE

EAGLE   ANDY   ADDER   GRIT

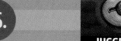 VS.

JUGGER   DRAKE CLONE

AREA PROPERTIES:

	●	●	●	●	A	N	✖
✖ AIRPORTS	-	-	-	-	-	1	-
▥ BASES	2	-	-	-	2	2	1
▥ CITIES	1	8	-	-	9	9	3
✖ COM TOWERS	-	-	-	-	-	2	-
▨ MISSILE SILOS	-	-	-	-	-	2	-
▨ SEAPORTS	1	-	-	-	1	1	-

BONUS POINTS: 80

OBJECT	#	PTS	TOTAL
▣ BLACK CANNONS	-	-	-
▣ BLACK CRYSTALS	-	-	-
▣ BLACK OBELISKS	-	-	-
▣ MINICANNONS	-	-	-
▣ OOZIUMS	2	40	80
▣ PIPE JOINTS	-	-	-

✖ BLACK HOLE INTEL

Your foe has beefed up its presence with a Black Boat, three Battle Copters and two Ooziums. In a bold move, the Black Hole Army will use the Fog of War to its advantage and go after the silos and Com Towers.

★ MARCHING ORDERS

Orange Star's Megatank has been swapped out for a Neotank, but Blue Moon hasn't lost or gained anything. Do not try capturing the Com Tower or Missile Silos until it's safe to do so.

Stem the flow of Black Hole Infantry coming through the mountain range with indirect-fire units.

Take note of enemy positions. On the third day, a sheet of fog will conceal their whereabouts.

As always, make it a priority to reach and launch the missiles before the other guys do.

Expect the Black Hole Army to send a Cruiser, Sub and Battleship through here.

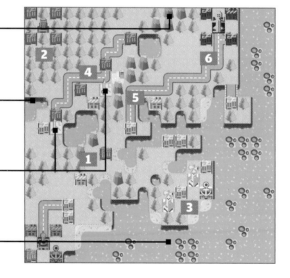

THE FOG HAS FINALLY ROLLED IN

Order the Orange Star Army to begin producing units on the first day. You'll need a pair of Recons to improve your forward vision after the Fog of War kicks in. Immediately convert real estate near your headquarters. Park your Battleship in the cove near the pair of Com Towers to provide fire assistance while sending your submersed Sub in as backup. Your Cruisers should be stationed nearby, as well, to confront the incoming Battle Copters. Use Adder for the first three days, then switch to Grit. After that, the enemy won't advance on your northwest front. Pick them off and clear the road for your forces to move out. Fear the Black Hole Tag Battle—it's crushing!

CO POWER STRATEGY

Early on, Eagle will have his power meter charged up before his partners. Use it when you can. Later on, he and Andy should team up for a Tag Battle to heal your forces and gain momentum. Adder's powers increase the movement range of all of Blue Moon's units. Grit's, on the other hand, charge your weapons with a firepower bonus and increase their effective range by one or two spaces, depending on the power.

MISSION TIMELINE

START

Days 1-4
SET UP AND MOVE OUT
1

Days 1-4
BLUE MOON TACTICS
2
Reposition your troops during the first three days and leave the enemy's fire zone. On the fourth day, switch COs to attack.

CO Power ★
Use Eagle's CO power.

Days 4-8
CONVERT THE NAVAL YARD
3
Capture the port, Com Towers and cities here. Escort your troops with your Battleship and Battle Copters.

CO Power ★

Days 8-12
BREAK THROUGH WITH BLUE MOON
4
By the eighth day, you should have removed all of the enemy's Rockets. Press onward to the east.

CO Power ★

Days 12-15
COMBINE YOUR FORCES
5
Converge your forces and combine them for maximum assault power. Capture the bases here.

Days 15-18
ELIMINATE OR CAPTURE THE ENEMY
6

VICTORY

MISSION 25

RING OF FIRE

JAKE RACHEL

VS.

KOAL KANBEI CLONE

AREA PROPERTIES:

	●	●	●	●	Ⓐ	N	✕
✕ AIRPORTS	-	-	-	-	-	1	-
▣ BASES	-	-	-	-	-	2	-
⌂ CITIES	7	-	-	-	7	11	8
◩ COM TOWERS	-	-	-	-	-	3	2
◿ MISSILE SILOS	-	-	-	-	-	2	-
⌑ SEAPORTS	-	-	-	-	-	-	-

BONUS POINTS: 120

OBJECT	#	PTS	TOTAL
▦ BLACK CANNONS	-	-	-
▦ BLACK CRYSTALS	-	-	-
▦ BLACK OBELISKS	-	-	-
▦ MINICANNONS	-	-	-
▣ OOZIUMS	3	40	120
▣ PIPE JOINTS	-	-	-

✕ BLACK HOLE INTEL

Your Black Hole buddies have removed a few units from each front and replaced them with heavier tanks and aircraft, in addition to a Black Bomb.

★ MARCHING ORDERS

You're down one Infantry unit up top (lucky you!), but you've gained Rockets and Artillery in lieu of one Anti-air unit and a pair of Battle Copters on the main front.

THE BATTLE ABOVE GOES ON. . . .

If you choose to let the AI fight for you, change the settings to defensive. Otherwise, take the helm and capture the Com Towers, but don't advance your forces—let the enemy come to you. Place your Artillery in front and a Missile in back. Stay put and fight!

☐ Avoid landing on the red squares. These are the danger zones where the volcano's fallout will hit.

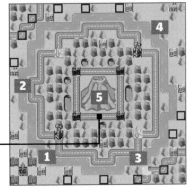

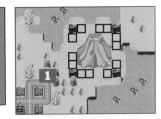

Concentrate your efforts on removing the Black Hole units outside of the mountain ring. Fire on the units inside only when you have an easy shot.

ALL DRESSED UP AND NOWHERE TO GO

You'll want to send up Anti-air, Artillery and Missiles to the secondary front on the first day of fighting. Follow that up with a few Mechs, along with a Bomber and an AA gun by the seventh day. Use Rachel's CO Power to put down the Black Hole resistance. On the lower screen, station your Rockets and Artillery around the island perimeter. Destroy anything that comes near you. You can mostly ignore the enemy units in the center—they can't escape. Travel around the island, laying waste to your foes and capturing Com Towers.

CO POWER STRATEGY

When you're ready to use your CO Powers, you'll gain quite an advantage over the dwindling Black Hole forces. Jake's Block Rock will increase vehicle movement range while kicking your firing range up a notch. This will come in handy, especially when the enemy has turned tail and moved just outside your grasp. Rachel's Covering Fire rains Orange Star missiles on your targets of choice, and can seal the deal near the end of the secondary-front fight.

MISSION TIMELINE

START

Days 1-4 ❶
SEND UP REINFORCEMENTS

Send up additional units to the secondary front and capture the Com Towers. Send Mechs overseas to take the HQ.

CO Power ★

Rachel should be at full power now.

Days 3-7 ❷
CAPTURE THE NEUTRAL BASE

Capture the base and manufacture an AA gun, then send it up top. Ward off the advancing enemy threat.

Days 3-7 ❸
CAPTURE THE NEUTRAL AIRPORT

Capture the airport and build a Bomber, then send it to the secondary front. Ward off the advancing enemy threat.

CO Power ★

Go, Jake!

Days 8-13 ❹
SWING UP TO THE NORTHEAST

Send strong units to the northeast and collect the real estate there. Watch for fallout from the volcano.

CO Power ★

It's time for a Tag Battle, kids.

Days 14-18 ❺
FINISH THEM!

VICTORY

SURROUNDED!

RACHEL   **NELL**   **SENSEI**   **GRIMM**

VS.

KINDLE   **ANDY CLONE**

AREA PROPERTIES:

	●	●	●	●	A	N	✖
✈ AIRPORTS	-	-	-	-	-	2	-
🏠 BASES	2	1	-	-	3	1	4
🏙 CITIES	4	5	-	-	9	17	4
📡 COM TOWERS	-	-	-	-	-	-	4
⚔ MISSILE SILOS	-	-	-	-	-	2	-
⚓ SEAPORTS	-	-	-	-	-	-	-

BONUS POINTS: 10

OBJECT	#	PTS	TOTAL
🔲 BLACK CANNONS	-	-	-
🔲 BLACK CRYSTALS	-	-	-
🔲 BLACK OBELISKS	-	-	-
🔲 MINICANNONS	-	-	-
🔲 OOZIUMS	-	-	-
🔲 PIPE JOINTS	2	5	10

✖ BLACK HOLE INTEL

Black Hole has added two Piperunners, two Neotanks, two Tanks, one Mech and three Infantry. Between the Piperunners and the Neotanks, you'll have plenty of targets to keep you busy.

★ MARCHING ORDERS

Orange Star has taken Blue Moon's Battle Copter, but the boys in blue have added a Mech and Recon to their forces. Destroy the enemy Piperunners first, then go capture all four Com Towers within the 24-day window.

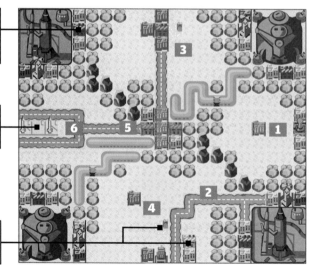

Though you might be tempted to grab the Com Towers first, capture the Black Hole bases to inhibit your enemy's ability to manufacture reinforcements.

If your nemesis reaches the Missile Silos first, you'll get hit hard. Either beat them to it, or prepare for injury.

Capture the airport and bases here before the bad guys; otherwise you'll have to fight for it.

WHERE'S A PLUMBER WHEN YOU NEED ONE?

Unless you destroy the Piperunners here, you'll likely get pummelled. Take out the first one using Rockets and a Recon. You'll want to convert the northern Black Hole base next, so send a Tank and Battle Copter escort alongside a Mech-loaded APC and take it over. Reposition your Artillery, a Neotank and a Md. Tank near the southeast Com Tower (see the screenshot below). On the following day, you'll be in range to squash the resident Black Hole forces. Once the area is yours you can retreat to your HQ and fend off the advancing enemy. Have Blue Moon place Artillery on the center city—when the Piperunners swing into range, let 'em have it! The fight is tougher this time, but if you take it slow and steady you'll come out on top.

CO POWER STRATEGY

Rather than save your CO Powers for a Tag Battle, activate each one individually, as it would take too long otherwise. Fire Rachel's Covering Fire only at clustered forces, or you'll waste it. You can send smaller units after larger ones with Nell's Lady Luck. Pump out lots of cheap reinforcements with Sensei's Airborne Assault. Use Grimm's Haymaker to really sock it to the Black Hole Army.

MISSION TIMELINE

START

Days 1-4
GRAB THE FIRST COM TOWER 1
Eliminate the Piperunner. Move small units north and larger ones south.

Days 1-4
BLUE MOON TO THE RESCUE! 2
Assist your Orange Star compatriots in the southeast. Set up defensive positions.

Days 1-4
TAKE THE NORTH-EAST COM TOWER 3
Switch to Grimm, then build Mechs and send them after the Black Hole Tank. Capture the airport. Send Recon after Infantry.

CO Power ★
Use each CO's powers individually this mission.

Days 4-8
NAB THE SOUTH-WEST COM TOWER 4
Clear the region of enemy units and snag the Com Tower.

Days 4-10
HOLD YOUR GROUND 5
The Black Hole Army will swoop in with a vengeance. Combine your forces and repel your foes.

CO Power ★
Again, use powers individually.

Days 10-15
CLAIM THE FINAL COM TOWER 6

VICTORY

MISSION 27 — FOR THE FUTURE!

RACHEL   JAVIER   DRAKE   COLIN   EAGLE   HACHI   **VS.**   VON BOLT

AREA PROPERTIES:

	●	●	●	●	Ⓐ	Ⓝ	�֎
✖ AIRPORTS	-	-	1	-	1	1	1
⌂ BASES	2	1	1	-	4	4	3
⌂ CITIES	7	6	6	-	19	8	8
✖ COM TOWERS	-	-	-	-	-	-	3
✓ MISSILE SILOS	-	-	-	-	-	2	-
▨ SEAPORTS	-	1	-	-	1	1	1

BONUS POINTS: 275

OBJECT	#	PTS	TOTAL
BLACK CANNONS	-	-	-
BLACK CRYSTALS	3	20	60
BLACK OBELISKS	1	30	30
MINICANNONS	4	10	40
OOZIUMS	2	40	80
PIPE JOINTS	13	5	65

✖ BLACK HOLE INTEL

The fun never ends! Black Hole is packing extra Ooziums, Piperunners, Tanks, Artillery and more. You'll have to contend with Black Crystals healing the enemy units, along with the dangerous Piperunners.

★ MARCHING ORDERS

You have the benefit of extra firepower, but not much. Use what you've got wisely to eliminate the Piperunners and Minicannons, as well as the various crystals that will make your life miserable.

> By the time you reach the Black Obelisk, you'll face a formidable welcoming party. Reach the silos and launch the missiles.

THE DARK CRYSTAL

You'll fight this battle much like you did the first time. Beef up your Orange Star forces and send them north, just out of range of the flanking Minicannons. Send your ground troops to capture the outside Com Towers, but do not go after the central one until your allies have destroyed the first row of protectors. Station your Tanks in front to fend off the incoming threats. Blue Moon will have to contend with the Piperunners. You can whale on the pipe joints to limit the Piperunner's movement, then bash away at the thing when it swings into range. Assist the mainland fight with nearby indirect-fire units.

Have Blue Moon and Green Earth forces bust through the pipelines to assist Orange Star.

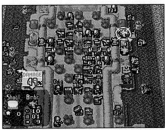

CO POWER STRATEGY

After you grab the three Com Towers, Javier's CO Powers will have a much greater effect. Between him and Rachel, you should be able to reduce the opposition significantly. Drake will lop 2 HP off the entire lot and slow their movement, while Eagle gets a second turn—very useful when you're blasting away at a Piperunner or Minicannon. Use Colin and Hachi to reinforce your army on the cheap.

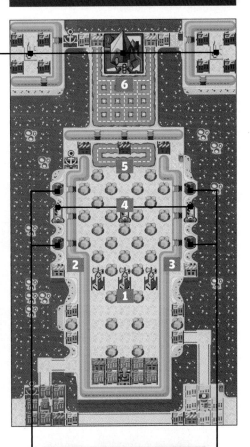

> The outside armies should take out the Minicannons and Piperunners by the third day so Orange Star can advance.

MISSION TIMELINE

START

Days 1-5 — 1
STRAIGHT UP THE MIDDLE
Set your Artillery and Rockets in back and your larger Tanks in front. Think defensively.

Days 1-5 — 2
BLUE MOON TACTICS
Keep your Battleship along the shore and attack the Minicannon with Artillery.

Days 1-5 — 3
GREEN EARTH TACTICS
Keep your Artillery and Bomber near the shoreline and attack the Minicannon.

CO Power ★

Days 6-11 — 4
DESTROY THE BLACK CRYSTALS
The enemy will crowd around the crystals to stop you from destroying them. Push your way in!

CO Power ★

Days 12-15 — 5
BREAK THROUGH THE PIPES
Convert the Black Hole bases and break through the pipes. Be prepared for a stiff fight.

CO Power ★

Days 16-20 — 6
DESTROY THE BLACK OBELISK
Steamroll over the Black Hole forces and destroy the *real* Black Obelisk.

VICTORY

MISSION 28: MEANS TO AN END

KANBEI **JAVIER** VS. **VON BOLT** **KINDLE**

AREA PROPERTIES:

	●	●	●	●	Ⓐ	Ⓝ	✖
✖ AIRPORTS	2	-	-	-	2	2	-
🏠 BASES	4	-	-	-	4	2	2
🏙 CITIES	2	-	-	-	2	20	-
🗼 COM TOWERS	-	-	-	-	-	4	-
✓ MISSILE SILOS	-	-	-	-	-	-	-
🚢 SEAPORTS	-	-	-	-	-	-	-

BONUS POINTS: 650

OBJECT	#	PTS	TOTAL
🔲 BLACK CANNONS	-	-	-
🔲 BLACK CRYSTALS	-	-	-
🔲 BLACK OBELISKS	-	-	-
🔲 MINICANNONS	-	-	-
🔲 OOZIUMS	16	40	640
🔲 PIPE JOINTS	2	5	10

✖ BLACK HOLE INTEL

The ominous blob is back, and it's brought some extra friends. Dotting the field are more Mechs in place of some Infantry. Up top, you'll notice an extra Neotank. Expect three new Ooziums every six days.

★ MARCHING ORDERS

You've been shafted on the secondary front: to replace your lost Cruiser, Recon and Tank you've gained three Mechs. But you have plenty of bases to help make up for the losses.

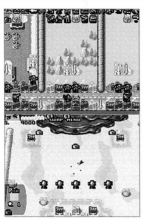

SET THE CO STRATEGY UP TOP

Kanbei and Javier pack superior firepower and great defense. Begin the battle with the AI set to Defense, then switch to Aggressive after you've destroyed most of the enemies. Your army will then pursue the Black Crystals.

THE BLOB IS BACK

Kanbei possess strong offensive and defensive traits, so he's a good choice to fight on the main front. Start building Infantry and Mechs, and begin capturing the real estate surrounding your HQ. Don't stop cranking them out, even as the enemy advances. Build a few Recons, a Transport Copter and a Battle Copter. Load up your men, fly south and claim all the bases, cities and Com Towers there. Eliminate the Black Hole forces in your way. Keep a strong front in the north and attack the Ooziums with multiple Recon units simultaneously. After you've won the secondary front, fire away at the three red eyes on the big Oozium. You've done it!

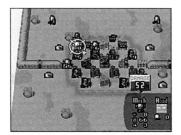

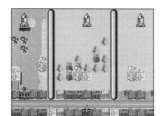

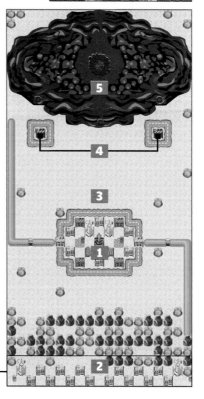

Take over the south to increase your daily earnings, boost your firepower, and produce air units.

MISSION TIMELINE

START

Days 1-6
BULK UP YOUR MILITARY
Build Infantry like they're going out of style. With Kanbei as CO, you'll have little problem taking over.

★ **CO Power**
Boost morale with Kanbei.

Days 1-6
OCCUPY THE SOUTH

Days 7-12
PUSH BACK THE ENEMY
Send your Anti-air units, Recons and Tanks to blast away at the creeping field of Ooziums in the north.

★ **CO Power**
Use Kanbei's power.

Days 13-18
CLAIM THE BASES
Snag these Black Hole bases to cease production of enemy reinforcements, but be wary of baby Ooziums. . . .

★ **CO Power**
After the secondary front is won, join together for a Tag Battle.

Days 18-24
DESTROY THE ULTIMATE OOZIUM
Either annihilate the beast immediately or sacrifice its offspring first for bonus points.

VICTORY

★ EXTRAS

- **SURVIVAL**
- **WAR ROOM**
- **VERSUS**
- **COMBAT**

EXTRA MODES MEAN EXTRA FUN

Congratulations! You did it! You beat the Hard Campaign and sent that stodgy Von Bolt to the netherworld. Unless you're one of those people who skips to the end of a book. In that case, shame on you! Either way, the following section contains information and strategy on additional gameplay modes. Strap on your helmet and get reading!

SURVIVAL MODE

There are three Survival modes for you to wrap your head around. Do you have what it takes to carry on?

NEW WAYS TO PLAY

There are three Survival modes, each containing 11 maps. Every Survival mode has specific rules you'll need to follow. At the end of a round, you'll be ranked on speed, power and technique as usual, for a maximum of 50 points per rating. Your overall rank will be assigned when you've completed all 11 levels of a mode. You'll earn points to spend in the Battle Maps shop every time you complete a map. Extra money, days and time will be added to your points.

CHOOSING THE RIGHT CO

Choosing the right CO for the job is essential for victory in Survival mode. Examine each commander's traits and CO Powers before you decide. Unlike in Campaign mode, you cannot swap your officers between levels, but you will carry over unused CO Powers to the next map—so if you can complete the current map without using your CO's unique attack, do so. Always select a pair of officers with powers that complement each other. To check an officer's compatibility with another CO, refer to the chart on page 128.

MONEY SURVIVAL

You will start Money Survival with 500,000G. You must complete all 11 challenges using the same pair of COs. You cannot earn additional funds, so you'll need to spend your cash on prudent purchases.

- **CHOOSING YOUR COs**
  Choose one CO who can purchase units at cheaper cost, but don't compromise your firepower in the process. Build your army using the frugal CO, then switch partners when it's time to go on the offensive. Team Hachi or Colin with a stronger CO like Hawke or Grimm. At the end of the round, switch back to the weaker commander in preparation for the next map.

- **PLANNING YOUR STRATEGY**
  Survey each map before you jump into the fray. Note your enemy's number, position and unit types, and plan your strategy before you start building. Consider inexpensive means to take down your opponents. You will find opportunities to accrue bonus points, but don't sacrifice funds in the process. Remember, when you park a damaged unit on a captured property it will regain HP, but it will cost you funds.

TURN SURVIVAL

In Turn Survival mode you have 99 days to complete all 11 missions. As in Money Survival, you cannot switch out your COs after making your selections. If you haven't finished the final level after 99 days, the game will end.

- **CHOOSING YOUR COs**
  Pair up COs who possess terrain skills with those who have power and defense skills. Jess, Adder and Koal have greater range and terrain advantages than other officers. Team one of them with a powerhouse like Flak, Grimm or Kanbei. Try different combinations of the aforementioned COs to complete Turn Survival in the fewest days. Save your CO Powers until you need them.

- **PLANNING YOUR STRATEGY**
  Sometimes it'll be faster (and easier) to capture your enemy's HQ rather than wipe out its army. Other times, the opposite holds true. In either case, use the appropriate CO for the task at hand and maximize your daily activities. You might be tempted to go after those sweet, low-hanging bonus points, but remember that you have a limited number of days to finish all 11 maps.

TIME SURVIVAL

As if Turn Survival weren't tough enough, Time Survival gives you a measly 25 minutes to emerge victorious from all 11 missions with the same pair of officers. But don't worry: time counts down only during your turns, not your enemy's.

- **CHOOSING YOUR COs**
  Select officers who are strong and fast. Eagle is an excellent choice for this mode due to his CO Powers that allow him to to move twice in a single turn. Andy, Drake and Kindle are solid partners for him. Andy can heal your units, whereas Drake and Kindle can devastate the enemy with powerful attacks and speed you to victory.

- **PLANNING YOUR STRATEGY**
  Keep an eye on the timer during this mode. Think fast and don't hesitate while the seconds tick away. If you need to clear your head, pause the game to stop the clock. If you employ Eagle as a CO, engage in a Tag Battle only if he's first in line and he's just made his last move; otherwise, he will have only one turn instead of two.

★ MONEY

MAP 1: SILO SWEEP

SPENDING GOAL: **1,800**G

ENEMY: JESS

Jess is strong and has superior firepower with vehicular units. But with all the Missile Silos around, this mission is a cinch. Build two Infantry units and move the Md. Tank to HQ, then end the turn. Next, move Infantry toward the silos. The following day, inch closer to the silos and move the Md. Tank to the Com Tower. After that, attack Jess's Neotank with your Md. Tank, and have your men launch the missiles. On the last day you should be able to finish off Jess's forces.

Consider using Hachi or Colin as one of your COs to lower the cost of building units. You'll need to conserve cash if you want to make it through all 11 levels.

BUILD: 2 INFANTRY

MAP 2: BAD PANGAEA

SPENDING GOAL: **22,500**G

ENEMY: SAMI

Construct Artillery at the eastern and northwestern bases, then pump out a Tank at the remaining one. Switch to your stronger CO. Send all units to destroy the Minicannon in the southwest. The following day, target the western-central Minicannon, then pursue enemy Infantry and APCs. You'll amass 10 points for each Minicannon you destroy. Continue shelling the remaining units with your forces.

BUILD: 3 ARTILLERY
1 TANK

MAP 3: CHOKEPOINT

SPENDING GOAL: **27,000**G

ENEMY: SASHA COLIN

Form two Infantry units to capture the Com Towers. The next day, build a Rocket at the western base and Artillery at the eastern one. Reposition both new units as depicted in the screenshot. Manufacture a Tank and move it near the Artillery. Assault the enemy Megatanks with Rockets and Artillery, then move on to other targets. Prepare to intercept units across the water with your Neotank and Tank.

BUILD: 2 INFANTRY
1 ARTILLERY
1 TANK

1 ROCKET

Don't use your CO Powers. Save them up for a Tag Battle on the fourth map.

MAP 4: COLD SHOULDER

SPENDING GOAL: **36,900**G

ENEMY: NELL

Hopefully, you've saved up your CO Powers from the previous encounter. Build three Infantry and move them east to capture the cities. Create two Recons and have them attack Nell's Infantry. Switch to your miserly officer. Your enemy will send in a Neotank, so you'll want to Tag Battle and build two Md. Tanks and one Neotank at a discount to counter. Switch back to your stronger CO to wipe out the opposition.

BUILD: 3 INFANTRY
2 RECON
2 MD. TANKS *

1 NEOTANK *

* You'll need to employ Hachi's CO Powers to produce these units within budget.

MAP 5: CROWDED PLAIN

SPENDING GOAL: **27,000**G

ENEMY: RACHEL

Construct two Rockets. Move your existing Rockets as shown in the screenshot. Blast the pipelines to earn bonus points. Lure the enemy Megatank into range with your Piperunner, but stay outside of its firing range. Resupply your Rockets at your bases, then attack the Megatank with all five of your units as it heads for your HQ.

BUILD: 2 ROCKETS

Don't use your CO Powers. Save them up for a Tag Battle on the seventh map.

MAP 6: NARROW ROAD

SPENDING GOAL: **28,800**G

ENEMY: KINDLE

Build two Infantry, then advance toward the Missile Silos while you crank out a pair of APCs. The strategy here is to reach all the available silos and turn them against Kindle's army, so load up your APCs and ship out your men to the two silo clusters in the west. Advance west with your other forces and grab bases as you go. Block the incoming Megatanks with your Infantry and shell them with your Artillery as you unload missiles on them from the silos.

BUILD: 10 INFANTRY
2 APCs
2 ARTILLERY

Don't use your CO Powers. Save them up for a Tag Battle on the seventh map.

MAP 7: TRIPLE THREAT

ENEMY: GRIMM

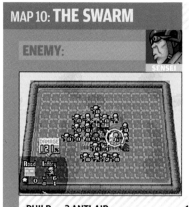

SPENDING GOAL: 40,000G

Build an APC and two Infantry. Load up the transport and reposition it behind the northern base. Also reposition your troops as shown in the screenshot. Allow the enemy Neotanks to attack. Using Hachi, engage in a Tag Battle and build three Neotanks of your own, then switch back to your stronger CO. Once you've eliminated most of Grimm's forces, head to enemy HQ and take out the Piperunner. Switch back to Hachi in preparation for the next map, and capture enemy HQ.

BUILD: 2 INFANTRY
1 APC
3 NEOTANKS *

* You'll need to use Hachi's CO Powers to contruct these units within budget.

MAP 8: THE GOOPING

ENEMY: EAGLE

SPENDING GOAL: 18,900G

Assemble Infantry on every base except the eastern one, where you'll build a Recon unit. Begin capturing the Com Towers the next day. Make the rest of the suggested Infantry at your bases, but save the southern base for a Tank. Pursue the enemy Infantry with your Recon and Tank. Continue capturing Com Towers to boost your firepower. Distract the Ooziums to clear a path for a trio of Infantry to invade your enemy's HQ. If the enemy produces a Tank, take it out.

BUILD: 10 INFANTRY
1 RECON
1 TANK

Don't use your CO Powers. Save them up for the tenth map.

MAP 9: SINGLE FILE ISLE

ENEMIES: OLAF GRIT

SPENDING GOAL: 17,100G

Build two Infantry and a Transport Copter. The following day, load your men into the whirlybird. March your other troops north toward the silo, but outside of enemy firing range. Build another pair of Infantry. On Day 3, advance your men to the silos while you fly your chopper over the water. By Day 4, you should be able to reach the enemy HQ. Capture it, using your T. Copter to block the enemy Tanks, then build a Battle Copter. Launch the missiles and finish off the enemy.

BUILD: 5 INFANTRY
1 TRANSPORT COPTER
1 BATTLE COPTER

MAP 10: THE SWARM

ENEMY: SENSEI

SPENDING GOAL: 63,000G

Manufacture two AA guns and a Battle Copter. On the following day, attack the enemy Mechs. Activate Hachi's CO Power to deploy cheap troops and to build two Megatanks and one Bomber. Switch to the stronger CO to maximize damage. You may need to spend some cash healing your units that are on bases, but you shouldn't have to build additional reinforcements. Hack away at the opposition until you emerge victorious.

BUILD: 2 ANTI-AIR   1 BOMBER *
1 BATTLE COPTER
2 MEGATANKS *

* You'll need to use Hachi's CO Powers to build these items within budget.

MAP 11: GRIT'S GAMBIT

ENEMY: GRIT

SPENDING GOAL: VARIES

The Fog of War has rolled in, so you'll need to protect your Recon and your men on the mountaintops. Grit's Super Snipe ability boosts his units' indirect-firing range, so watch out when he goes on the offensive. Employ Hachi's CO Power to build cheap units, then use your stronger CO to attack your enemy's army. Continue pushing it back until the battlefield is littered with smoking remnants. Keep Mechs on mountaintops, and Recons in front for increased vision.

IF YOU HAVE 50,000G OR MORE LEFT AND SUFFICIENT POINTS, YOU SHOULD EARN AN S RANKING. SPEND WISELY, BUT HAVE A LITTLE FUN, TOO!

KEEP ON CHUGGIN'

Once you've completed Money Survival mode, you can purchase Money Champion mode. It's a tougher version of the original, and lets you spend extra cash on units across limitless maps. How far can you stretch that budget?

TURN

MAP 1: CONVOY CAPE

TURN GOAL: 5 Days

ENEMY: DRAKE

Day 1
Load Infantry into Landers. Reposition Landers on both sides of the island, outside of Sub and Cruiser range.

Day 2
Move a Lander close to enemy HQ. Retreat with the other one.

Days 3-5
Unload Infantry and capture enemy HQ. Distract enemies with your boat.

MAP 2: CANNON LAND

TURN GOAL: 10 Days

ENEMY: KOAL

Days 1-4
Capture cities, build Recons and move to HQ while avoiding Minicannon fire. Create Infantry and grab a neutral base.

Day 4
Craft a Piperunner at the northern base. Build Artillery at the south base.

Days 5-7
Move the Piperunner through Minicannon and Black Cannon space to the east. Attack the Black Cannon with your Artillery. Make Rockets and destroy the cannons.

Days 8-10
Attack enemy Infantry with your Piperunner to conclude the mission.

MAP 3: MR. FIX-IT

TURN GOAL: 10 Days

ENEMY: ANDY

Day 1
Move two western Battleships toward the Missile Silo. Repair the big boats and attack the enemy Infantry.

Days 2-5
Continue healing your Battleships and attacking the enemy. Advance your Infantry to the silo.

Day 5
Keep Infantry hidden in the trees and move in to launch the missile.

Days 5-10
Finish repairing the Battleships, then move into firing position and whale on the enemy units.

MAP 4: AIRCRAFT HUNT

TURN GOAL: 3 Days

ENEMY: SENSEI

Day 1
Move your AA guns south and attack the pair of Battle Copters. Sail your Carrier and release its payload.

Day 2
Reposition AA guns to the north and destroy enemy copters. Use Missiles, Battle Copters and a Carrier to attack.

Day 3
Finish off Sensei's forces.

MAP 5: RAIN OF PAIN

TURN GOAL: 5 Days

ENEMY: SONJA

Day 1
Move your Subs and Battle Copters inland to increase visibility. Keep the Black Boats away from land, and attack with your Battleships.

Days 2-4
Attack the enemy with your copters and Battleships and clear one island at a time.

Day 5
Use your CO Powers to finish the job, or save them up for the next map.

MAP 6: LONE WOLF

TURN GOAL: 10 Days

ENEMY: KOAL

Days 1-4 *
Capture the eastern base. Build Infantry and Artillery and launch the nearby missiles. Create a Md. Tank on day four.

Day 5
Launch another missile. Reposition your Infantry to the northwest. Attack the opposition with your Md. Tank.

Days 6-10
Continue launching missiles. Assault Koal's forces with your Md. Tank and Artillery until you win.

* Provided you saved your CO Powers from the last mission, you can win this conflict in the first few days with a Tag Battle.

MAP 7: FENCED IN

TURN GOAL: 5 Days

ENEMY: MAX

Days 1-3
Hide your Stealth Fighters near the pipeline breaks. Bust through the pipeline and prepare to attack.

Days 2-3
Move in your Bombers and Battle Copters but stay out of range of the enemy Carriers.

Days 3-5
Move all air units in and destroy all the enemy units to end the mission.

MAP 8: RIVER RAID

TURN GOAL: 5 Days

ENEMY: JAVIER

Day 1
Move your APC and Lander to the shoreline and block in the enemy. Send your remaining units west and attack enemy Battleships with your Neotank and Md. Tanks.

Days 2-3
Continue heading west with your APC and Lander, and push the enemy back. Finish off the Battleship with your Artillery and Rockets. Send your tanks after the Black Boats, then Cruisers.

Days 4-5
Corner Javier with your Lander, then start a Tag Battle to finish him off.

MAP 9: CRYSTAL FIELD

TURN GOAL: 10 Days

ENEMY: KANBEI

Days 1-4

Advance to fire on the crystals, but stay ouside of enemy attack range.

Days 4-7

Destroy all the crystals, then move your Rockets forward and attack the Artillery.

Days 7-10

Load tanks and Mechs into the T. Copter and APC, and engage enemy Rockets with your own.

MAP 10: FIVE MILE ISLE

TURN GOAL: 10 Days

ENEMY: JAKE

Days 1-2

Position Mechs as shown in the screenshot. Repair your Battle Copters to absorb enemy punishment.

Days 3-7

Advance your Mechs at an even pace. Shield them with your Battle Copters, but do not engage your foes.

Days 8-10

Move your forces east and grab Jake's headquarters.

MAP 11: FOREST FRENZY

TURN GOAL: ?? Days *

ENEMY: SONJA

Days ?? *

You'll have to deal with limited visibility and a seemingly endless barrage of Black Bombs as Sonja attacks your troops. Leave your Md. Tanks in the rear and press forward with your Recons. Block the bombs with your AA guns and Recons. Use your Tag Battle when it's advantageous.

IF YOU HAVE 25 DAYS LEFT AND PLENTY OF BONUS POINTS, YOU SHOULD EARN AN S RANKING.

WHERE ARE YOU GOING, CHAMP?

Now you can purchase Turn Champion mode from Hachi's shop. You'll have a few extra days at your disposal, so see how long you can last before you use up your final turn.

⭐ TIME

TIME AVAILABLE: 25:00

MAP 1: RED HEART

ENEMY: JUGGER

TIME GOAL: 0:30

Attack the Neotank with all of your available Mechs in the vicinity. Combine your remaining forces that are out of range; keep them grouped so they'll be close enough to the Neotank to attack it the next day. On the following turn, finish off the Neotank.

MAP 2: FROZEN PIPES

ENEMY: OLAF

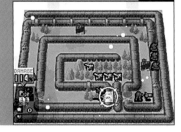

TIME GOAL: 1:30

Destroy the pipe joints near the Bomber and Neotank. Reposition the three Piperunners clockwise as shown in the screenshot. Once you've cleared a path, send in the Black Bomb and hit the enemy. Finish off your opponent with your Bomber and Piperunners. (Continue moving in Piperunners for help, and take out as many pipelines as you can within the time limit.)

MAP 3: CAPE SPLINTER

ENEMY: LASH

TIME GOAL: 1:30

You'll need Eagle's CO Power to finish this map inside the time goal. Send your Black Bombs around Lash's cluster of units as shown in the screenshot. Advance your Md. Tank and regular Tank. Attack on the fourth day, using your bombs followed by your tanks. Activate Eagle's CO Power and attack again. Pursue the remaining forces and obliterate them before they retreat to the crystal to heal.

MAP 4: LAKE FEVER

ENEMY: ANDY

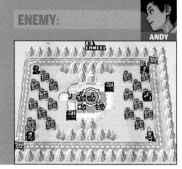

TIME GOAL: 1:30

Build two Infantry units and send them toward the silos. Then produce two more. On the next day, continue moving toward the silos, and pump out another pair to capture the Com Towers. Create two Megatanks. Capture the towers, launch the missiles and reposition your Megatanks near enemy shores. Build Rockets at the corner base. Attack the opposing army with your Rockets and Megatanks until it is destroyed.

MAP 5: OPEN ROAD

ENEMY: SAMI

TIME GOAL: 0:30

You'll need to be quick to finish this map in under 30 seconds. Load Infantry into an APC as shown in the screenshot and head east. Park north of the Recon. Leave your Recon units in place, as they are currently concealed in the woods. With your APC, move east along the road to the next Recon in the field. On the following day, you should reach your enemy's HQ and deploy your troops unscathed. Grab the property and win the round without the enemy moving.

MAP 6: THE MIDDLEMAN

ENEMY: HAWKE

TIME GOAL: 1:30

Attack the four Minicannons in range of your Md. Tanks. Reposition your Artillery behind each Md. Tank and create two Recons. On the next day, finish off the bottom pair of Minicannons with your Artillery. Send your Recons after enemy Infantry. On the following day destroy another pair of cannons. Eliminate the Mechs and pair of Neotanks with your four Md. Tanks. Trap and annihilate the remaining Neotank with your Md. Tanks.

MAP 7: STEALTH FIGHT

ENEMY: OLAF

TIME GOAL: 1:30

Load your T. Copter and cruise to the mountains southwest of your HQ while staying out of enemy firing range. Fly your cloaked Stealths next to the enemy Carriers. On the following day, destroy the Carriers and continue moving your copter south. Distract the Battleship with your APC. Attack the enemy Md. Tank while you swing the T. Copter to enemy shores. Park the chopper in the mountains and deploy your troops near enemy HQ for the final assault (but only after Olaf has used his CO Power).

MAP 8: TACTICAL DECOY

ENEMY: JAVIER

TIME GOAL: 2:00

Javier will toss a lot of missiles your way, so spread your forces out into six small groups to minimize widespread damage. Do not join injured units together. Lead a small, spread-out pack with a Md. Tank and attempt to stop your enemy from launching the last pair of missiles. Activate a Tag Battle once you're in range to put the hurt on Javier.

MAP 9: LAST STAND

ENEMY: COLIN

TIME GOAL: 1:30

Fall your Rockets back behind HQ and move your Megatank in front. Reposition your Infantry, APCs and Neotank as shown in the screenshot. Wait for the enemy to attack, but don't move your units from their positions. Hit the advancing forces as they come into range. You sould be able to waste them all without moving a single unit.

MAP 10: PURSUIT PLAINS

ENEMY: LASH

TIME GOAL: 2:00

You'll need Eagle's CO Powers to finish this map quickly. Send your pair of Infantry units after the Rockets and AA guns. Create two Recons and use Eagle's CO Power that you saved from previous battle. Move the Recon in and engage the enemy Infantry and Megatank. Chase down your foes with your Recon and Infantry as they retreat to the crystal. Build a pair of APCs and load them with Infantry, then head toward Lash's HQ for the capture and the win.

MAP 11: FOG HUNTER

ENEMY: GRIMM

TIME GOAL: ??? *

Build Infantry and capture what properties you can. Create and load APCs with Infantry then move east. Build and load a Lander with a Megatank and Neotank. Load two Mechs into the Black Boat. Deploy your tanks and engage in a Tag Battle to hurt Grimm's forces. Launch the missile and grab HQ.

***IF YOU HAVE NINE OR MORE MINUTES LEFT AND ENOUGH POINTS, YOU SHOULD GET AN S RANKING.**

ONE LAST TIME!

Once you have triumphed in Time Survival, you can purchase Time Champion mode. It's similar to the previous mode, though you'll have extra time to get through as many maps as you can.

HACHI

WAR ROOM MODE

You'll find a host of challenging battle scenarios against multiple commanding officers inside the War Room.

RULES AND REGULATIONS

The War Room allows you to tailor your fights. You'll square off against one or more COs on the maps of your choosing. When you finish a map victorious, you'll earn points to spend in the shop, as well as boost your CO's rank. The upper screen displays a condensed version of the current map and includes information on how many cities and bases there are. Additionally, you'll be able to see your next opponent on the top screen. The touch screen is where you'll determine the battle settings and choose how many COs you'll compete against. As before, your performance will be ranked.

CHOOSING THE RIGHT CO

As always, be sure to take note of your opponent before diving into a battle. You'll want to select a CO whose abilities effectively counter those of your enemy (or enemies). Check the upper screen to see if the battlefield contains ports, Com Towers or airports—some COs fare better with certain units than with others. Pick the right CO for the job to save yourself some needless headaches.

MULTIPLE COs

You can select how many COs you'll fight by pressing the L and R Buttons. Tap the Control Pad up or down to scroll through the list and choose the battlefield. The X and Y buttons let you change the page. Consult the list below when you're ready to tweak your team's settings. The small person icon represents the number of COs on your team, and the skills data determines whether your officers will have their skills enabled. The EXP selection denotes what bonus multiplier you'll have factored into your score, if any.

🔲 Skills:OFF EXP×2.5 **ONE CO/SKILLS OFF/EXP x2.5**	🔲 Skills:OFF EXP×1.5 **TWO COs/SKILLS OFF/EXP x1.5**
🔲 Skills:ON EXP×2.0 **ONE CO/SKILLS ON/EXP x2.0**	🔲 Skills:ON NO BONUS **TWO COs/SKILLS ON/NO BONUS**

DS CO BATTLES

After you've selected DS Battle with the L and R Buttons, you can choose skill settings using the Control Pad as before. The small GBA icon indicates that you can change the AI strategy to General, Offense, Defense or Aggressive. The person icon giving the thumbs-up allows the computer to call the shots as it sees fit. Similar to the multiple-CO settings, the skills information shows whether your officers will have their skills enabled. The bonus multiplier will change depending on the AI and skill settings you've chosen.

🔲 Skills:OFF EXP×2.5 **AI ON/SKILLS OFF/EXP x2.5**	🔲 Skills:OFF EXP×1.5 **AI OFF/SKILLS OFF/EXP x1.5**
🔲 Skills:ON EXP×2.0 **AI ON/SKILLS ON/EXP x2.0**	🔲 Skills:ON NO BONUS **AI OFF/SKILLS ON/NO BONUS**

WAR ROOM MAPS

There are 56 War Room maps in all, including 12 that are unlockable. To the right of each map name is the officer or officers you'll face on that battlefield, along with the color of the army they'll control.

TWO COs MAPS

MAP NAME	ENEMY CO
SPANN ISLAND	ANDY
MOJI ISLAND	KOAL
DUO FALLS	MAX
SOLE HARBOR	DRAKE
PIVOT ISLE	EAGLE
LAND'S END	LASH
KITA STRAIGHT	SAMI
POINT STORMY	OLAF
RIDGE ISLAND	GRIT
MIAL'S HOPE	SENSEI
BOUNTY RIVER	JUGGER
TOIL FERRY	HAWKE
TWIN ISLE	JESS
DIRE RANGE	COLIN
EGG ISLANDS	KANBEI
TERRA MAW	SONJA
PAY DIRT	COLIN
LONG ROAD	JESS
NEST EGG	SENSEI
THE TRIDENT	NELL
BANKER HILLS	HACHI
MISSILE PLAINS	VON BOLT
LITTLE LION	ANDY
MEGALOPOLIS	KANBEI
PIPELINE	JESS

You'll need to purchase Little Lion, Megalopolis and Pipeline from Hachi before you can play them. Consult the Battle Maps section on page 124.

THREE COs MAPS

MAP NAME	ENEMY COs	
LOST BASIN	SONJA	SAMI
RIVERS FOUR	LASH	SONJA
RING ISLANDS	GRIT	OLAF
LAST MISSION	NELL	ANDY
STAMP ISLANDS	EAGLE	DRAKE
RISKY VALE	KANBEI	MAX
RABBIT ISLAND	EAGLE	DRAKE
WATERY DOWNS	SONJA	LASH
FORTRESS ISLE	ANDY	HAWKE

You must purchase Rabbit Island, Watery Downs and Fortress Isle before you can fight on them. See page 124 for the list of Battle Maps and other items for sale.

FOUR COs MAPS

MAP NAME	ENEMY COs		
THE RING	JESS	DRAKE	EAGLE
STRONG LAND	KOAL	LASH	JUGGER
TREBLE RIDGE	NELL	MAX	GRIT
FOUR ACRES	GRIMM	JAVIER	SASHA
FINAL BATTLE	KINDLE	KOAL	JUGGER

You can acquire the Treble Ridge, Four Acres and Final Battle maps at the store. Turn to page 124 for a full list of maps and items you can purchase.

DS MAPS

MAP NAME	ENEMY COs	
JELLY ISLAND	GRIT	OLAF
WHIPLASH	EAGLE	DRAKE
SILO NATION	SONJA	KANBEI
RISKY DUO	ADDER	FLAK
HELIX PENINSULA	MAX	ANDY

The final three levels—Silo Nation, Risky Duo and Helix Peninsula—are available for purchase at Hachi's store. Page 124 has the details.

MAX

GRIT

VERSUS MODE

Who says warmongering is antisocial behavior? Battle against up to four human opponents using your DS and a single game card!

RULES AND REGULATIONS

Versus mode allows you to battle up to four players with a single game card. In Normal Battle, choose from any of the maps listed below and on the following page. You'll need to purchase some battlefields in the store before you can play them. DS Battle lets you choose from all but the maps marked with a star. You can import maps that you've contructed in the Design Room and set up a custom battle against the CPU or a friend.

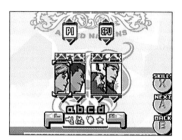

SETTING UP YOUR TEAM

Now that you have selected the map you want to fight on, it's time to pick your COs. After you've appointed your leaders, you can choose your opponent and decide whether the CPU will control that team. If your officers have acquired skills, you can press L and R to choose up to four slots in which to enter skills. Press X to choose the skill for each slot. When it comes time to battle, just select the appropriate slot.

SETTING UP THE MAP

Before you begin the conflict, you'll have to tweak the battlefield conditions. You can change the following settings: Fog, Weather, Land, Funds, Turn, Capt, Power, Visuals and CPU/AI. Experiment with different combinations to change the difficulty and flavor to suit your mood.

VERSUS MAPS

There 150 maps in Versus mode, 27 of which are waiting to be purchased. The maps marked with a star are not available for play in DS mode.

CLASSIC MAPS

BEAN ISLAND	**LOST RIVER**
CRATER ISLE	**VOLCANO ISLE**
TRIANGLES	**TURTLE ATOLL**
BALL ISLANDS	**SQUASH ISLAND**
CORAL LAGOON	**CUBE KEYS**
PUZZLE TRIO	**MIRROR ISLANDS**
FIST PENINSULA	**SHARK STRAIT**
DEER HARBOR	**ROYAL CHANNEL**
ALARA RANGE	

Each map highlighted in grey must be purchased before you can play it. To see a complete list of maps, turn to page 124.

⊛ Map marked with a star are unavailable for play in DS Battle mode. They are accessible only in Normal Battle.

* Each map marked with an asterisk is playable only if you have Advance Wars and Advance Wars 2: Black Hole Rising. Consult the Battle Maps section on page 124 for more information.

DEPLOYED MAPS

BRACE RANGE		**BATTLE CUBE**	⊛
RIVER RANGE		**BIG DADDY**	
MOON ISLE		**GRID ASSAULT**	⊛
MINT PLATEAU		**CROSSROAD**	⊛
JEWEL CANAL		**TRIFECTA ISLES**	
WRENCH ISLAND		**OCEAN PRISON**	
RAPID FERRY		**NARROW RIDGE**	
BUNDLE CITY		**DEADLAKES**	⊛
SCARAB ROAD		**NO-EXIT ISLES**	⊛
POINTING RIVER		**ARROW POINT**	⊛
LIAISON WOOD		**CRATER REEF**	⊛
DELTA HEIGHTS	⊛	**LOST ROAD**	⊛
POEM CAPE	⊛	**CAPITAL CLASH**	⊛
BLUE LAKE	⊛	**ISLANDS AGOGO**	⊛
COIL RANGE	⊛	**GRAND BATTLE**	⊛
LEAF HAVEN	⊛		

TWO COs MAPS

LITTLE ISLAND	TRIBE ISLANDS
SUN CANAL	VISION BRIDGE
BEAKER RIVER	PISTON DAM
STAR ISLANDS	HAT HARBOR
EON SPRINGS	SWAN COVE
PORTAL BRIDGE	GO ISLANDS
SABRE RANGE	HOURGLASS ISLE
ASPHALT MAZE	PIPES APLENTY
COG ISLE	FRIGID FINALE
ZERO WOOD	HACHI'S LAND *
SWITCHBACK	NELL'S LAND *
RUBY KEYS	STURM'S LAND *
RAINY HAVEN	LASH'S LAND *
RAIL STRAIT	

THREE COs MAPS

PYRAMID CAPE	✪	LIAR'S COVE	✪
BEAD ISLANDS	✪	NAIL CANAL	✪
CLOVER KEYS	✪	ATLAS RIVER	✪
KEYHOLE COVE	✪	EEL CHANNELS	✪
FORK RIVER	✪	JAB PENINSULA	✪
MANTIS RIVER	✪	THRON ISLANDS	✪
CHANNEL CITY	✪	PORTSMOUTH	✪
INK CANAL	✪	ARCHIPELAGOS	✪
SHIELD HILLS	✪	WYRM'S EYE	✪
PERIL MAZE	✪	KNOTTED KEYS	✪
GEM CREEK	✪	FAN ISLE	✪
GLASS HEIGHTS	✪	GRIDLOCK GLEN	✪
DEVIL'S INLET	✪	KIDNEY ISLAND	✪
SHEAR PORT	✪		

FOUR COs MAPS

FOUR CORNERS	✪	WEB RIVER	✪
ROCKET CAPE	✪	CAP NARROWS	✪
CROP RIVER	✪	JAY ISLANDS	✪
TWEEN ISLE	✪	CHAIN CANAL	✪
RIVAL ISLANDS	✪	SPRING LAKES	✪
LOOP ROAD	✪	TATTER RIVER	✪
PLUS CANAL	✪	ISLAND X	✪
ISLAS FIVE	✪	ALAKULE	✪
PATRIOT COVE	✪	TRAITOR RIVER	✪

FOUR COs MAPS, CONTINUED

FABLE HILLS	✪	WORM CANAL	✪
SOUTH CAPE	✪	BROKEN LAND	✪
GLORY ISLANDS	✪	ROUGH TERRAIN	✪
PIPE MAZE	✪	DEEP FOREST	✪
LOCK RIDGE	✪	SCRAMBLE ISLE	✪
HEARTLAND	✪	DANGER POOL	✪
BADLANDS	✪	DARK CITY	✪
MARINE CROSS	✪	CLOVER POND	✪
AXLE ROADS	✪	CROSS CAPE	✪

WAR ROOM MAPS

SPANN ISLAND		MISSILE PLAINS	
MOJI ISLAND		STAMP ISLANDS	✪
DUO FALLS		RISKY VALE	✪
SOLE HARBOR		THE RING	✪
PIVOT ISLE		STRONG LAND	✪
LAND'S END		LITTLE LION	
KITA STRAIGHT		MEGALOPOLIS	
POINT STORMY		PIPELINE	
RIDGE ISLAND		RABBIT ISLAND	✪
MIAL'S HOPE		WATERY DOWNS	✪
BOUNTY RIVER		FORTRESS ISLE	✪
TOIL FERRY		TREBLE RIDGE	✪
TWIN ISLE		FOUR ACRES	✪
DIRE RANGE		FINAL BATTLE	✪
EGG ISLANDS		JELLY ISLAND	
TERRA MAW		WHIPLASH	
LOST BASIN	✪	SILO NATION	
RIVERS FOUR	✪	RISKY DUO	
RING ISLANDS	✪	HELIX PENINSULA	
LAST MISSION	✪	JELLY ISLAND DS	
PAY DIRT		WHIPLASH DS	
LONG ROAD		SILO NATION DS	
NEXT EGG		RISKY DUO DS	
THE TRIDENT		HELIX DS	
BANKER HILLS			

COMBAT MODE

Still looking for more action? Try Combat mode on for size. In this new game type, you'll fight intense battles in real time.

BUILDING YOUR TEAM

To begin Combat mode, you must select your CO from the list of available officers. Your opponent will change based on your selection. You have limited funds with which to purchase Mechs, Recons, Tanks and Artillery. Once you're ready for battle, press the Start Button. Control your selected unit with the Control Pad, use the A or Y Button or the touch screen to fire, and press the L Button to select your CO Power. You can control only one unit at a time. If destroyed, that unit will not be usable on future maps during the current game session. To safeguard against losses, place your active unit on a captured property to heal it. You can capture real estate (either neutral or belonging to your enemy) simply by moving onto that property. After you seize a base, you will receive an extra unit of the same type that captured it. You'll earn points by destroying enemy units, pipelines, Minicannons and Black Cannons. Once you capture your enemy's HQ, you will not receive points dispatching remaining units, however. As you blow up mountains, look for the icons shown on the right; they'll boost your stats. The game ends when the timer runs out or you lose your last unit.

 REPAIR
Restores 2 HP

 ARMOR
Makes you invincible temporarily

 POWER
Attack rises a small amount

 BOMB
Damages other units

 SLOW
Cuts other units' speed in half

MAP 1

Select a Tank as your first unit. Pursue the moving enemy troops first, as the ones out of range won't move until you advance on their position. Section them off for a quick defeat.

MAP 2

Begin this level with a Mech. Your vision will improve as you pass over the mountains. Attack your foes when they stop off at a property and try to heal—they usually won't retaliate. Capture cities when you can.

MAP 3

You can fire over the mountains and rivers and hit your enemies at a distance using your Artillery. Earn additional Artillery by capturing a base.

MAP 4

Your opponent doesn't possess an HQ, so you'll have to obliterate every last unit to win. Guard your headquarters and take out each enemy as it advances. Don't leave yourself open to attack by multiple units!

MAP 5

Though a Recon unit would seem like a good choice for this Fog of War situation, instead select a Tank or Artillery and capture a base to earn another unit. Guard your HQ until you've dispatchd most of your opponents then move onward.

MAP 6

Blast the troops from behind the pipeline with your Artillery. Neutralize the three Minicannons by attacking, then backing up. Repeat this approach as neccessary, but be ready for incoming enemy troops and the Black Cannon on the other side of the pipe.

TRY THIS ON FOR SIZE!

After you complete Combat Mode, you can purchase the hard version from Hachi, where you'll play for more points. Prepare to get brutalized!

APPENDICES

- **BATTLE MAPS**
- **UNIT DATA**
- **CO DATA**

QUICK-REFERENCE CHARTS GALORE

The final section of the guide is your one-stop shop for information at a glance. You'll find lists of items and maps for purchase, details on each officer and invaluable data regarding the units you'll have at your disposal.

BATTLE MAPS

Go on a shopping spree in the Battle Maps shop, and personalize your copy of Advance Wars: Dual Strike any way you see fit.

READING THE CHARTS

The charts on the following pages list all of the items available for purchase in the Battle Maps shop. You'll need to amass some cash and satisfy certain game requirements to unlock and acquire the goodies you desire. If you own any of the previous Game Boy Advance versions of Advance Wars, you can unlock additional maps and wallpapers. Simply insert the GBA game pak into the bottom slot of your Nintendo DS with Advance Wars: Dual Strike in the game card slot on top. Turn on your DS and follow the prompts.

AVAILABILITY: IMMEDIATE

COLOR EDITORS	PRICE	COLOR EDITORS	PRICE
ANDY	150G	SONJA	150G
SAMI	150G	SENSEI	150G
OLAF	150G	EAGLE	150G
GRIT	150G	DRAKE	150G
KANBEI	150G	JESS	150G

MAPS	PRICE	MAPS	PRICE
LITTLE LION	500G	CAPITAL CLASH	500G
MEGALOPOLIS	500G	ISLANDS AGOGO	500G
PIPELINE	500G	GRAND BATTLE	500G
RABBIT ISLAND	500G	PIPES APLENTY	500G
WATERY DOWNS	500G	FRIDGID FINALE	500G
FORTRESS ISLE	500G	FAN ISLE	500G
TREBLE RIDGE	500G	GRIDLOCK GLEN	500G
FOUR ACRES	500G	KIDNEY ISLAND	500G
FINAL BATTLE	500G	MARINE CROSS	500G
SILO NATION	1,000G	AXLE ROADS	500G
RISKY DUO	1,000G	WORM CANAL	500G
HELIX PENINSULA	1,000G	BROKEN LAND	500G
TRIFECTA ISLES	500G	ROUGH TERRAIN	500G
OCEAN PRISON	500G	DEEP FOREST	500G
NARROW RIDGE	500G	SCRAMBLE ISLE	500G
DEADLAKES	500G	DANGER POOL	500G
NO-EXIT ISLES	500G	DARK CITY	500G
ARROW POINT	500G	CLOVER POND	500G
CRATER REEF	500G	CROSS CAPE	500G
LOST ROAD	500G		

AVAILABILITY: MISSION 09

COLOR EDITORS	PRICE	COLOR EDITORS	PRICE
RACHEL	150G	COLIN	150G
MAX	150G		

AVAILABILITY: MISSION 22

MAP EDITORS	PRICE
OOZIUM	1,000G

COs	PRICE	COs	PRICE
SASHA	600G	JAVIER	600G
GRIMM	600G		

COLOR EDITORS	PRICE	COLOR EDITORS	PRICE
SASHA *	150G	JAVIER *	150G
GRIMM *	150G		

*You must already own this CO to acquire the Color Editor.

AVAILABILITY: AFTER NORMAL CAMPAIGN MODE

MODES	PRICE	MODES	PRICE
HARD CAMPAIGN	1,000G	GALLERY	2,000G
SOUND ROOM	2,000G		

COs	PRICE	COs	PRICE
NELL	2,000G	HAWKE	1,000G
HACHI	2,000G	JUGGER	3,000G
FLAK	1,000G	KOAL	3,500G
LASH	1,000G	KINDLE	4,000G
ADDER	1,000G		

COLOR EDITORS	PRICE	COLOR EDITORS	PRICE
NELL *	200G	HAWKE *	200G
HACHI *	200G	JUGGER *	300G
FLAK *	200G	KOAL *	300G
LASH *	200G	KINDLE *	300G
ADDER *	200G		

*You must already own this CO to acquire the Color Editor.

AVAILABILITY: AFTER HARD CAMPAIGN MODE

CO	PRICE
VON BOLT	5,000G

COLOR EDITOR	PRICE
VON BOLT *	300G

*You must already own this CO to acquire the Color Editor.

AVAILABILITY: AFTER NORMAL COMBAT MODE

MODE	PRICE
HARD COMBAT	1,500G

COs	PRICE	COs	PRICE
FLAK	1,000G	ADDER	2,000G
LASH	1,500G	HAWKE	2,500G

AVAILABILITY: AFTER STANDARD SURVIVAL MODE

MODES	PRICE	MODES	PRICE
MONEY CHAMPION *	1,000G	TIME CHAMPION *	1,000G
TURN CHAMPION *	1,000G		

*You must complete the standard version of the corresponding mission to unlock it.

AVAILABILITY: INSERT ADVANCE WARS GAME PAK

MAPS	PRICE	MAPS	PRICE
STURM'S LAND *	1G	LASH'S LAND *	1G

*Both Advance Wars: Dual Strike and Advance Wars must be inserted at same time.

EXTRA	PRICE
ADVANCE WARPAPER 2 *	1G

*Both Advance Wars: Dual Strike and Advance Wars must be inserted at same time.

AVAILABILITY: INSERT ADVANCE WARS 2 GAME PAK

MAPS	PRICE	MAPS	PRICE
NELL'S LAND *	1G	HACHI'S LAND *	1G

*Both Advance Wars: Dual Strike and Advance Wars 2 must be inserted at same time.

EXTRA	PRICE
ADVANCE WARPAPER 1 *	1G

*Both Advance Wars: Dual Strike and Advance Wars 2 must be inserted at same time.

GALLERY PHOTOS

Here is a list of the photos you'll find in the gallery. While some are unlocked at the start of the game, others depend on particular accomplishments.

GALLERY LIST

#	PICTURE	REQUIREMENTS
1	WORLD MAP	-
2	JAKE	-
3	RACHEL	-
4	ANDY	-
5	MAX	-
6	SAMI	-
7	NELL	-
8	HACHI	-
9	SASHA	-
10	COLIN	-
11	GRIT	-
12	OLAF	-
13	JAVIER	-
14	JESS	-
15	EAGLE	-
16	DRAKE	-
17	GRIMM	-
18	SENSEI	-
19	SONJA	-
20	KANBEI	-
21	JUGGER	-
22	KOAL	-
23	KINDLE	-
24	VON BOLT	-
25	FLAK	-
26	LASH	-
27	ADDER	-
28	HAWKE	-
29	RACHEL'S HAT	WATCH THE MISSION 09 ENDING
30	TOAST	WATCH THE MISSION 22 ENDING
31	PARTY 1	WATCH THE MISSION 22 ENDING
32	PARTY 2	WATCH THE MISSION 22 ENDING
33	HANDSHAKE	WATCH THE MISSION 22 ENDING
34	DISMISSED!	WATCH THE GAME ENDING
35	REPORT	WATCH THE GAME ENDING
36	PROMISE HILL	WATCH THE GAME ENDING
37	FLOWERS	WATCH THE GAME ENDING
38	THREE VILLAINS	WATCH THE GAME ENDING
39	ORIGINAL SEVEN	SELECT "YES" ON THE FINAL MISSION
40	SALUTE	SELECT "NO" ON THE FINAL MISSION
41	DRIVE	CLEAR THE HARD CAMPAIGN

UNIT DATA

		ANTI-AIR	APC	ARTILLERY	INFANTRY	MECH	MEDIUM TANK	MEGATANK	MISSILE LAUNCHER	NEOTANK	OOZIUM	PIPERUNNER	RECON	ROCKET LAUNCHER	TANK	AIRCRAFT CARRIER
ANTI-AIR	MAIN	45	50	50	105	105	10	1	55	5	30	25	60	55	25	-
	SUB	-	-	-	-	-	-	-	-	-	-	-	-	-	-	-
ARTILLERY	MAIN	75	70	75	90	85	45	15	80	40	5	70	80	80	70	45
	SUB	-	-	-	-	-	-	-	-	-	-	-	-	-	-	-
INFANTRY	MAIN															
	SUB	5	14	15	55	45	1	1	25	1	20	5	12	25	5	-
MECH	MAIN	65	75	70	-	-	15	5	85	15	30	55	85	85	55	-
	SUB	6	20	32	65	55	1	1	35	1	20	6	18	35	6	-
MEDIUM TANK	MAIN	105	105	105	50	45	55	25	105	45	30	85	105	105	85	10
	SUB	7	45	45	105	95	1	1	35	1	20	8	45	55	8	-
MEGATANK	MAIN	195	195	195	50	45	125	65	195	115	45	180	195	195	180	45
	SUB	17	65	65	135	125	1	1	55	1	30	10	65	75	10	-
MISSILE LAUNCHER	MAIN	-	-	-	-	-	-	-	-	-	-	-	-	-	-	-
	SUB	-	-	-	-	-	-	-	-	-	-	-	-	-	-	-
NEOTANK	MAIN	115	125	115	50	45	75	35	125	55	35	105	125	125	105	30
	SUB	17	65	65	125	115	1	1	55	1	20	10	65	75	10	-
PIPERUNNER	MAIN	85	80	80	95	90	55	25	90	50	15	80	90	85	80	60
	SUB	-	-	-	-	-	-	-	-	-	-	-	-	-	-	-
RECON	MAIN	-	-	-	-	-	-	-	-	-	-	-	-	-	-	-
	SUB	4	45	45	70	65	1	1	28	1	20	6	35	55	6	-
ROCKET LAUNCHER	MAIN	85	80	80	95	90	55	25	90	50	15	80	90	85	80	60
	SUB	-	-	-	-	-	-	-	-	-	-	-	-	-	-	-
TANK	MAIN	65	75	70	35	30	15	10	85	15	20	55	85	85	55	1
	SUB	5	45	45	75	70	1	1	30	1	20	6	40	55	6	-
AIRCRAFT CARRIER	MAIN	-	-	-	-	-	-	-	-	-	-	-	-	-	-	-
	SUB	-	-	-	-	-	-	-	-	-	-	-	-	-	-	-
BATTLESHIP	MAIN	85	80	80	95	90	55	25	90	50	20	80	90	85	80	60
	SUB	-	-	-	-	-	-	-	-	-	-	-	-	-	-	-
CRUISER	MAIN	-	-	-	-	-	-	-	-	-	-	-	-	-	-	5
	SUB	-	-	-	-	-	-	-	-	-	-	-	-	-	-	-
SUBMARINE (ABOVE OR UNDERWATER)	MAIN	-	-	-	-	-	-	-	-	-	-	-	-	-	-	75
	SUB	-	-	-	-	-	-	-	-	-	-	-	-	-	-	-
BATTLE COPTER	MAIN	25	60	65	45	50	25	10	65	20	25	55	55	65	55	25
	SUB	6	20	25	75	75	1	1	35	1	20	6	30	35	6	-
BOMBER	MAIN	95	105	105	110	110	95	35	105	90	35	105	105	105	105	75
	SUB	-	-	-	-	-	-	-	-	-	-	-	-	-	-	-
FIGHTER	MAIN	-	-	-	-	-	-	-	-	-	-	-	-	-	-	-
	SUB	-	-	-	-	-	-	-	-	-	-	-	-	-	-	-
STEALTH FIGHTER (VISIBLE OR HIDDEN)	MAIN	50	85	75	90	90	70	15	85	60	30	80	85	85	75	45
	SUB	-	-	-	-	-	-	-	-	-	-	-	-	-	-	-

Nothing spells fun like poring over charts! These pages provide valuable intel on every unit in the game. Familiarize yourself with the details of each one.

Battleship	Black Boat	Cruiser	Lander	Submarine (Above Water)	Submarine (Underwater)	Battle Copter	Black Bomb	Bomber	Fighter	Stealth Fighter (Visible)	Stealth Fighter (Hidden)	Transport Copter
-	-	-	-	-	-	105	120	75	65	75	-	105
-	-	-	-	-	-	-	-	-	-	-	-	-
40	55	50	55	60	-	-	-	-	-	-	-	-
-	-	-	-	-	-	-	-	-	-	-	-	-
-	-	-	-	-	-	7	-	-	-	-	-	30
-	-	-	-	-	-	-	-	-	-	-	-	-
-	-	-	-	-	-	9	-	-	-	-	-	35
10	35	30	35	10	-	-	-	-	-	-	-	-
-	-	-	-	-	-	12	-	-	-	-	-	45
45	105	65	75	45	-	-	-	-	-	-	-	-
-	-	-	-	-	-	22	-	-	-	-	-	55
-	-	-	-	-	-	115	120	100	100	100	100	115
-	-	-	-	-	-	-	-	-	-	-	-	-
15	40	30	40	15	-	-	-	-	-	-	-	-
-	-	-	-	-	-	22	-	-	-	-	-	55
55	60	60	60	85	-	105	120	75	65	75	-	105
-	-	-	-	-	-	-	-	-	-	-	-	-
-	-	-	-	-	-	-	-	-	-	-	-	-
-	-	-	-	-	-	10	-	-	-	-	-	35
55	60	60	60	85	-	-	-	-	-	-	-	-
-	-	-	-	-	-	-	-	-	-	-	-	-
1	10	5	10	1	-	-	-	-	-	-	-	-
-	-	-	-	-	-	10	-	-	-	-	-	40
-	-	-	-	-	-	115	120	100	100	100	-	115
-	-	-	-	-	-	-	-	-	-	-	-	-
50	95	95	95	95	-	-	-	-	-	-	-	-
-	-	-	-	-	-	-	-	-	-	-	-	-
5	25	25	25	90	90	-	-	-	-	-	-	-
-	-	-	-	-	-	105	120	100	85	100	-	105
65	95	25	95	55	55	-	-	-	-	-	-	-
-	-	-	-	-	-	-	-	-	-	-	-	-
25	25	25	25	25	-	-	-	-	-	-	-	-
-	-	-	-	-	-	65	-	-	-	-	-	95
75	95	50	95	95	-	-	-	-	-	-	-	-
-	-	-	-	-	-	-	-	-	-	-	-	-
-	-	-	-	-	-	120	120	100	55	85	85	120
-	-	-	-	-	-	-	-	-	-	-	-	-
45	65	35	65	55	-	85	65	120	45	55	55	95
-	-	-	-	-	-	-	-	-	-	-	-	-

READING THE CHARTS

The units along the left edge denote the attacking unit, and the units across the top of the chart are the intended targets. Each group is color-coded to match its working environment: green=land, blue=sea, orange=air. You'll notice that the Oozium and the Black Bomb are not listed as attacking units. That's because an Oozium will destroy any unit it comes in contact with, provided it is directly aligned with the target. A Black Bomb will dish out 5 HP of hurt on its foes.

Some forces, such as the Mech, have various weapons at their disposal. When a Mech confronts a Tank, it will use its most powerful weapon. But when it squares off against Infantry, it will switch to more-appropriate munitions (Machine Guns) instead of utilizing Bazookas and the like. Damage information is subject to change based on battle conditions, which CO is leading the army, and whether CO Powers are in effect.

SONJA

CO DATA

Which CO pairings are the most effective? Which ones carry penalties? The handy chart below indicates the Attack percentage for each pairing.

	ADDER	ANDY	COLIN	DRAKE	EAGLE	FLAK	GRIMM	GRIT	HACHI	HAWKE	JAKE	JAVIER	JESS	JUGGER	KANBEI	KINDLE	KOAL	LASH	MAX	NELL	OLAF	RACHEL	SAMI	SASHA	SENSEI	SONJA	VON BOLT
ADDER						105				105							110	105									
ANDY				115						105									110	105				105			90
COLIN							105											90			105			130			90
DRAKE					115					90			105														90
EAGLE		115		115						70			105					90				120					90
FLAK	105																	110									
GRIMM												105													105	110	90
GRIT			105																110		115						90
HACHI																											90
HAWKE	*	105		90	70						90				80			110									
JAKE												110			90					120				105			90
JAVIER						105							110	110											105		90
JESS				105	105					90	110	110															90
JUGGER															110	105											
KANBEI										110															105	130	90
KINDLE										80	90			110			110										
KOAL	110													105	110						65						
LASH	*			90	110					110										80						105	
MAX		110						110												105		105					90
NELL		105																	105			130	105				90
OLAF			105					115										80									90
RACHEL										120						65			130					105			90
SAMI		105		120															105	105						110	90
SASHA		130				105				105												105					90
SENSEI						110				105				105												105	90
SONJA														130				105						110	105		90
VON BOLT		90	90	90	90	90	90	90	90		90	90	90		90				90	90	90	90	90	90	90	90	

*Luck is increased by five. Additionally, Attack value increases when Adder initiates a Tag Battle.